IN SEARCH OF
SISTERHOOD

Also by Paula Giddings

When and Where I Enter: The Impact of Black Women on Race
and Sex in America

IN SEARCH OF
SISTERHOOD

DELTA SIGMA THETA AND
THE CHALLENGE OF THE
BLACK SORORITY MOVEMENT

PAULA GIDDINGS

Amistad
An Imprint of HarperCollins*Publishers*

First Quill edition published 1994.

Reprinted in Perennial 2002. Reprinted in Amistad 2006.

Designed by Jaye Zimet

Library of Congress Cataloging-in-Publication Data

Giddings, Paula.
    In search of sisterhood: Delta Sigma Theta and the challenge of the Black
sorority movement / Paula Giddings.
      p. cm.
    Includes index.
    ISBN: 978-0-688-13509-6
    ISBN-10: 0-688-13509-9
    1. Delta Sigma Sorority—History. 2. Afro-American women—Societies,
etc.—History. I. Title.

LJ145.D615G53   1988
378'.198'5508996—dc19   88-11128
                                              CIP

---

24 25 26 27 28 LBC 73 72 71 70 69

P R E F A C E

In 1984, soon after I had published *When and Where I Enter: The Impact of Black Women on Race and Sex in America,* I received a call from Hortense G. Canady, the national president of Delta Sigma Theta. She congratulated me on the book—and then offered me two propositions. The first was to invite me to Delta's seven regional conferences where I would have the opportunity to talk about the book, and offer it for sale to those who attended the meetings. It was a gesture of support, something that Black sororities are well known for. And Delta, especially, has had a long tradition of supporting women in the arts. The second proposition was for me to write a history of the organization in time for its seventy-fifth anniversary in 1988. I had to weigh that proposal more carefully, both as a writer interested in Black women's history, and as a Delta who had some knowledge of the obstacles I would encounter.

Writing the history would give me an opportunity to explore the inner workings and dynamics of a major Black women's organization—something that I could not do in *When and Where I Enter.* . . . Such organizations are an important, yet much neglected, subject in both Black and women's studies. As one of the largest Black women's groups in the world, with some 125,000 members, Delta was certainly a major one. The fact that its membership also included significant historic and contemporary figures such as Mary Church Terrell, Sadie T. M. Alexander, Patricia Roberts Harris,

Barbara Jordan, Leontyne Price, and many other women who were
leaders and pioneers in their fields, made it more so.

As a college-based group, its history also would shed light on the
experience of Black women in higher education—a driving force in
our history. Barred from most occupations, Black women had few
choices besides domestic work or the "women's" professions, such as
teaching or social work. Education, then, was the dividing line between a life of drudgery and crude exploitation, and the greater quality of life and status derived from professional work.

That such aspirations were not sanctioned by society defined the
nature of Black women's organizations. Most are what sociologists
call social movement organizations whose purpose is to change individuals within them and/or the society. Like other Greek-letter
groups, Delta Sigma Theta was founded by young college women
with the idea of creating social bonds or a sense of sisterhood among
its members. Its primary focus, then, has been on transforming the
individual. At the same time, however, its founding in 1913, a time
of both racial and feminist ferment, also imbued it with a secondary
purpose: to have an impact on the political issues of the day, notably
the woman suffrage movement. By 1925, the organization made its
first public pronouncement against racism and four years later created a Vigilance Committee whose purpose was to enlighten the
growing membership about political and legislative issues and thus
prepare them to become agents of change. This aspect of Delta distinguished its beginnings from the other sororities, both Black and
White, that preceded it. It also makes contemporary Black sororities, in general, different from most of their White counterparts.

The history of Delta is better understood when seen in the light
of the principles that govern social movement organizations. For example, they must be able to adapt to changing environments: in this
case, the ever changing exigencies of race relations and the attitudes
toward women. Consequently, Delta has had to alter its purposes
and goals throughout the years—and must continue to do so—as
well as its internal structure to accommodate them. This makes the
Black sorority a particularly dynamic organization.

At the same time, however, changes cannot occur too abruptly or
without the consensus of an increasingly diverse constituency. For
like other social movement organizations, its viability is dependent
on the growth of its membership, which in turn, is largely determined by the number of its members who feel that the sorority's
goals are in harmony with their own.[1] This makes it complex as well
as a particularly democratic organization, for if power becomes too

concentrated, it invites apathy—the kiss of death for a social movement organization.

Social movement organizations are also dependent on the attitudes of the larger society toward both the movement that they represent and the organization itself.[2] The more legitimate it is seen in the broader society, sociologists say, the more potential supporters become actual supporters. The ideal condition for organizational growth "is a strong sentiment base with a low societal hostility toward the movement and the organization."[3] This, too, has important implications in terms of its public activities and the need to maintain not only respect but a deep loyalty of its members.

The sorority, I knew, would also be an interesting subject to study because it is an "exclusive" or closed membership organization. Undergraduate members must be in college. All members must be invited to join, and undergo a final selection process that includes both quantifiable criteria, for example, grade point average, and/or subjective assessments regarding achievement and character. Against the long experience of discrimination and exclusion in the broader society, and color and class distinctions within the race itself, debates regarding the various criteria for membership have, historically, been particularly emotional and intense. Behind the internal debates, of course, is how the organization sees its mission and itself—a vision that has constantly reshaped itself during different periods of Delta's history.

Despite the inherently controversial nature of an exclusive Black organization, it also has certain advantages. For one thing, a closed membership group is better able to take on new goals.[4] For another, it is less subject to membership declines and conflicts in the face of competing social movements. This is even more true for an organization with "solidarity" incentives, one that emphasizes coherence, or, in this case, sisterhood, within its membership. And because the focus of its leaders is mobilizing its membership for tasks—rather than attracting members through a charismatic leadership style—there is greater diversity in the kind of women who lead the organization, and more emphasis on getting those tasks done.

While there was no question that the sorority had historic importance, I also knew that there would be difficulties in writing the history. Systematic efforts to organize its archives were still in the early stages, and documentation is scattered and incomplete. And I was afraid that many of those who had a long-standing and thorough knowledge of the sorority would be reluctant to reveal its inner workings and problems. I was not willing to write a public relations tract, and I wondered about how much freedom I would have to get beneath the skin of the sorority and write about its weaknesses as well as its strengths. Concerning the latter, President Canady assured me that she would welcome constructive criticism, and that it was important to give a realistic picture of the organization—and she noted as much to the membership. Her style of leadership convinced me that the organization would be supportive, and that I would have a free reign—which turned out to be true.

The last thing I considered was my own personal view of the sorority. I had become a Delta during my sophomore year at Howard University. At that time, 1967, fraternal organizations were being widely criticized for their emphasis on social activities—which seemed all the more frivolous during the Black Power years—and their exclusiveness in a period when middle-class notions were under intense attack. However, for me, who never found socializing very easy, the ready-made parties and get-togethers with the sorors and fraternity men were an attractive feature of the Greek-letter groups. Growing up in Yonkers, New York, I had never felt a sense of belonging to a community, and the sorority paved the way for lifelong friendships. But more importantly the groups were concerned with more than the frivolities of campus life. Most of the student leaders belonged to them—including those who were poised to close down the university in the following year in an attempt to make it more responsive to the Black Power movement. Additionally, on Howard's campus, the fraternities and sororities functioned with the power of well-heeled political parties when appointive and elective positions were to be filled. Among the sororities, the Deltas held, to my mind, most of the coveted ones such as the editorship of the literary magazine that was beginning to reflect the more race-conscious poetry and prose of the period. Finally, the coeds whom I most admired, and liked, were Deltas, and I was anxious to be a part of the sisterhood that they shared.

Later, I would experience the down side of sorority life. Friends of mine would be rejected for what I thought petty, personal reasons, and be devastated by it. The pledge period was an intense one. There was little sleep, constant fear of "big sisters"—who had extraordinary power over the pledgees—hazing, and other unpleasantries. On the one hand, the experience accomplished what it intended: a sense of bonding among the pledgees, and a profound understanding of one's own weaknesses and strengths under stress. On the other hand, there were the excesses, the mean-spiritedness, even the revelation of the sadistic side of human nature, that are inevitable by-products of the pledge period. Hazing that might produce any physical harm was strictly forbidden by the national organization, but it could occur. A paddling incident during my own pledge period cast a shadow over the whole sorority experience.

It was one of the reasons why I ceased to be an active member or join any of the alumnae groups after I graduated. But there were other reasons, too. I became involved in my own career as a writer and editor. In any case, I was never much of an "organization" person. Also, although I was aware that the Deltas had a long and honorable history of serving their community and helping individuals, I was not convinced that the demands put upon its graduate members were equal to the results the group achieved.

However, by the mid-seventies, when I was an editor at Howard University Press I was invited to become a part of a newly established arts and letters commission. It was headed by a past president, Jeanne Noble, and was cochaired by no lesser Deltas than Leontyne Price and Lena Horne. As will be written about in more detail, the commission was an effort to support Black women in the arts, and one of its projects was a book and author luncheon for poets Nikki Giovanni—also on the commission—and the venerable Margaret Walker, who had co-authored a book for Howard University Press. But its most ambitious project was the production of a full-length feature film with political import to counter the influence of the "blaxploitation" movies that offered little but stereotypical images of Blacks. However, the film encountered some major difficulties that caused much turbulence in the sorority. Soon afterward, I accepted an offer to work for a newsmagazine in Paris for two years, and, upon my return, I didn't not renew my financial membership in the organization.

So, when President Canady proposed my writing the history, I paused. I didn't have to make a decision until after attending the regional conferences, and it was there that I decided to pursue the project. I had forgotten that feeling of well-being and sisterhood that pervades those meetings. This is not to say that the usual intercourse among people competing for office, attention, and power wasn't taking place, but something larger was happening as well. It struck me that Black women may be among their freest, their happiest, and, in some ways, their most fulfilled when they are together in their organizations. A psychologist whom I once interviewed, Kathy White, used the term "beloved organization" when we discussed this dynamic; and it is the sorority, I am convinced, that is the most beloved of all. These feelings are even true, I have found, of many of those who are inactive, or have been disappointed or hurt by sorority life.

The challenge of the sorority, one made all the more difficult by the pathos of the Black women's experience in North America, is to maintain that sense of sisterhood while striving, organizationally, for a more general purpose: aiding the Black community as a whole through social, political, and economic means. As one can see from the rules that govern the social movement organization, this idea can be a difficult one to realize. But the effort to resolve the tension between the goals of the organization, and those of the sisterhood, through strengthening social bonds within the context of social action has been an interesting and engaging experiment. One that can be seen as a model for Black organizational life, and which adds contour and dimension to the history of Black women in this country.

ACKNOWLEDGMENTS

I would like first to express my appreciation to immediate past national president, Hortense G. Canady, and the national board of Delta Sigma Theta for giving me the opportunity—and support—to write about Delta's history. They, among many others in the Delta organization, gave me their time and cooperation in this effort. My special thanks to our two living founders: Bertha Pitts Campbell, who at her home in Seattle not only granted me an interview, but took me shopping, and to lunch and dinner. (*I* was the one who needed a nap at the end of the day.) I also spoke to Naomi Sewell Richardson in her home in Washingtonville, New York, and found that both she and Mrs. Campbell still possessed the sense of humor and fun that they had as students at Howard. Thanks also to members of the Mid-Hudson Valley chapter who took part in the interview with Mrs. Richardson, and shared earlier ones with me for this book.

All of the national presidents gave of their time to talk to me about the organization. I especially benefited from the help of Anna Johnson Julian, who was among those who read the manuscript, despite recovering from surgery. The generosity of Louise Thompson, Hilda Davis, and Elsie Brown Smith is also appreciated. Thanks also to Yvonne Catchings, chair of the Archives and Heritage Committee for her help; Charlie Mae Brown Smith who coauthored a book about founder Frederica Dodd, and also went out of her way to send me additional material about her and the other founders from Texas; and Rae Pace Alexander Minter, Irene McClellan King, Benetta Hicks, Jean S. Porter and Jessie Nave Carpenter for sending me additional materials; Norlishia Jackson, who helped me find photographs and was an important source of information. The unpublished manuscript of Helen G. Edmonds was an invaluable guide to the writing of the history. And last, but not least, a special thanks to the already overworked national headquarters staff, who graciously acceded to yet more demands from this writer.

A number of university archivists responded promptly to my requests for Delta material. They included, Howard University, where Paul Coates and Janet Sims Wood are *always* so helpful, and where Dr. Owen D. Nichols, secretary of the board of trustees was good enough to comb the archives' board meeting minutes to send me information. Also my appreciation to the universities of Pittsburgh, Iowa, Wilberforce, Syracuse, Nebraska, Butler, West Virginia State, Kansas, Ohio State, Cincinnati, Fisk, Michigan, and Illinois for responding to my requests. My thanks also to those who helped me at the Chicago Historical Society in Chicago and the Schomberg Collection in New York City.

CONTENTS

INTRODUCTION

THE IMPORTANCE OF THE BLACK SORORITY: SOME CONSIDERATIONS

On January 13, 1913, twenty-two young women attending Howard University, in Washington D.C., chartered Delta Sigma Theta sorority. Seventy-five years later it has become one of the largest Black women's organizations in the world, with over 125,000 members in 730 chapters in the United States, Africa, and the Caribbean. Throughout its history, Delta has shaped and been shaped by its members—many of whom rank among the most important figures in American history. The activist, and suffragist Mary Church Terrell wrote the sorority's official "Delta Oath" in 1914, which is still recited at formal meetings. She also led the young coeds in their first public act as an organization: marching down Washington's Pennsylvania Avenue (with the Delta banner aloft) in the famous woman suffrage demonstration on the eve of Woodrow Wilson's inauguration. And when, thirty-seven years later, Terrell became one of the leading plaintiffs of the celebrated "Thompson Restaurant case"—which ultimately led to desegregated public accommodations in Washington—the Deltas, in coalition with other Greek-letter organizations, helped "man" the picket lines and filed an amicus curiae brief in support of the plaintiffs.

Terrell's colleague, Mary McLeod Bethune, the educator, a member of Franklin D. Roosevelt's Cabinet, and the founder of the National Council of Negro Women (NCNW) was a frequent speaker at Delta conventions, and an important source of information about what was happening at the highest levels of government. She helped shape the sorority's social action agenda in the thirties and forties, and Delta, in turn, provided vital support to the NCNW in its early years. At one Delta convention enough money was raised to hold repossessors of NCNW's national headquarters at bay. Delta was an early member of the council's board of directors and many officers of the sorority also served in executive capacities in Bethune's organization.

The sorority has always been an important source of leadership training for Black women, whose opportunities to exercise such skills in formal organizations are few. Patricia Roberts Harris, who became the first Black woman to be appointed an ambassador, to become dean of Howard University's School of Law, and to head the Cabinet post of secretary of housing and urban development, was in 1953, Delta's first executive director. On the eve of her appointment as ambassador to Luxembourg in 1965, she said that "while there are many things in my life which have prepared me for what I am about to do, it is largely the experience in Delta Sigma Theta which gives me the most security."[1] Similiar sentiments are heard from women like Barbara Jordan, who served as chair of the sorority's National Finance Committee and was among the Deltas who lobbied Capitol Hill before becoming a United States congresswoman from Texas. It was on one of those occasions when, looking up at the arched ceilings of the Capitol, she told the then national president, Geraldine P. Woods, that one day she, too, would have an office there.

In addition to opportunities for leadership, the sorority has also historically been both a supporter, and magnet, for Black women in the arts. Throughout our history, even the most brilliant talents could depend on little financial support for study, and few opportunities to perform, publish, or have the benefit of an empathetic audience that appreciated the meaning of their achievement. There was a mutual appreciation, for example, for writers like Alice Dunbar-Nelson, the poet, journalist, and suffragist who was the widow of Paul Laurence Dunbar when she became a member of the sorority. At a historic Delta national convention in 1924, Nelson and another soror, the soprano Florence Cole Talbert—one of the earliest Black singers to perform operatic roles in Europe—wrote the lyrics and the music, respectively, for what was adopted as the official Delta Hymn. At the same convention, Delta, which began giving scholarships in the early twenties, granted its first foreign study award of $1,000 to the Harlem Renaissance artist Gwendolyn Bennett. Others to receive support in critical phases of their careers included the concert artist Dorothy Maynor, whose extraordinary gifts were recognized by Boston Symphony conductor Serge Koussevitsky; Mattiwilda Dobbs, who became one of the first Blacks to sing at the Metropolitan Opera House; and another promising operatic artist—Leontyne Price. Delta-sponsored concerts featuring such artists were frequent. On one particularly memorable occasion, a chapter sponsored a concert featuring Price and Paul Robeson. Several decades later, the diva of divas would cochair the sorority's Commission on Arts and Letters with another soror of considerable talent and verve, Lena Horne. The involvement in arts and letters has been a particularly deep one for Delta—it is a tradition that began with several of Delta's founders who were drawn to various forms of artistic expression in the days before there were many such role models. Founder Osceola Macarthy Adams, for example, a member of the Howard Players Theater group as early as 1911, went on to a professional career as an actress, drama teacher, and director. In the latter capacity, she directed the theater debut of two "green" actors who, hope against hope, wanted to make their mark on the national consciousness: Harry Belafonte and Sidney Poitier.

Of course it is more than well-known names, or historic firsts, that make up the meaning of the seventy-five-year-old organization. When, in 1913, those twenty-two students organized Delta Sigma Theta, they added an important and vital dimension to the "Black sorority idea"—an idea that filled such a compelling need, that gained such wide currency among college-educated women, it became a full-fledged social movement. In many ways it was a movement that was part and parcel of the general fraternal movement that began with the appearance of Phi Beta Kappa at William and Mary College in 1776, saw the first women's sororities in the mid-nineteenth century, and reached new peaks in the early twentieth century. By 1912, there were 256,000 members in forty such organizations in the country,[2] including the Black fraternities, Alpha Phi Alpha (1906), Kappa Alpha Psi (1911), Omega Psi Phi (1911); and the sorority Alpha Kappa Alpha (1908). Soon following was the establishment of Delta Sigma Theta (1913), Zeta Phi Beta (1920), and Sigma Gamma Rho (1922) sororities, and Phi Beta Sigma fraternity (1914). Both the Black and White groups shared in common, Greek names; a closed, or exclusive rather than inclusive, membership; and the culture of "secret societies" replete with rituals, oaths, and symbols. Members of all the groups had to meet particular criteria and go through "novitiate" periods where they were subjected to hazing and the discipline and orders of the organization. All were created out of the desire to form social bonds with like-minded students.

However, the particular needs of Black students in general, and women in particular, made the history of Black Greek-letter groups distinct both in degree and kind from those of their White counterparts. The growing but still small numbers of Afro-Americans attending universities in the early twentieth century created a special sense of urgency to form the social bonds with each other that was inherent in the nature of Greek-letter societies.

From 1826, the year that the first Black attained a degree from an American university, to 1905, 7,488 Blacks had earned academic or professional degrees—the bulk of them in the turn-of-the-century years.[3] Though the number is not broken down by sex, disproportionately few were women. Jeanne Noble, in her important study "The Negro Woman's College Education" (1956), noted that in 1900, twenty-two women received B.A. degrees from Black universities—which educated the majority of Blacks, and particularly Black women. By 1910, that figure was 227.[4]

Racism, sexism, and the sense of racial obligation were also forces that helped shape the Black Greek-letter groups. It is interesting to note that the two earliest fraternities were actually established on predominantly White campuses: Alpha Phi Alpha at Cornell University and Kappa Alpha Psi at the University of Indiana. All of the others were born on Howard University's campus. But the early growth of the fraternal organizations, in most instances, was on predominantly White campuses—where there was a greater need for a haven against discrimination. In Delta's case, though the second chapter was organized at the predominantly Black Wilberforce University in Ohio, in 1914, twenty-seven of the next thirty chapters would be established on non-Black campuses—including the Universities of Pennsylvania, California (at Berkeley and Los Angeles), Pittsburgh, Michigan, Iowa, Nebraska, Chicago, Cornell, and Syracuse, among others. In such places even the idea of a sorority house had special implications. On many predominantly White campuses, they served not only as centers for social activity, but as the only on-campus housing for Black students, who were allowed to matriculate at the schools but not live in their dormitories.

The racial environment in which they were conceived also made the groups very conscious of scholarship and achievement, making them closer to honor societies such as Phi Beta Kappa than the more socially oriented White groups. For many, in fact, who for assorted reasons would never have the chance to hold a Phi Beta Kappa key, the criteria-based membership in a fraternity or sorority became its own evidence of academic distinction. At least one of the Black Greek societies, Alpha Phi Alpha, was originally conceived as a literary and study group on Cornell's campus, and only later evolved into a full-fledged fraternity.

For Black college students, scholarship had a double-edged purpose. It offered proof of their intellectual abilities in a society that doubted them; and as benefactors of a college education—a scarce commodity in the Black community—there was the racial obligation to achieve both on the campus and beyond it and so better lead the others. There was another dimension to these aspirations too: the right to attain the same intellectual training as that of the best of their White peers. For this reason, Black fraternal groups—conceived at a time when an academic education was widely seen as dangerous, futile, or impractical, for Blacks—had a decidedly liberal arts bent. Their development was more than an imitation of the White Greek-letter groups that excluded them. Even the Greek appellations were, in part, a defiant response to the notion that a "Negro would never learn to parse a Greek verb or to solve a problem in Euclid,"[5] as former Vice-President and states' righter John C. Calhoun once opined. Black Greek-letter societies were also calculated to strike a blow against proponents of industrial, nonacademic education for Afro-Americans. The latter included Blacks like Booker T. Washington, who believed the study of classical subjects was of little practical use. Unlike him, those in the Black fraternal groups did not see the irony in, as the Tuskegee educator once noted, "the black boy studying Greek, while the Greek boy is blacking shoes."[6]

For Black women, these circumstances had even deeper implications. The tremendous need for instructors who were not only teaching "a whole race trying to go to school"—as Washington once described the Black hunger for education—but providing important role models, did encourage Black women to study beyond high school. But most were attending normal institutions: two-year schools with limited curricula aimed at preparing teachers. Encouragement diminished as aspirations increased, especially during the late nineteenth and early twentieth centuries when the technological revolution was challenging women's traditional roles. Mary Church Terrell, who became the first Black woman to serve on a citywide board of education—in Washington, D.C.—and who was educated at Oberlin College in the late nineteenth century, wrote that "it was held by most people that women were unfit to do their work in the home if they studied Latin, Greek and higher mathematics . . . I was ridiculed and told that no man would want to marry a woman who studied higher mathematics . . . Most of my friends," she continued, "tried to dissuade me from studying for an AB degree."[7] Tellingly, Terrell's choice of subjects at Oberlin was called "the gentleman's course"—which she would complete, defiantly, and then pursue further study in Europe.

Black sororities were also liberal arts oriented and the small numbers of Black women in four-year institutions who sought social bonds and shared experiences gave a particular resonance to their organizations. (The first group of initiates of Alpha Kappa Alpha numbered nine: the total number of women in Howard's Liberal Arts School.) In general, the sororities often held their members to even stricter academic standards than their male counterparts, although all had similar criteria. For Black women though, who also saw community service and racial uplift as a vital part of their mission, those standards were often a source of conflict. Especially in the South, where the overwhelming majority of Black people lived, segregation, poverty, and racism prevented many potentially brilliant students from attending prestigious liberal arts institutions. Not until the 1920s were there significant numbers of public high schools in the South, even for Whites. Should the lack of opportunity exclude them from membership? If not, how could they attain the true "honor society" dimension of the sororities? When did selectivity go beyond the notion of excellence to embrace elitism and snobbery?

The debate touched on an always explosive issue among Blacks: the question of class and color. After all, it was often the Black descendants of White slaveholders who had the earliest opportunities to attain a liberal arts education and learn the social graces. Another layer of complexity was added because of the association of class with morality. The latter has been a particular preoccupation of Black women because of the widely held stereotypes about their sexual behavior—stereotypes that had horrible and far-reaching consequences. The sorority's constant redefining of the meaning of class and achievement within its own ranks has been an underlying theme in its history.

Black sororities have also had to grapple with how the concept of service is translated into political activism. The sorority may be unique among Black purposive organizations as it was not conceived to transform society but to transform the individual. The sorority is a sisterhood, and an enabler that helps individuals to grow through cooperation, leadership development, "culture" and exposure to the leading figures and issues of the times. Individually, many members of Black sororities were also active in the NAACP and a host of civil rights organizations on either end of the political spectrum; and organizationally, they have lent financial aid and other means of support to such groups. But the role of the sorority itself in Black political life has been less clear—and in highly charged times of Black militancy, such as the sixties, it has often been thrown into a crisis of identity and relevance as a primarily social organization. Especially in such periods its exclusive membership, its reluctance to be a vanguard for positions considered radical for the times (even those concerning education), and its primary concern for social bonding have drawn sharp criticism from those both within and outside the sorority. This is compounded by the perennial problem of chapters, many of which are small and made up of women with little experience in exercising the political mandates of the national leadership.

On the other hand, the sorority's emphasis on being an individual rather than societal transformer insulates its members from the kind of polarization, dependence on outside resources and disruption that other organizations have faced. Unlike civil rights organizations, for example, which had to alter its goals and leadership style when *de jure* integration was achieved, the sorority has been relatively immune from having to undergo such changes. Partly for this reason it has not only survived but grown while many other organizations have failed to do so. In 1908, with the founding of the first Black sorority, there were nine women who belonged to a Black Greek-letter organization. Today, over a quarter of a million women belong to the three major college-based sororities—Delta Sigma Theta, Alpha Kappa Alpha, and Zeta Phi Beta—and their numbers continue to grow. Their viability—despite the changes that two world wars, the Great Migration, the Great Depression, and de jure desegregation have wrought—attests to their continuing importance in Black life. So too, does the fact that unlike predominantly White Greek-letter organizations, association with Black groups does not end with graduation from college. The lifetime commitment to the ideals of the organization is stressed, and the majority of Delta's active members are non-students.

Throughout its seventy-five-year-old history, Delta Sigma Theta has maintained a stable yet dynamic organization that has consistently rendered service to its community. Its leadership is democratically elected by its membership, imbuing it with a legitimacy to represent and speak for a significant constituency of Black women. There are few Black organizations with a more skilled or more coherent membership, or that is less dependent on outside sources, than the Black sorority. Because of these very reasons, there is a challenge inherent in the Black sorority idea—a challenge that no one understands better than the sorority itself. Its history shows that its vision of itself and what it must do grows with each succeeding decade. From a self-contained group of college students, the sorority took on the goals of public service and support for those organizations that sought political change. Its mandate for the next century, following its own evolutionary path, is to continue its ever-increasing abilities to render public service, and to enlarge its concept to embrace and directly impact on public policy. This can't be done by fiat, but rather must be accomplished through a transformative vision internalized by the membership—a vision that will allow it to realize its extraordinary potential and continue to attract committed women.

In 1913, twenty-two young women, barely out of their adolescent years, founded a sorority that today touches the lives of thousands of women. This book is a history of how that organization was born, the ideas of those twenty-two women, of its struggles, and its attempts to fashion a meaningful life for the community and for themselves from the raw material of denial. It is the history of one group's search for sisterhood.

When I look at you, I see myself. If my eyes are unable to see you as my sister, it is because my own vision is blurred. And if that be so, then it is I who need you either because I do not understand who you are, my sister, or because I need you to help me understand who I am.
  —Lillian P. Benbow,
    National President, Delta Sigma Theta,
    1971–1975

PART ONE

CHAPTER 1

WORLD OF THE FOUNDERS

On a sweltering August 2 in 1981, ten thousand members of Delta Sigma Theta sorority marched down Pennsylvania Avenue in Washington, D.C. The women, all wearing white, and many of them carrying parasols to fend off the sun, were commemorating—at this, their thirty-sixth national convention—Delta's first public act as a sorority. On March 3, 1913, just two months after their inception, the Deltas had participated in the historic woman suffrage parade on the eve of President Woodrow Wilson's inauguration.

Two members of the Black sorority who participated in the commemoration march remembered the suffrage parade that had taken place sixty-eight years before: Sadie T. M. Alexander, then eighty-three years of age, and Bertha Pitts Campbell, who was ninety-two. In 1913, Alexander was preparing to enter the University of Pennsylvania, from which, in 1921, she would become the first Black woman to receive a Ph.D. degree.* While an undergraduate, Alexander was elected the first national president of Delta Sigma Theta, guiding its transition from a loose federation of chapters to national organization.

*Subsequently she became the first Black woman to pass the Pennsylvania Bar and the first Black assistant solicitor general of that state.

Only Campbell garnered more attention as she marched down Pennsylvania Avenue on that August day. Despite her years, she refused to ride in the limousine provided for her, and only half humorously urged then national vice-president Hortense Canady to go faster or she would "walk on her heels." Campbell was the only person who had actually participated in the 1913 march. She had marched as one of the twenty-two founding members of Delta Sigma Theta sorority. The experiences that brought her there mirrored those of a fortunate few in her generation.

Soon after Bertha Campbell was born, on June 30, 1889, her family moved from their home in Winfield, Kansas, to Montrose, Colorado, a mining town about 180 miles southwest of Denver. It must have been a painful decision for her parents, Ida and Hubbard Sydney Pitts, to leave their wheat-filled land in Kansas. The state possessed the hopes of her Mississippi-born father as it did for thousands of southern Blacks who migrated there after the Civil War. Wheat farming was benumbing work, with a growing season that sometimes lasted two hundred days a year, but the Pittses were successful farmers—until the windswept droughts made it difficult to make ends meet. When Ida became pregnant with their third child, Bertha, they were compelled to go elsewhere. The family decided on Montrose because Ida's mother, Eliza Butler, was there, and Hubbard (or H.S. as he was called) could find a job as a cook in the gold, granite, and coal mines that had attracted a population of about a thousand. It was a young town, founded in 1882, and was an emerging service center for miners and railroad workers. In November of 1889, the couple and their three children, Charles, Minnie, and Bertha, arrived there, and it would be the birthplace of two more siblings, Huey and Timmy.

Eliza Butler, Ida's mother, would have the most profound impact on Bertha, who would eventually live with this short, slim woman who was among the first generation of Blacks who knew both slavery and freedom. Campbell still recalls her saying that "education is the gateway to everything,"[1] and Campbell took those words seriously. In 1903, she became the only Black student to enroll in Montrose High School, and five years later delivered the valedictory address to the class of 1908. In that year, she graduated summa cum laude, and was offered a full four-year scholarship to Colorado College in Colorado Springs, some 160 miles from Montrose. And Campbell would have attended that thirty-four-year-old institution if it hadn't been for a woman who was a trustee of the nearby Congregationalist church, which was attended by the Pitts family. The trustee had just been to the nation's capital and had seen Howard University. "Oh, Bertha," the woman told her, "it's the nicest school in Washington."[2] She was also partial to the college because it was named after General O. O. Howard, a Congregationalist and Civil War hero who had been president of the university from 1869 to 1873. The general also had headed the Freedmen's Bureau, a government agency that aided newly emancipated Blacks. According to Campbell, the trustee also believed that it would be beneficial for her to be part of a Black community, an experience she had not had, since her family were the only Blacks in Montrose, and Colorado College would not be much better. Campbell protested that her family would be unable to afford Howard in lieu of the scholarship she had already received, but was told that perhaps the Church could offer her one. Campbell did get the financial support and in 1909 she found herself preparing to attend Howard.

For the twenty-year-old Coloradoan, the Howard adventure began with a three-day train trip—including one luxurious meal in the train's dining car and a long stop in Chicago before reaching Washington, D.C. When she arrived on the campus, she must have been pleased at what she saw. Howard University, chartered in 1867, "for the education of youth in the liberal arts and social sciences," stood on twenty acres of "the highest elevation in Northwest Washington, and the most attractive part of the city," noted the *Howard University Record,* the official organ of the university.[3] The campus looked over a small lake-sized reservoir, and the grounds of the National Soldiers Home that furnished a park. There were abundant shade trees and modern brick buildings that were "heated by steam and lighted by electricity," boasted the *Record.* One might also have been relieved to know that the campus and its surroundings had an enviable record of "healthfulness." No disease "has ever become epidemic in the institution," the publication proudly noted, "and there has never been on the grounds a death from typhoid."[4]

Spread across the campus grounds were Freedmen's Hospital, the Main Hall, Clark Hall, the Manual Training and Arts Building, the Memorial Chapel, and the medical and law schools. There was also Miner Hall, named after Myrtilla Miner, a White woman who in 1851 established an academy for Black girls in Washington, D.C., despite much opposition. It was here that Bertha Pitts and all of the female students would reside while at Howard.

The female students' residence was built at the same time as the university's main building, in 1869. No effort was spared, said the *Record,* "to give it a home-like atmosphere and to make it a center of intellectual and moral culture for the young women placed in charge of the institution."[5] The rooms in the four-story building were arranged in suites with accommodations for two or three girls each. On the basement level were the dining rooms; each had an outside entrance for young men. And on the other floors were a reception parlor, a music room, and sewing room. In these Victorian times there was also an effort to make it as "nearly as possible 'representative of a Christian home under the guidance of maternal care, sympathy and love,'" observed historian Rayford Logan in his history of the university.[6] Miner Hall, he observed, would remain under the "superintendence" of a lady matron. Students, Campbell would soon find out, were expected to show respect for order and morality, and were even liable for any misbehavior during vacation periods *away* from the campus. For the women students, especially, social rules were strictly enforced. They were not to take walks, ride in any vehicles, correspond, or engage in any outdoor games with the opposite sex without approval from the matron, who even acted as a kind of censor. She was the "instrumentality," as Logan noted, through which all mail sent or received by Miner Hall students passed.[7] Of course, going off campus without an approved chaperone was out of the question. And spending the night elsewhere, even on holidays, was only possible with parents' permission. As Delta founder, Naomi Sewell Richardson, recalled, punishment for any infraction was severe. "If Miss Hartley [the matron] saw smoke coming from a girl's room—even if she didn't see her smoking—but saw smoke coming out of the window of her room, then she was immediately dismissed from the university." The omnipresent matron was also always there to "greet" a student returning to the dorm after a holiday. Richardson remembered how once, a young lady came back after Thanksgiving, and the matron smelled liquor on her breath. The student said she had made a mince pie, said Richardson, "and you know how you make a mince pie—you usually put something more than water in it. Right away the matron accused her of drinking and the student was immediately dismissed."[8]

All of this was calculated, of course, to ensure not only ladylike behavior, but undistracted attention to one's studies. Bertha Campbell must have been impressed by, and perhaps a little anxious about, the high academic requirements of the school. In the College of Liberal Arts and Sciences, there was an array of courses in English, mathematics, Latin, Greek, French, German, physics, chemistry, biology, history, philosophy, and the social Sciences "such as are given in the best approved colleges," noted the *Howard University*

Journal.[9] There was also a School of Manual Arts and Applied Sciences, the Commercial College—offering business, commercial law, and bookkeeping courses—the Academy—a high-grade preparatory school—and the professional schools of theology, medicine, and law. Of particular interest to Campbell, as well as most of the women students, was the Teachers College that was at this time experiencing a period of growth.

By the turn of the century, there was a great deal of attention and emphasis focused on developing Black teachers who would join the missionarylike movement to educate the first generations of Blacks born beyond the pale of slavery. For Black women, being an educator at once made them part of this racial uplift movement, gave them status, offered an opportunity to work in one of the few professions open to them, and gave them the means to overcome some of the restrictive attitutdes toward the middle-class woman's role as silent and subservient homemaker. By the time Campbell came to Howard, it had already followed the lead of such schools as Columbia University in establishing a Teachers College that offered a more professional, comprehensive, and varied program than the two-year normal school.[10] As the *Record* described it, the function of the Teachers College was "to supply a very definite demand for advanced professional training for teachers and a more serious study of educational problems."[11] One of those problems was literacy, and it was Howard, Logan reminds us, that was among the first institutions of higher learning to express concern about remedial reading, and that identified the term.[12] No longer would the training of teachers be given an inferior status, promised the *Record:* "The training of the educator for all grades of instruction or of supervision from the elementary school up shall not be inferior to that of persons of other professions." Indeed, an education major had to complete 120 semester hours of courses, including history, principles of education, psychology, methods of teaching, actual teaching under observation, along with areas of specialization and elective courses.[13] As the *Record* noted, "[The student] will not sacrifice anything of the culture of the Liberal Arts Course, but through all of the four years of this course will be growing professionally in efficiency and spirit."[14] The word "spirit" is key. The growth in the education department, and the progressive ideas in pedagogy that it was offering along with the improving facilities and new buildings gave this class of students a new esprit de corps, as a student wrote in the *Journal*. Such a development affirmed the notion that "there is no reason why

[Howard] should not continue in her growth until Harvard and Howard be synonymous."15

Certainly, Campbell would soon find out, Howard's cadre of professors included some of the most brilliant scholars in the nation. Her philosophy instructor was Alain L. Locke (1886–1954), who was only three years older than she and had earned his B.A. degree from Howard. Locke, the first Afro-American Rhodes Scholar, did graduate work at Oxford University and the University of Berlin. After World War I, he would become the leading critic and interpreter of the Harlem Renaissance movement. She would also study with the even younger Ernest E. Just (1883–1941), educated at Dartmouth and the University of Chicago. Just, a biologist, would formulate new concepts of cell life and metabolism and receive the coveted Spingarn Medal from the NAACP in 1914. The well-known writer, Benjamin Brawley (1882–1939) would instruct Campbell in English. In 1913 he would publish *A Short History of the American Negro* and six years later *Women of Achievement*. And then there would be the venerable Kelly Miller (1863–1939), a mathematician trained at Johns Hopkins, dean of the Liberal Arts School, and a cosponsor of a new organization that made its appearance in 1911: the National Urban League. There were other professors of renown as well, those like Charles H. Houston in the law school, characterized by Thurgood Marshall as the "First Mr. Civil Rights Lawyer"; Lorenzo Turner, linguist and sociologist; and the historian Charles H. Wesley.

Fortunately, Bertha Campbell already had the academic discipline and confidence to take on the four-year curriculum. But how would she relate to the other students? Would she make meaningful friendships? Would she get along with her roommate and other students who came from different backgrounds? Some of these questions began to be answered when she met her roommate in Miner Hall. She was a young, attractive woman from Columbus, Georgia, who had attended school in Savannah, Atlanta, and Macon, and graduated salutatorian of her class from Ballard Normal School in the latter city. Her name was Winona Lucile (Cargile) Alexander, a wholesome if sassy enough student to earn the title "Most Flirtatious of Her Class," one year. Coincidentally, their birthdays were only one day apart; Alexander's was on June 21, though she was three years younger than her roommate. Unlike Campbell, Alexander was not a first generation college student. Her father, an African Methodist Episcopal (AME) minister, and her uncle had attended Howard before her. But both must have been awed by finding themselves in such a cosmopolitan city and heavily populated campus.

Alexander had graduated from a class of ten girls and one boy. And the well over one thousand students attending Howard was greater than the whole population of Montrose.

But the immensity of it all would become more manageable as the two young women found themselves becoming part of a growing circle of friends, linked by happenstance and a common conviction. Unbeknownst to them, they would form a core of what would become one of the largest organizations of Black women in the world. A core that would also include twenty other women: Osceola (Macarthy) Adams, class of 1913; Ethel (Cuff) Black, class of 1915; Zephyr (Chisom) Carter, class of 1913; M. Edna (Brown) Coleman, class of 1913; Jessie (McGuire) Dent, class of 1913; Frederica (Chase) Dodd, class of 1914; Myra (Davis) Hemmings, class of 1913; Olive C. Jones, class of 1913; Jimmie (Bugg) Middleton, class of 1913; Pauline (Oberdorfer) Minor, class of 1914; L. Vashti (Turley) Murphy, class of 1914; Naomi (Sewell) Richardson, class of 1914; Mamie (Reddy) Rose, class of 1913; Eliza P. Shippen, class of 1912; Florence (Letcher) Toms, class of 1913; Ethel (Carr) Watson, class of 1913; Wertie (Blackwell) Weaver, class of 1913; Madree (Penn) White, class of 1914; Edith (Motte) Young, class of 1913; and Marguerite (Young) Alexander, class of 1913.

Bertha Campbell would strike up one of her closest friendships with Zephyr Carter, who hailed from El Paso, Texas. Both were fun-loving and possessed a ribald sense of humor. Once Campbell's brother sent her a suit, but the jacket was too large: "Not enough bust," she recalls. Her friend, Zephyr, however, was a better "candidate" so, as Campbell remembered, "I gave her the jacket and she wore it and I wore the skirt."[16] Carter would become close to Naomi Richardson, from Washingtonville, New York, who became a target of her sense of fun. Richardson recalled how "jolly" she was and how Zephyr was a self-appointed member of the "Dust Club": a club for coeds who seemed unable to attract a suitable boyfriend. "After you were at Howard a certain length of time, you were expected to have a male friend," said Richardson, "so one day, Zeffie met me in the bathroom and she asked me if I had a male companion yet. 'No,' I said, 'my mother and father didn't send me to Howard to get a boyfriend.' So she laughed and said, 'Well, if you don't have a boyfriend, be at the Dust Club meeting tomorrow night. I'm declaring you an official member.'"[17]

Three other close friends of the young Richardson were Wertie Weaver, Ethel Black, and Frederica Dodd. Weaver was from Kansas City, Missouri, and like Richardson, celebrated her birthday in September, though the former was two years older. Naomi liked to kid the Missourian over the fact that all during her years at Lincoln High School the only college that Wertie had heard about was Tuskegee, until friends told her about others. After graduation Naomi and Wertie would both go to teach in East St. Louis together, and continue to correspond and visit with each other. Ethel Black was from Wilmington, Delaware, and could boast of grandparents who were second generation free Blacks and property owners. Her maternal grandfather had fought in the Civil War, and her father was an entrepreneur in Black banking and retail enterprises. Her background might have prompted the following note, written humorously to Richardson, to keep their "high finance" books straight: "On account with Miss Naomi Sewell," Black's note began, "25¢, a ticket for a recital, 10¢ carfare, 9¢ a sheet in the laundry, 12¢ hairnet, 5¢ a pickle and 5¢ a cracker. 49¢ total. If there be any more, speak now or forever hold your peace. Ethel." These were not insignificant amounts when you considered that an advertised "first-class" lunch at the nearby Georgia Avenue Cafe was $0.15, a pair of shoes could be gotten for $2.50 and suits sponged and pressed for $0.25.

Ethel Black had arrived on the Howard campus after graduating with the highest scholastic average from the Industrial School for Colored Youth in Bordentown, New Jersey. The high school, like so many in the postwar period, had to accommodate students of all levels as there were so few of them; and its curriculum was not an advanced one. So Black had applied to the Howard Academy in 1909, where she certainly must have met three other future Deltas—Jimmie Middleton, from Lynchburgh, Virginia, whose parents were graduates of Shaw University and whose father, a physician, was, she said, the first Black to pass the Virginia State medical board tests; Edna Coleman, from Washington, D.C., whose father, Sterling Nelson Brown, was a former slave who had a distinguished career as professor of religion at Howard for thirty-one years; and Ethel Watson, who had come from Parkersburg, West Virginia, where she had attended the Sumner School, whose principal advised her parents to send her to Howard. All three young women were of the Academy class of 1909, of which Edna Coleman was valedictorian.

Frederica Dodd, another of Richardson's early close friends, was one of the most popular in the circle. She was stunningly attractive, and is described as having a coppery, smooth complexion and "hair that was straight a few inches from the roots and then turned into shiny, lush waves."[18] She wore little makeup and was a conservative dresser. Bertha Campbell remembers her as "very aristocratic in her speech and carriage, and soft-spoken in manner." She was born in Dallas, and her father was one of the early Black lawyers in Texas. Her mother, the descendant of a slave woman and the master's son, was educated in a Quaker, then a normal school and became a teacher. She was well known in the Dallas community, where the Fannie C. Harris Elementary School was named after her. Dodd attended the Dallas Colored School Number 2, and arrived at Howard University in 1910. She and Naomi Richardson would continue to correspond and visit each other over the next four decades, and the Texan would also have enduring friendships with two others from her home state, Jessie Dent and Myra Hemmings.

Dent was from Galveston and had graduated from East District High School, one of the first Black high schools in the state of Texas. Myra Hemmings was from Gonzales, Texas, though her family had moved to San Antonio while she was still a child; she graduated from Riverside High School in 1909. During her train ride to Howard, she would meet another young student also bound for the same destination by the name of Mamie Rose. Rose was coming to Washington from a small town called Beta, in South Carolina. Their encounter was an especially friendly one, and led to their becoming roommates in Miner Hall.

Of the group of twenty-two, Hemmings had, perhaps, the most outstanding leadership ability. Naomi Richardson describes her as very "sober, but friendly, and somewhat older than the rest." She was the kind of student that the others looked up to, Richardson recalled. Bertha Campbell was more direct: Myra, she said, "was a blustery one. Myra'd take over everything. . . . She worked for Miss Childers, worked for the director of singing, and of course, she felt she was as big as Miss Childers. . . . She tried to impress us with her bigness."[19]

Lulu Vere Childers, a graduate of the Oberlin Conservatory of Music, was appointed instructor of music at Howard in 1896. Childers would soon become a full-fledged professor, teaching both instrumental and vocal courses, as well as directing the Choral Society. She had tremendous influence and a reputation that extended beyond the campus. One of her students who graduated in 1917, Lillian Evans, or Madame Evanti as she became known, was, according to Logan, probably the first Black opera star of the twentieth century, and the first Black to sing at La Scala in Rome. On the campus, the Choral Society was extremely popular, of the extracurricular events, ranking second only to football.[20] The choir sang stirring renditions of Handel's *Messiah,* and the Black composer Samuel

Coleridge-Taylor's *Hiawatha's Wedding Feast.* Vocalists such as Roland Hayes and Florence Cole Talbert were also featured. The future founders had come to Howard at a time when music and the performing arts were beginning to be taken quite seriously by the administration, and that development would have an impact on many of their lives. In the years just preceding the Harlem Renaissance, there was already the conviction, as Kelly Miller stated, that "our colleges and universities must find some way to relate their motive to the awakening of the Negro's artistic powers."[21] Already, for example, plans had been made to develop a conservatory of music, headed by Childers, which was established in 1913.

Another member of Childers's choir was a student by the name of Pauline Minor, who one year would room with Naomi Richardson. Minor was born in Charlottesville, Virginia, and, by her own submitted biography to the sorority, did not know who her parents were or the exact date of her birth. She was reared by an aunt and uncle and graduated from the Philadelphia High School for Girls in Pennsylvania in 1910. As a member of the Union Baptist Church in Philadelphia, she sang in the choir, and through the influence of the dean of the Howard Teachers College, Lewis B. Moore, was given a church scholarship to the university. She was an excellent student and musician; those who knew her were not surprised when she graduated valedictorian of the Teachers College in 1914, or went on to become a mezzo-soprano recitalist and published hymn-writer.

In fact, an unusual number of the circle of twenty-two were involved in the arts at Howard. Ethel Black was also a member of the choir. Washingtonian Olive Jones, who would graduate with the majority of the twenty-two in 1913, would be a music teacher in the Washington public school system. Edith Young, from North Carolina, was known as an excellent pianist and dedicated her adult life to the education of her daughters at the Oberlin Conservatory of Music in Ohio.

However, it was drama that seemed to catch the fancy of most of the future Deltas. Leading this list was Osceola Adams, a Georgian from Albany, who was considered the most dramatic and elegant among them in manner, speech, and dress. She had a true artistic temperament, which emerged, unfortunately, when the first picture was taken of the twenty-two as a group. Although she was angry at the missed opportunity, Bertha Campbell recalled that "she wasn't there because she didn't want to come. She didn't want to be around all the time."[22] But she did want to perform on the stage and Howard was the beginning of a notable career in the theater. Adams was a leader of the Howard College Dramatic Club, which was directed by a man who came to Howard in 1910 and was destined to play a significant role in the first year of the sorority, Professor T. Montgomery Gregory. Zephyr Carter, who had her own kind of verve, was also in the dramatic group and gained campuswide fame for her role as Mistress Quickly in Shakespeare's *The Merry Wives of Windsor.* Also in that production was Edna Coleman, as her sister, Mrs. Elsie Brown Smith, recalls. The occasion was an especially memorable one, because in those times acting was not considered a respectable avocation for proper young women and the play was one of the few occasions on which the Brown younger sister was allowed to attend a theater.[23] In another production, *For One Night Only,* the cast included Adams, Carter, and another young woman destined to join their circle: Vashti Murphy.

Murphy, like Coleman and Jones, was from Washington, D.C. She was attractive and often pictured with a stylish hat. The Washingtonian had graduated from that city's famed M Street High School, the first public high school for Blacks in the United States, and during this period, unquestionably the best. The M Street School, later known as Dunbar High School, was the proud alma mater of such achievers as Sadie T. M. Alexander, Dr. Charles Drew—who developed the means to preserve blood plasma in blood banks—the lawyers Charles H. Houston, and his protégé William P. Hastie, who became the first Black governor of the Virgin Islands and later an outstanding judge. Its principals included a future judge, Robert H. Terrell, husband of Mary Church; and Anna J. Cooper, scholar, activist in the Black women's club movement, and writer.

After graduation, Murphy went on to Normal School Number 2 (later the Miner Normal School), which was associated with Howard. The "culture" of the normal school in the early twentieth century included not only pedagogy, but manners befitting a teacher. As a commentator noted, "Normal school students were taught correct posture when standing or sitting. In chapel, you sat stiffly erect. As the speaker of the day arose to speak, you leaned forward slightly as evidence that you were attentive."[24]

Upon completion of her studies, Murphy was appointed to teach in the Washington public schools in 1908. Shortly after she began teaching, however, she was struck by a devastating tragedy. She had lost her mother eight years before and within eighteen months of her teaching appointment, her father, sister, and brother also died. Nevertheless, her determination to succeed was undiminished. According to her daughter, Bettye Moss, after a year's experience in the classroom, she realized that her career would be limited with just a normal school diploma. And she might have been encouraged by the fact that in 1909, Howard's board of trustees approved the recommendation that tuition scholarships be given to the normal school graduates.[25] She enrolled in the Howard University evening school. Though several years older, Murphy had probably known the other Washingtonians, especially Eliza Shippen, who was from a well-known family in the District and whose father had attended Howard. After attending elementary school in Long Island, New York, Shippen had followed a similar path, graduating from both the M Street School, and, the first in her class, from Normal School Number 2 in Washington, D.C. Another District native was Florence Toms, the last survivor of six children in her family, who graduated from the Armstrong Manual Training High School with a ceremony made particularly memorable by her being awarded a diploma and scholarship by President William Howard Taft.

Of the "D.C." group, Murphy, despite the fact she was older, attended evening school, and was a shy, private person, enjoyed campus social and extracurricular activities. Of the latter, there were more than a few. In addition to the Choral Society and the Dramatic Club, there were six literary societies and debating clubs, which, as the *Record* stated, "through exercises, debates, oratorical contests, and renditions of choice dramas, provide for the student a training the value of which cannot be overestimated."[26] There were student chapters of the YWCA, "devoted to the development of Christian character in [their] members, and the prosecution of active Christian work,"[27] and a variety of student publications. Additionally, there was the opportunity to attend lectures by noted figures both on and outside the campus.

Many of the band of twenty-two would come to meet and know each other through these activities. Both before and after they formed their own organization, they were zealous in their pursuit of all of the opportunities campus life offered—opportunities that were now only opening for women. As Jimmie Middleton noted to the historian Helen Edmonds, "As positions in campus life opened to women, Delta girls were always in the vanguard of those seeking to fill them; in fact no aspect of Howard University's campus life open to women was unattended by the presence of some soror."[28] Madree White, for example, was the first female student to be on the staff of the *Howard University Journal*. As its associate editor, White, the young woman whose family had moved from Atchison, Kansas, to Omaha, Nebraska—where she graduated from Central High School with honors—would play an important part in documenting Delta's inception.

Along with Winnie Alexander, she was also a member of the College Classical Club, which opened its meetings with a prayer in Latin and discussed various topics in classical literature. On one occasion, Madree White read a paper entitled "The Ideal Orator As Discussed by Quintilian" (a Roman rhetorician known for his beautiful Latin style) and Alexander closed the discussion with a review of *Current Classical Literature*.[29] The Kansan was also the reporter for a group called the Arts and Science Club, whose purpose was to "act as a bond between the young ladies in Miner Hall and those in the city, in order that a true college spirit may be developed and fostered."[30] The president of the literary and social club was Mamie Rose, the young woman from Beta, South Carolina, who grew up in Mount Vernon, Illinois; the treasurer was Ethel Watson, from Parkersburg, West Virginia; and the critic, Zephyr Carter—all future Deltas.

The energetic Kansan also managed to find time to take part in a number of declamation contests, in which students matched their oratorical skills against one another. Naturally, Osceola Adams would participate in them and one year she performed John Greenleaf Whittier's "Polish Boy." Winnie Alexander once tried her hand at "A Second Trial", by S. W. Kellogg and White did "A Man Without a Country" by Edward Everett Hale.[31] Mamie Rose was cited for her awards as a dramatic reader.

Myra Hemmings, in addition to her duties with Miss Childers, was also a member of the Alpha Phi Literary Society, which presented programs such as the one honoring Samuel Coleridge-Taylor, the great musical composer of African descent. The program included piano selections from a distinguished future soror, who would miss being a founder by one year, Eva B. Dykes.

In addition to the arts and letters activities, there were also campus organizations such as the YWCA, which would have an important relationship with the sorority for decades to come. Winnie Alexander was in the Y cabinet in 1912 and 1913; Ethel Black was chairperson of its collegiate committee (1911–1912), and both White and Frederica Dodd served as president during their undergraduate years. These were important years for the Y's national organization, which in 1913 appointed its first "Colored Secretary," Eva Bowles. Addressing the YWCA student group, Coralie Franklin Cook, who would become one of the first honorary members of the sorority and a leading clubwoman and suffragist, read a letter from Bowles to the group. "The YWCA of Howard University," Bowles wrote, "is an ideal source from which we may find leaders for our women in the community life to which they will go when they leave school."[32] It was a message that formed the cornerstone of the young women's organizational lives. As teachers they would have a special role in that community life, and not surprisingly, the Teachers Club was also a popular one. Eliza Shippen, who would graduate magna cum laude in 1912, was a member, as was Pauline Minor, who was the president of the organization one year. Her achievements were cited in the NAACP's *Crisis* magazine, edited by W.E.B. Du Bois.[33]

The Crisis, in fact, devoted many of its pages to the activities and achievements of Black college students. The NAACP itself was only formally established in 1910, the same year that a student branch was organized at Howard. The presence of the student chapter may have been an issue of some controversy. The primary role of Du Bois in the formation of the civil rights organization had given it a radical image in the eyes of many. It certainly was widely perceived to have been created as a counterweight to the influence of Booker T. Washington—who had been a member of Howard's board of trustees since 1907—and his philosophy of industrial education and the forbearance of political inequality. In *The Souls of Black Folk,* published in 1903, Du Bois had written about the need for an intellectual vanguard—the "talented tenth"—to lead the fight for racial equality. And at Howard, he had his allies. Alain Locke, for instance, believed that the chief aim of Black education was to train a "racially inspired and devoted professional class with group service as their ideal."[34] Kelly Miller similarly believed that the race would not progress unless its educated leaders recognized their "racial responsibility and duty" and assumed their "rightful place in race leadership which their culture calls for and which the situation demands."[35] Such professors daily imparted these views to their students. Madree White recalled how Miller impressed upon her "that the talented tenth owed it to people who had made possible the special opportunity they'd had, to go back to that community and [help] to leaven the lump."[36]

By the late nineteenth century there were some "leavening influences" that promoted the progress of Blacks in general and Black women in particular. Though the numbers were still small, Black women had broken into the legal and medical professions. In fact, the first women of any color to practice medicine in the South were Black. There were nationally known journalists, the most famous of which was Ida B. Wells, who had initiated the first antilynching cam-

paign in 1892. Other leaders had emerged, particularly through the
National Association of Colored Women, founded in 1896, and stud-
ded with school founders, writers, former abolitionists, and successful businesswomen.

Nevertheless, the young women knew that as Howard students,
they were among the precious few Blacks able to attain a higher
education with a liberal arts curriculum. By the end of 1910, only
4,238 Blacks had received a bachelor of arts degree (79 had received
master's degrees and 11, doctorates).[37] Though figures for women
are not available, it can be assumed that they made up a very small
percentage of the above number. In 1910, for example, 227 women
received B.A. degrees, at a time when 80 percent of Black women in
the work force were performing arduous work on farms and as cooks
and washerwomen. At Howard, one of the largest of the schools
educating Black women, there were 25 women in its class of 1910.
The numbers were increasing by the time the 22 were at Howard;
and so too were the racial obligations they were taught. Some of
them would express that conviction through the student chapter of
the NAACP. Vashti Murphy, Winnie Alexander, Zephyr Carter, and
Madree White—who served as vice-president of the chapter in 1913
and 1914—joined its student branch. Carter, in fact, would be cited
by *The Crisis* magazine as the "leading spirit in the organization."[38]

W.E.B. Du Bois was a frequent lecturer in Washington, and was
a familiar figure on Howard's campus. At least on one occasion he
was invited before the Social Science Club to lecture on socialism, a
topic of much interest in those times when the exploitive nature of
expanding—and largely unchecked—industrialism was rearing its
head in this country. And in another, Russia, it had already lit the
fuse for an incipient socialist revolution. That Howard was dependent on a largely conservative Congress for federal funds made such
subjects inherently controversial, and the school was periodically
chastised and threatened for its liberal stance. Other programs, including one that featured the representative of a striking waiters
union in Washington, D.C., and another on woman suffrage, seemed
to make the club the most political and progressive of the student
organizations. And with the decidedly political bent of many of the
circle, it is no surprise that a number of them would be a part of it.
Zephyr Carter was a member and so was Vashti Murphy. Winona
Alexander served as its secretary one year; and Madree White, as
vice-president, had presided over the 1912 meeting where the address on woman suffrage was heard.

The young women also enjoyed the special events off the campus: The combination of political interests and social restrictions made them something to look forward to. The most important was "Howard Night," sponsored by the Bethel Literary and Historical Society at the city's Metropolitan AME Church. The chief aim of Howard Night, according to the *Journal,* was to bring the university "into closer touch with the city and to establish a higher appreciation of the importance of the university in the National Capitol."[39] During these evenings, the church would be filled to capacity. The center aisles on the main floor of the church were reserved for the visitors, friends, and guests. To the left and right of the middle aisles sat the professional-school students. The undergraduates sat in the gallery, and each class wore its own insignia, and sang its own class song during the course of the evening. Of course the most important element of Howard Night was the speeches they heard from those well known to them, like Terrell who was president of the Bethel Society. Others read from their works, talked about the evils of segregation, and reported on lynchings.

Howard Night added an important dimension to the college experience for its students. They were exposed to the city and its leaders. They had the opportunity to hear a variety of views on the great issues facing Blacks and the nation during these years. And it would help them further understand the complexities of racism and discrimination in a cosmopolitan place like Washington. For the young Bertha Campbell, who was spared the cruder aspects of discrimination in Montrose, the experience of not being able to eat in the city's "White" restaurants, or try on a dress before buying it, was a new one. Naomi Richardson wasn't quite as put out by it all. Washingtonville, New York, was as "prejudiced as anyplace in Mississippi, Alabama, or Georgia," she said. The racial situation might have seemed particularly ironic to Madree Penn White who had refused scholarships to the University of Iowa and the University of Nebraska, situated in the more tolerant West, to attend a Black school in a rigidly segregated city, where, by 1913, ninety-two thousand Afro-Americans resided. Of course, a number of the future sorors came from the South. Two were from Georgia, two from Virginia, one each from West Virginia, South Carolina, and North Carolina. Published news stories that promoted the worst stereotypes about Blacks and separate accommodations would be nothing new to them. The same was true for the four students from Texas, and the five "home girls" from D.C. The others from Wilmington, Chicago, and Kansas City were no strangers to racism either.

But with the university as a supportive ally, they now, at least, had a means and opportunity to analyze racial problems through their exposure to the great men and women of their time. They had also been privy to the ideas of woman suffrage, particularly from activists in the city such as Mary Church Terrell, and Nannie Helen Burroughs—founder of the National Training School for Girls and secretary of the Women's Auxiliary of the National Colored Baptist Convention—who were stressing the specific need for Black women to get the vote because of their greater vulnerability and the disenfranchisement of Black men in the South. The NACW, of which Terrell was the first president, had suffrage clubs in almost every major city in the country. What may have been more curious, and in its way more frustrating, was Howard's seeming inability to be as progressive on the woman question. Indeed, the university, tolerant of radical ideas when it came to race, was way behind when it came to the social freedoms of its female students or even the rights of its women on the faculty. The suffocating restrictions imposed on the women were in marked contrast to the ideas they heard from those like Du Bois, who during the years that the circle of twenty-two were students (and before he published them in his 1920 edition of *Darkwater*) told them that changed economic conditions demanded a "change in the role of women," and that women were "entitled to a career the same as men."[40] Entitled, and able, he could have added, for the Industrial Revolution that had begun in earnest by the turn of the century, had provided such work-saving innovations as sewing machines, gas-lighting, and refrigeration—devices that freed women to spend more time outside the home. Yet, as late as 1913, Howard's board of directors would vote that any female teacher who "thereafter married while teaching at the university would be considered as having resigned her position."[41]

All of this may have accounted for the new signs of restlessness among the women students. In 1912, for example, thirty-three coeds took the uncharacteristically bold step of formally requesting the president to appoint a dean of women who would have "general supervision" over them and "direct them in all womanly activities."[42] The request would not be granted for another decade.

These weighty issues, as well as the joy of sharing the heady experiences of college life, no doubt made joining a women's sisterhood an attractive proposition. So as soon as they were eligible, they looked to the newly formed sorority Alpha Kappa Alpha, or AKA, as it was known. It had been organized during the 1907–1908 academic year, and was the brainchild of a junior, Ethel Hedgeman, member of the class of 1909.[43] Born in St. Louis, Hedgeman had a background very much like that of the circle of twenty-two. She graduated with honors from Sumner High School in St. Louis, and was active in campus organizations, including the choir and the YWCA. She was encouraged by a member of the faculty, Ethel Robinson, who had graduated from Brown University, and shared her experiences of sorority life there with the young Hedgeman. Eight other students in the Liberal Arts School were approached and became interested in the idea of a sorority.

By January 15, 1908, Hedgeman was elected temporary chairperson of the organization and appointed committees to decide on the name, motto, and colors of the sorority. There was also a need for a constitution, of course, and that project was given to a student who would become AKA's first president and subsequently a force in Black women's education and Howard's first dean of women: Lucy (Diggs) Slowe. Within a week, the young women presented the plans for the organization to the Howard administration, including Dr. Wilbur P. Thirkield, the school's president, and Deans Lewis B. Moore and Kelly Miller. They received permission to function as a recognized campus group by the end of the month, becoming the first Black sorority in the nation, and the second Greek-letter organization established on Howard's campus.

Preceding AKA was the fraternity, Alpha Phi Alpha, which had evolved from a study group to a full-fledged fraternity on the campus of Cornell University, in Ithaca, New York, in 1906. A year later the second chapter of the fraternity was established at Howard. A number of influences, no doubt, were brought to bear on the establishment of the two organizations. There was the larger fraternity movement that had begun in 1776 with Phi Beta Kappa and by 1912 would number forty such organizations with a student membership of 256,087.[44] Sororities had started later, in the mid-nineteenth century, and had become more popular as increasing numbers of women attended college. The underlying ideas of Greek-letter life, which were scholastic, inspirational, and fraternal, had a particular appeal and urgency among Black students whose opportunities made them exceptions in their own communities and the object of neglect or hostility in the majority society. Women, experiencing new circumstances not only as Blacks but as females in a changing society, would also feel these things keenly. These ideas would be in even sharper relief at a Black institution whose curricula and exposure were roughly the same for men and women but whose social life was more sharply circumscribed and reflective of a previous era. So, it was no accident that the first Black fraternity was established at a predominantly White university, or that the first Black sorority emerged at a coeducational one like Howard.

In February of 1908, seven more students of the class of 1910 were admitted and are considered as part of the founding group of the sorority. As yet there was no initiation ritual, oath, or creed associated with the sorority, recalled Jimmy Middleton.[45] And it seemed to yet be conceived as an organization whose inner workings were for "women's eyes only," as the formalities were attended by a male member of the administration, probably George W. Cook, the dean of the Commercial College. To be eligible, one had to have completed at least the freshman and first half of the sophomore year, and have maintained an academic average of 75 percent.

The first efforts of the sorority, noted AKA historian Marjorie Parker, were "focused on their own talents, and were cultural in nature. "In the spring of 1908, for example, the group of sophomores who had been invited to join the original founders gave a concert in Rankin Chapel and used the proceeds of the concert to purchase badges for the entire group.[46] The young women's active participation in such organizations as the YWCA also identified them with projects of service and social uplift.

By 1912, a new generation of sorors had become members of the organization. The original group of the AKA founders received their diplomas in 1908 and 1909. The second tier of seven students belonged to the class of 1910. In the academic year 1911–1912, the circle of twenty-two would be eligible for membership, and being the kind of students they were, AKA would be an organization that was attractive to them. "All of us wanted to join," observed Bertha Campbell, "you didn't have to do much persuading."[47]

C H A P T E R   2

THE FOUNDING

There was change in the air in 1912. Change at Howard, change in the intensity of the women's movement: for the circle of twenty-two, it was a year of new possibility.

In the fall, returning students discovered that Wilbur P. Thirkield, president of the institution since 1906, had suddenly resigned to become a Methodist bishop. When his plans to leave became known, three of the university's deans, Kelly Miller, Lewis B. Moore, and George W. Cook, vied for the office, in the hopes that Howard was finally ready for a Black president. Nevertheless, their bids proved to be premature. In July it was announced that Stephen M. Newman, a White Congregationalist minister who was president of Kee Mar College, a small women's institution in Hagarstown, Maryland, would be Howard's new presiding officer. Nevertheless, Newman quickly invested the deans with new powers in order to "keep the peace." During his administration, Moore, Cook, and Miller gained enough autonomy in conducting Howard's affairs that they became known as the Triumvirate.

Although it would take some time for its tangible results to be seen in programs and curricula, the change in administration began a rising tide of Black consciousness at the university. Alain Locke proposed a provocative course in interracial history and Carter G.

Woodson, who would establish the Association for the Study of Negro Life and History in 1915, attempted to establish a course to study Black problems. In 1912, plans would be finalized to establish the long talked about conservatory of music; a new library would soon be the benefactor of trustee Jesse E. Moorland's extraordinary Afro-American collection. A new hospital was being built on the campus and the curriculum was deepening, especially in education. All of which seemed to give students a new zeal and sense of racial mission that had evolved into confidence. "That the Negro is a race endowed with untold energy, fifty years of unparalleled achievement in a civilization, the greatest since that of Rome, . . . is too much rehearsed to need comment here," wrote a student in the *Howard Journal* that year. "Every school boy and girl writes of our leaders, of our contributions to medicine, to the ministry, and all the other broad fields of human endeavor."[1] There was also a new pride in "the New Howard, the progressive Howard, the Howard of to-day . . . A visitor would find new life, vim, energy and dash, and not those proverbial, shrivelled, head drooped, monk-like leaders of auld lang syne," the lead article in the same October issue noted. Even the new facilities and buildings on the campus were a sign that "Howard is right in line to do the classical, scientific or whatever work is expected of her, second to no other institutions."[2]

Outside the campus, the issue of woman suffrage was heating up as states, in rapid succession, began to once again enfranchise women after a decade-long respite. By 1912, the organized suffrage movement was in full swing, with its leaders looking forward to the presidential election in the following year as a time to make a dramatic statement for women's enfranchisement. Washington, D.C., became not only a center of Black intellectual and social development, but of feminist activity as well.

At this high point of the Progressive Era, Howard, Afro-Americans and women were on the move—and so were the twenty-two young coeds who saw themselves an integral part of the developments swirling around them. They were proving their worth academically. They were participating in the fullness of extracurricular life. And they were showing their leadership abilities in those organizations as well as their respective classes. Madree White held the positions of class journalist, vice-president, and treasurer during her tenure at Howard; Bertha Campbell and Winona Alexander also were also elected vice-president, as was Vashti Murphy; and Osceola Adams was elected class secretary one year. And, true to form, many also rose to the top of the AKA leadership after they joined. An article in the October 18 issue of the *Howard Journal* announced the election of officers that took place at the October 11 meeting: Myra Hemmings, president; Ethel Black, vice-president; Edith Young, secretary; Jessie Dent, corresponding secretary; Winona Alexander, custodian; Frederica Dodd, sergeant at arms; and Pauline Minor, treasurer.

There are differing accounts of the exact sequence of events that took place within the organization in 1912; common to all, however, is that that year marked a growing dissatisfaction among the group. All of the officers, or course, were undergraduates, yet, by 1912, a great many of the AKAs had graduated and left school to begin their careers and/or family lives. For them, the vibrant issues of the times, or "the new Howard" would not have the same currency that it would with the undergrads. If still associated with Howard at all, many of the older students were dividing their time between student teaching in the city and the campus, observed Delta historian Mary Elizabeth Vroman. Another issue, indicated by Naomi Richardson, was the rivalry between the students of the Teachers College and those in the Liberal Arts School. In its earlier years, the AKAs were almost entirely made up of the latter. Many of the new officers and younger members of the sorority, however, including Minor, Young, Dent, Middleton, Shippen, Campbell, and Richardson were enrolled in the Teachers College. Richardson recalled the members of the two different schools voting against each other on various issues in a partisan way.

There were other dissatisfactions on the part of the younger group. In this time when the power of nationwide movements were being felt, there was a desire to form a link with other like-minded students across the country. Yet, according to Delta historian Edna Morris, the sorority "had no legal entity, was unincorporated, and had neither a charter nor the power to form other chapters."[3] In fact, there was no means to even maintain ties between graduates and undergraduates. Then there was concern that the name, Alpha Kappa Alpha, seemed to be more of a derivation of Alpha Phi Alpha than having any particular meaning of its own. Students like Edna Coleman thought the Greek titles for the AKA officers, such as Basileus, Anti-Basileus, Grammateus, Epistoleus, and Tamiouchos, unnecessarily pompous.

The restlessness of the younger women might also have been partially stimulated by their association with fraternity men, especially those of the newest fraternity to be established on Howard's campus,

Omega Psi Phi, which emerged in 1911. Among its founding members were three men who were so close they were called the Three Musketeers: Frank Coleman, who would have an outstanding career as a physics professor; Oscar Cooper, who would enter Howard's medical school after graduation and was a lab assistant to Ernest Just—also instrumental in Omega's founding—and Edgar Love, who would enter the School of Theology after graduation. All three were members of the class of 1913. The young men had had a less than easy time establishing their fraternity on campus. Then-President Thirkield had grudgingly allowed them to organize, but with the provision that they not attempt to form chapters on other campuses. According to Herman Dreer, the Omega historian, the men would not acquiesce to this demand, and finally won out.

Two of the fraternity founders were particularly close to several of the circle of twenty-two. Edith Young dated Edgar Love, who was deemed trustworthy enough for Myra Hemmings to confide to him their group's dissatisfaction and eventually their reorganization plans. Frank Coleman became engaged to Edna Brown around this time, and would marry her after their graduation. It is not unlikely that the men shared their own ordeal with the university's administration—and their insistence that the organization become a national one. This also may shed light on Jimmie Middleton's recollection of the close association that she and her close friends and college roommates, Osceola Adams and Marguerite Alexander—a Chicagoan who would subsequently cofound a chapter with Adams in that city—had with male friends who challenged them to form an organization similar to the fraternity that they had established.[4]

In any case the younger women had a desire to establish a national organization, enlarge the scope of activities of the sorority, change its name and symbols, and be more politically oriented. "A group of us felt that it was time for another sorority," recalled Naomi Richardson. "We had broader views. We wanted to reach out in the community. We wanted to be more than just a social group. We wanted to do more, when we graduated, for the community in which we were going."[5] Observed Bertha Campbell, "We wanted to change some ideas, we were more oriented to serve than to socialize."[6] Delta historian Edna Morris wrote, "Having received inspiration from the nation-wide feminist movement of 1912, the members of this group realized that they must do something to meet the challenge of the changing times."[7] Jimmie Middleton likened the decade of 1910–1919 to that of the sixties in terms of its spontaneity of action and the fight against indignities—for women in the former decade, and race in the latter.[8]

However, the number of these ideas that reached clear fruition in 1912 is not known. Of greater certainty is that the dissatisfaction and concerns of the younger AKAs were first seen in their desire to change the name of the sorority. It was Madree White, characterized by Bertha Campbell as "the inspiration to the whole Delta movement," who first went to AKA president Myra Hemmings to discuss the change of name, motto, colors, and symbols of the sorority. It was White's idea to make the violet the official flower: It connoted modesty, and even more poignantly, she thought, the violet, like Africans, had gone to the four corners of the earth. The purple and gold varieties signified the special bond that they had with the Omegas. The colors, crimson and cream, were chosen to symbolize courage and purity, respectively.

Hemmings was receptive to the idea, and according to the recollections of Ethel Black, the AKAs, including a number who had graduated, were contacted and asked if they would agree to the change.[9] The response from all contacted was that they would accept the changes. President Hemmings appointed Madree White to chair a committee to draft a constitution and set of bylaws, and to select the Greek-letter symbols and formulate an initiation ritual. For the name and symbols, members of the committee consulted a professor of Greek, Edward P. Davis. They arrived at the name Delta Sigma Theta, which denoted a phrase that had a particular meaning to its members.

In the fall of 1912, a sorority meeting was called whose agenda would be the proposed reorganization. Present were the undergraduates, and one member who had graduated that June, magna cum laude, and who had been president of the sorority in 1911. Nellie Quander was her name and she has been described as small-built, dynamic, firm, resourceful, and scholarly by Marjorie Parker, AKA historian. Bertha Campbell remembered her as a "go-getter," and Jimmie Middleton characterized her as a "chronic dissenter."[10] Quander, a native Washingtonian who was teaching in the city belonged to a family that was very close to the Browns; they were among the most active in the Reverend Sterling Brown's church. As Parker wrote, when the unknowing Quander heard of the proposed agenda and changes, she "was surprised, indeed her word was 'horrified,'"[11] at the undergraduates' plans. Unwittingly, the undergraduates may have added insult to injury by offering the graduates honorary membership in the new organization. Quander is said to have stormed out of the meeting and immediately contacted as many of the graduate members as she could to fight the planned reorganization. According to Ethel Black, she went even further. Quander was able to persuade the undergraduates to table their approval of the changes, then gave them a deadline to drop "Delta Sigma Theta" and return to the fold.

None of the twenty-two undergraduates acquiesced, however, and the deadline passed. This caused not a little trepidation in the group. Now they were no longer AKAs and had yet to get the approval of the board of trustees to become Deltas. "We did a little campaigning among the board members, who were on campus for one of their scheduled meetings," said Black. One with whom they talked was George C. Cook, "who was Howard University itself; and I believe . . . Dean [Lewis B.] Moore, and anyone else in the area to work for the approval of the name Delta Sigma Theta. You can imagine our anxiety," she continued. "Happily they agreed to the setting up of a second sorority on campus. With the change of the name, new ideas and objectives were brought into the organization," Black concluded.[12] A spate of organizing meetings ensued, many of them at the house of Edna Coleman, who lived at Sixth and Fairmont Street, N.W., considered the campus in those days. As her younger sister, Elsie Brown Smith, (a founding member of Beta Sigma, now the Washington Alumnae Chapter) remembered, "Delta was born in our living room."[13]

There is some debate as to how to characterize the split between the two organizations. Parker describes the undergraduates who sought changes as "dissenters." Florence Toms concludes that the "Delta girls did not necessarily secede from AKA but effected the dissolution of the former organization when twenty-two undergraduates, the entire active membership, constituting a sovereign body voted unanimously to reorganize."[14] Helen G. Edmonds, a historian who wrote an unpublished history of Delta, observed that "since the lone dissenter was a schoolteacher and theirs was an undergraduate organization dedicated to fostering scholarship on the college campus and cementing closer bonds among undergraduate students of like cultural and social tastes, they agreed that AKA should cease to exist." It was Miss Quander, Edmonds concludes, who "*seceded* from the group"[15] (emphasis in original).

Of more immediate concern to the undergraduates was to establish their new organization not only as an official one on the campus but as a legal, incorporated body. Those who remained in AKA had the same idea, and the rush to become the first to incorporate was the beginning of many competitive activities between the two groups. As Morris describes the sequence of events, "Each sorority knowing the intentions of the other to apply for a charter and file articles of incorporation, lost no time in performing whatever duties were necessary preliminary to filing for application."[16] The Deltas completed the requirements first, becoming as Johnson concludes, "the first sorority composed of undergraduate Negro women to apply to the trustees of any university for the right to become an incorporated body."[17] Her careful wording was due to the fact that although the Deltas seemed the first to apply for a charter, and received it on January 13, 1913, they were not the first to receive it. Though the undergraduates had submitted the application before the Christmas holidays, in December of 1912, the trustees didn't consider it until January 1913, when school reopened. According to Jimmie Middleton's recollections, when the charter application went through the university secretary's office, it was held up for a day, so that the AKA application would clear first—thus giving them the distinction of being the first sorority to be chartered (by about twenty minutes). Whether the delay was an intentional one is a matter of speculation, of course. But it is interesting to note that the university secretary and business manager was George W. Cook. And Cook, some years before, had had a close professional relationship with Lucy Slowe— the first president of AKA, who was his assistant, correcting papers for his English course and chaperoning undergraduate women students.[18]

In any case, it was at the midterm meeting of the trustees of Howard University when the application of Delta Sigma Theta sorority was considered and approved by the university. "On the Motion of Dr. Richards, seconded by Dr. Waring," reads the board of trustees' minutes of February 6, 1913, "permission was granted the Alpha Kappa Alpha Sorority and the Delta Sigma Theta Sorority to incorporate with the understanding that they omit the provision that they be permitted to organize chapters in other institutions." How they got around the limitation of organizing additional chapters is not entirely clear, although succeeding chapters were required to attain their own charters from the respective states in which they were established. The certificate of incorporation was issued on February 18, 1913, and noted that "the particular purpose and object of [Delta Sigma Theta] shall be to establish and maintain a high standard of morality and scholarship among women generally and especially among the women of the School of Liberal Arts of Howard University." By previous agreement, the officers of Delta would be the same as those elected in 1912 as AKAs, with the addition of Zephyr Carter in the office of reporter.

With its official founding date of January 13, 1913, a new Black women's organization was born. It had begun with a simple idea of changing a name and grew to one of looking toward a new direction and meaning of fraternal life. In the beginning its aims and objectives, as Osceola Adams later recalled, was outlined only in the broadest terms. They knew that they wanted to have "a more forceful influence in the lives of women students than any previous organization," Bertha Campbell noted.[19] They knew that they wanted to work "toward developing the sorority as "not only a social group but a working group," said Naomi Richardson, "and as each went off into her own community, she was to work as much as possible in that community to help and to organize."[20] Although there was regret that there "were some very good members who didn't feel they wanted to leave AKA," said Richardson, the twenty-two had more in common, and potential conflict among the group was greatly diminished. "There were, of course, many differences of opinion, and conflicting notions as to how things should be done," observed Adams, "but regarding matters of principle and ideals, there was a rare degree of unanimity."[21] That they had also come together under somewhat trying experiences also gave them a greater sense of camaraderie. As Florence Toms opined, "The new sorors banded themselves more closely together with the determination to succeed and exemplified a better esprit de corps, unhampered by the influence of teachers and housewives who belonged to the former organization but had little in common with the goals and aims of college students."[22]

Of course, it wasn't long before the inevitable rivalry between the two groups surfaced. In a February 1913 issue of the *Howard University Journal,* two articles were published denoting the claims of each group. Under the heading ALPHA KAPPA ALPHA, an article about the organization squarely confronted the charges of being merely a social sorority with little continuity between its graduate and undergraduate members. The article also sought to make it clear which of the two groups had historical precedent. "The Alpha Kappa Alpha Sorority of Howard University has the distinction of being the first and the only chartered sorority existing in a university which we can claim as being distinctly our own," it said pointedly. It "intends to prove that a college sorority need not be a factor merely in the social life of the student, but it shall lay its emphasis upon the promotion of the intellectual standards and the mutual uplift of its members. In this regard the graduate members have accepted a brief management of the sorority, and they shall always stand ready to help their sorority. . . . Undoubtedly, the Sorority is the strongest tie binding the women graduates to their beloved Alma Mater."[23] At the end of the article was a list of officers, or boule, in their Greek nomenclature, naming Nellie Quander as Basileus, along with three other AKA founders who had graduated and were teaching in Washington or Baltimore.

The members of Delta Sigma Theta countered with a more pithy article of their own. Under the headline, A SORORITY ORGANIZED, it stated: "Realizing that there was no true sorority in Howard University, and desiring to form one which would measure favorably with any secret organization, anywhere, the active members of an existing club by unanimous consent reorganized into a chartered organization to be known as the Alpha Chapter of the Delta Sigma Theta sorority of Howard University."[24] This too was followed by the names of the officers.

Competition would manifest itself in other ways. It was said that special kudos awaited the member of one sorority who managed to attract the boyfriend of a student belonging to another. However, the center ring was reserved for a "safer" pursuit: scholarship. For the two organizations, scholarship was also a quantifiable means of their competitiveness. In these years, the arena of rivalry was that of the grade point average, though other qualities of "finer womanhood" were also important. So it was for many reasons that the AKAs instituted at Howard the Alpha Kappa Alpha Sorority Prize "to be awarded to the young woman maintaining the highest scholastic average graduating with an A.B. or B.S. degree, after having successfully completed a four-year course at Howard University and who must at least have maintained *cum laude* grade."[25] The winner would receive a ten-dollar gold piece, not an inconsiderable sum for a student in 1913. If the award motivated women generally, its meaning would be a special one to the Deltas. Helen Edmonds wrote that "Delta women of the period declared that they studied night and day to maintain superiority in numbers on the university's honor roll; and when they could not manage that they settled for nothing less than parity."[26] Jimmie Middleton added that their "conscientious efforts" were not limited to the honor roll. The AKA prize was, as one can imagine, a real plum for the Deltas.

On both counts the Deltas seemed successful. In the very year following the establishment of the AKA prize in 1913, Eva B. Dykes won it. And at least for the next few years, the new sorority would outscore the old when it came to grades. This was verified by Numa P. G. Adams, a member of Alpha Phi Alpha fraternity and a chemistry professor who subsequently became the first Black dean of the Howard Medical School (and husband of Osceola Macarthy). In a campaign to prove that members of Greek-letter groups benefited from their associations, he kept a comparative record of their averages and published them in the *Journal*. The conclusions showed that peer pressure resulted in higher grades among the fraternity and sorority members. When taken group by group, the sororities outscored the fraternities, and in the 1914–1915 school year, the Deltas had the highest average of any of the Greek-letter organizations.* In addition, there was a significantly higher percentage of Deltas on the university's honor roll, which required an average of 80 percent or above.† Also in 1915, of the thirty-one active members of the sorority, twenty-one were on the honor roll. And as Mary Elizabeth Vroman found, the Deltas outscored the other groups for both semesters in 1916 as well.[27]

THE SUFFRAGE MARCH

Grade-point averages were not the only thing on the young women's minds, however. They always had been anxious to become involved with the greater issues of their times, and the opportunity presented itself in 1913. There was much excitement in the Washington, D.C., air during the early months of that year. The quest for woman suffrage was reaching a new pitch as states, individually, began to give women the vote. In those days, enfranchisement of women was the dominant issue among proponents of women's rights. It was believed that the ability to vote for elected officials was the key to assuaging every aspect of women's inequality. For Black women as a group, the issue was even more compelling. "If White women needed the vote to acquire advantages and protection of their rights," noted Adella Hunt Logan, the leading suffragist of the Tuskegee Woman's Club, "then Black women

*The average for Delta Sigma Theta was 76.82 in the first semester and 79.90 in the second. For AKA the figures were 75.98 and 77.84, respectively.
†In the first semester, 56.52 percent of the Deltas were on the honor roll; in the second semester, the percentage was 64.52. For Alpha Kappa Alpha, the percentages were 34.78 and 50.00).

needed the vote even more so."[28] As women were more vulnerable to sexual exploitation and stereotypes of immorality, the vote was seen as a means of protection. Black women needed the ballot "to reckon with men who place not value upon her virtue, and to mold healthy sentiment in favor of her own protection," opined Nannie Helen Burroughs, founder of the National Training School for Girls and secretary of the Women's Auxiliary of the important National Colored Baptist Convention.[29] Enfranchisement would also be a boon to education, as a result of greater influence with legislators and school boards; and it would help them in the work force—an important consideration because the vast majority of Black women of every economic class had to work. Finally, the issue was an especially compelling one because in the years after Reconstruction, Black men in the South, who had been enfranchised in 1870, were no longer a political force. Through violence, "legal," and extralegal means, they were systematically disenfranchised. Granting of the vote to women, especially in the South where in some states they would be the largest class of voters, would mean race empowerment and in the opinion of such southern senators as Ben "Pitchfork" Tillman of South Carolina, the end of White supremacy. "Votes for women," observed W.E.B. Du Bois, "means votes for Black women."[30]

Nevertheless, as the Deltas undoubtedly knew, Black women suffragists had few allies. Many Black men were fearful of the social implications of empowering women. The predominantly White suffragist organizations such as the Congressional Union and National American Women's Suffrage Association (NAWSA)—the most prominent among them—were reluctant to advocate suffrage for Black women because of the White supremacists within their ranks; or, in view of the power of racist congressmen, because of political expediency. Consequently, they were reluctant to include Black women's concerns on their organizational agendas—or in their public demonstrations.

This was evident before the parade started. NAWSA and the Congressional Union told Ida B. Wells that she and her Alpha Suffrage Club, the first Black suffrage club in the state of Illinois, would not be able to march with the Whites from the state in the prescribed alphabetical order; they would have to march at the rear of the line. Whether the venerable activist would acquiesce to such an insult remained to be seen.

The young Deltas must have been aware of some of these tensions, if only through their association with Mary Church Terrell, who would become one of their first honorary members and author the official Delta Oath. She and her husband, Robert Terrell—a municipal judge and professor at the Howard University School of Law during this period—were, in the words of Rayford Logan, "among the most noted Negro leaders of social, cultural and intellectual life in Washington."[31] What precise role Mary Terrell played in the Deltas' initial decision to participate in the suffrage march is unknown. Jimmie Middleton, however, recalled that she urged their participation.[32] It was a weighty decision on the part of the young sorors. There were rumors that the demonstration would be met by derision and maybe even violence on the part of the onlookers. And as Black women they knew that they could be even more of a target. "Don't be demonstrating, they won't let you because you're colored," Bertha Campbell remembered hearing. "If they [White women] get the vote, we will too, someday."[33]

There was also concern about the attitude of a strict Howard administration. Would they allow the young women off campus to take part in a potentially dangerous exercise? Could such a demonstration, which challenged a newly elected President, affect Howard's dispensations from the government? And what about the attitudes of the professors? It may have been known that for all of his other progressive ideas, Dean Kelly Miller was unsympathetic to woman suffrage. He believed that "there may be some argument for suffrage for unfortunate females, such as widows and hopeless spinsters, but such status is not contemplated as a normal social relation."[34]

Despite all of these drawbacks, the young students, much to their credit, decided to forge ahead. Advocating suffrage for women was "a part of our program and this was our first opportunity to put our program into action," noted Florence Toms.[35] Indeed, the parade scheduled for March 3 would take place less than two months after Delta's founding date. According to Naomi Richardson, it was Osceola Adams who first began rallying her new sorors to take part in the demonstration. Adams of course had not only a keen political sense but a penchant for high drama. Surprising to many, the administration gave its okay—perhaps owing to the influence of the Terrells. But there was another—and ironic—problem to solve: A male chaperon would have to be found to accompany them off the campus. After some searching, a professor by the name of T. Montgomery Gregory expressed his willingness to help them out. Gregory had come to Howard in 1910 and was, for many years, the director and "inspiration" for Howard's Dramatic Club—a favorite of many of the Deltas. He also had a close relationship with Edna Coleman's family, and was a frequent visitor to their home. Her sister remembers that he had a special foundness for Mrs. Brown's apple pie. And so, the founders of Delta Sigma Theta were ready to engage in their first public act as a group and one that would leave an indelible mark on their memories.

There was tremendous excitement among them. Florence Toms confided that she was told by her family, not to march, but was forced to defy the order because she was drafted to hold the banner since she was the tallest. She was anxious, if exhilarated by the experience. Naomi Richardson said that she was too naïve to be frightened. "I just wanted to march, be involved," she said.[36] When they reached Pennsylvania Avenue, the path of the demonstration, and began marching, it must have been an awesome sight for these young women. Thousands participated (news estimates ranged from 5,000 to 10,000), representing states, countries, organizations, colleges. News reports described the marchers: women from all walks of life, in every conceivable color and fashion. Floats added to the pageantry, as the women and male sympathizers walked to the Pan-American Union building while some 250,000 onlookers cheered them on. But there was also the negative side to the experience. Bertha Campbell described how, when they marched down the street, "the men threw things at us. They were saying 'Go back to the kitchen.' There was a lot of police and you didn't dare step onto the sidewalk."[37] Reporters on the scene described the full extent of the behavior of the mob. *The Baltimore Afro-American* described

> *five thousand women, marching in the woman suffrage pageant today, practically fought their way foot by foot up Pennsylvania Avenue through a surging throng that completely defied Washington police, swamped the marchers, and broke their procession into little companies. The women, trudging stoutly along under great difficulties, were able to complete their march only when troops of cavalry from Fort Myers were rushed into Washington to take charge of Pennsylvania Avenue. No inauguration has ever produced such scenes, which in many instances amounted to nothing less than riots.[38]*

Another story noted:

> *The women had to fight their way from the start and took more than one hour in making the first ten blocks. Many of the women were in tears under the jibes and insults of those who lined the route. At Fourth Street progress was impossible. The Commissioner called upon some members of a Massachusetts National Guard regiment to help clear the way. Some laughed, and one assured the Commissioner they had no orders to act as an escort. At Fifth Street the crowd again pressed in and progress was impossible. The Thirteenth Regiment, Pennsylvania National Guard, was appealed to and agreed to do police duty. . . . Very effective assistance was rendered by the students of the Maryland Agricultural College, in guarding the women marchers. It was where Sixth Street crosses the avenue that police protection gave way entirely and the two solid masses of spectators on either side came so close together that three women could not march abreast. It was here that the Maryland boys formed in a single file on each side of the "Pilgrims" and became a protecting wall. In front a squad of the boys locked arms and formed a crowd-breaking vanguard. Several of the "war correspondents" were forced to use their fists in fighting back the crowd. . . . The parade itself, in spite of the delays, was a great success. Passing through two walls of antagonistic humanity, the marchers, for the most part, kept their tempers. They suffered insult, and closed their ears to jibes and jeers.[39]*

If the White suffragists had reason to be frightened by the scene, Blacks had more to worry about, especially since they could depend on little support from the organizers. But Black women handled themselves admirably. Some may have seen the indomitable Ida B. Wells slip out from the crowd to join the Chicago contingent, and march in her rightful place. And so did the Deltas, emphasized Madree White, "thus helping to break down the tradition of Negroes [taking] their place at the tail end."[40]

And although Toms reported that the Delta participants were indeed criticized for their activities, none regretted what they had done. "Yes, we marched and we did receive criticism, but we expected that," she observed. "Those were the days when women were seen and not heard. However we marched that day in order that women might come into their own, because we believed that women not only needed an education, but they needed a broader horizon in which they may use that education. And the right to vote would give them that privilege." The demonstration, she continued, "was not only city-wide, it was nation-wide, it was international and it was the day we launched our program."[41] It was a day, as Madree White would write, to "exult" over the fact "that in those years Delta took a stand."[42] It was also a day in which other leaders would praise their comrades-in-arms. "In spite of the apparent reluctance of the local suffrage committee to encourage the colored women to participate, and in spite of the conflicting rumors that were circulated and which disheartened many of the colored women from taking part, they are to be congratulated that so many of them had the courage of their convictions and that they made such an admirable showing on the first great national parade," editorialized W.E.B. Du Bois in *The Crisis*.[43] The new sorors of Delta Sigma Theta were proud that his words included them.

CHAPTER 3

EXTENDING THE VISION: NATIONALIZING AN IDEA

Eliza Shippen had graduated from Howard in 1912, and thirteen more members of the original circle of twenty-two were preparing to graduate the following spring. In May of 1913, Myra Hemmings, who had the distinction of being the president of both the AKA and Delta sororities, stepped down from office, and, not surprisingly, Madree White was elected to take her place. It was under the administration of White, who had been so important to the founding of the new sorority, that the first initiation ceremony, conceived by her committee just a few months before, took place.[1]

The torch was passed to fifteen students who were inducted into the Delta membership: Alberta and Ceretta Desmukes, Grace Coleman, Eva B. Dykes, Edith M. Chandler, Louise Denny, Beatrice Hardy, Jemima Harris, Eulalia M. Lane, Ruby A. McComas, Clara M. Oliver, Meta A. Redden, S. Edessa Toles, Ruth A. Tuell, and M. Frances Gunner. Most were members of the classes of 1914 and 1915, and a number of them seemed to possess the same zest for all aspects of university life as the founders. Grace Coleman, sister of

Omega founder Frank Coleman, was elected Delta president in 1914, as well as class secretary. Eva B. Dykes, the gifted student who had won the AKA ten-dollar gold prize, had been her class secretary in 1910, and was also a talented musician. She was the pianist for the Alpha Phi Literary Society, and her musical abilities were also sought beyond the campus. In January of 1914, she was the accompaniest for Jacob Jones, who performed before the Bethel Literary and Historic Society.

The second group of initiates also possessed the characteristic fun-loving, wholesome spirit of their predecessors, as seen in a *NIKH* description of Alberta Desmukes:

> *Alberta Desmukes, "Bert." Born in Gonzales, Texas. This demure Miss has pretty well succeeded in evading most of the male sex, and remains unconquered. Most of her time has been spent in applying herself to her studies so that she may become an efficient teacher, but how long she will continue in this mood cannot be told. The hubbub of student life has not greatly upset Alberta and she has remained a serious earnest student, but, withall, filled with a great sparkle of life. She is an active member of Delta Sigma Theta Sorority and finds much pleasure in pursuing her duties in that organization. Her address, which some will be delighted to learn, is 209 0 St., N.W. Washington, D.C.[2]*

The "pleasure" of sorority activities was also enjoyed by the others, as noted in the *Howard Journal*. Many, no doubt, attended the second annual reception of Omega Psi Phi, in December of 1913, which was "thronged with guests" who with "eager eyes" scrutinized their fraternity house where it was held.[3] In January of 1914, there were the social activities that accompanied the sixth annual convention of Alpha Phi Alpha, said to be "unquestionably the best in the history of the fraternity." And, of course, there was Delta's own annual banquet, which in November of 1913 was reported to be hosted by Vashti Murphy who, "in her own inimitable way officiated as toastmistress scattering on all sides laughter and good cheer." The evening was described as "a renewal of the best womanhood and college ideals and aims. Miss Nannie Burroughs and Mrs.

Coralie Franklin Cook were among the honorary members present. Among the graduate members were Misses Lee Shippen, Olive Jones and Florence Letcher. . . . In all there were present about 45 members who spent together a social evening full of pleasure and profit."[4]

But, social activities were not enough to satisfy the young women in the year that they had already participated in the suffrage parade. In December of 1913, they were the only Howard student group to send a delegate to the Intercollegiate Socialist Society conference, held from December 29 through 31 in New York City. Reporting on the event, the *Howard Journal* observed that the society was founded in 1905 "to promote an intelligent interest in socialism among college men and women." Some sixty-five colleges were members of the organization, including Yale, Harvard, Radcliffe, Simmons, and Columbia. The Delta delegate—and the only Black student present—was M. Frances Gunner, one of the newly initiated members who was vice-president of her class, an associate member of the *Journal,* vice-president of the Howard NAACP chapter, and a future chapter president of the sorority. At the meeting, Gunner heard speakers such as suffragist Harriot Stanton Blatch, daughter of suffragist Elizabeth Cady Stanton, who spoke on "Suffrage and Socialism"; and the NAACP founders William English Walling and W.E.B. Du Bois. The latter's discussion of the economic "history of the race since the war" was met by "thunderous applause,"[5] the *Journal* noted, bringing about a heated debate over whether race prejudice was primarily a function of economic problems or social prejudice. Gunner's opinion about the matter was specifically sought out, and one can imagine both the trepidation and the exhilaration the young women must have felt by being in the spotlight among such prominent figures. Though which side she took was not recorded in the article, the racial significance of the conference and of socialism, itself, was expressed. "As Socialism is one of the most discussed subjects of the day and is a growing factor in the life of all civilized nations, it behooves the broadminded student to devote some time to an impartial study of its principles and work," wrote the author of the article, which though not named was probably Gunner herself. "Particularly should the young colored student be interested in it because of its fair and open attitude toward racial issues," the article concluded.[6]

The Deltas' interest in the political issues of the day was also reflected in the induction of their first honorary members—nonstudents who were invited into the organization because of their outstanding achievements. Mary Terrell was invited as an honorary member as was Coralie F. Cook. Both women were active in the Washington Colored Women's League, established in 1892, and the first Black women's organization established that would become a part of the national Black women's club movement manifested as the National Association of Colored Women's Clubs, founded in 1896. In that year Terrell was named as the first president of the organization that predated both the NAACP and the National Urban League and was a potent force in the development of social institutions in the Black community and in the woman suffrage and other political movements. Coralie Cook was also an ardent suffragist and like Terrell a member of the National American Women Suffragist Association and a friend and associate of Susan B. Anthony's. The students had heard her address them on several occasions about participation in the YWCA and other groups. Other early honorary members included Nannie H. Burroughs, founder of the National Training School for Girls in Washington, D.C., secretary of the powerful Women's Auxiliary of the National Colored Baptist Convention, and associate editor of the *Christian Banner,* a Philadelphia newspaper.

In addition to women of such national reputation, Deltas also inducted women who were important figures on college campuses. The very first honorary member invited into the organization was Mrs. Gabrielle Pelham who had been Howard's director of music between 1905 and 1907 and was a graduate of Adrian College in Michigan. Her husband, Robert Pelham, was a well-known newspaperman, who cofounded the Detroit *Plaindealer,* and subsequently became publisher and editor of the *Washington Tribune.* He was also the founder of the Capital News Service, which furnished syndicated news items to over a hundred weekly newspapers throughout the country. Both of Pelham's daughters would be active with the sorority; one of them, Dorothy, would serve as national president from 1923 to 1926.

As in academic achievement, honorary members could also be a source of competition between the two sororities. In 1913, AKA proudly announced that their first honorary member was Jane Addams, the well-known social reformer of Hull House in Chicago. Among the faculty members, Mrs. Kelly Miller, wife of the powerful Howard dean, was also inducted.

LIFE AFTER HOWARD

By the spring of 1914, all of the founders, with the exception of Ethel Black (who because of illness would not graduate until 1915) would leave the universe of the Howard campus to pursue their professions and adult lives. They were not only among the 68 graduates who would earn their bachelor's degree from Howard, which now had an enrollment of 314 students, including 55 women in the Liberal Arts School; they were also a part of national history. The year marked the "largest colored class in modern history," *The Crisis* boasted.[7] In 1914, 291 degrees were conferred upon Afro-Americans nationally according to Charles S. Johnson. *The Crisis* also noted the fact that Eva B. Dykes led her class, graduating summa cum laude; as did Pauline Minor in the Teachers College. Though Dykes was selected as the "Most Versatile" in the year-end class vote, neither she nor Minor would win the "Most Brilliant" title. That went to Grace Coleman, who graduated magna cum laude and planned to do graduate work in the classics. For her part, Dykes would continue her studies at Radcliffe, where she became the first Black woman to complete her requirements for a Ph.D. She actually received it soon after Sadie T. M. Alexander, the first to actually earn the degree, was granted hers. Madree White was named the "Most Popular" of the class and came in third for "Who Has Done the Most for Howard." They were a well-rounded group.

Ten of the original founders would also pursue graduate study at a time when master's degrees were still rare among Blacks. Through 1936, a total of fifteen hundred had been granted to Afro-Americans.[8] Only Shippen would earn a Ph.D, which she received from the University of Pennsylvania in 1944.

As would be expected, most of the founders taught after graduation with the exception of Mamie Rose, who was a homemaker, and Marguerite Alexander who became a French and Spanish correspondence secretary for a Chicago business firm. In these years, even teaching could be filled with hazards, and not a little drama, as Naomi Richardson recalled.

Along with Wertie Weaver, Richardson had received a recommendation, from Dean Lewis B. Moore, to be appointed to the East St. Louis public school system after graduation. The schools were, of course, segregated and Richardson remembers that the building to which she was assigned wasn't large enough for all of the children, so one-room schoolhouses were built in back of the main building to accommodate them. She taught third, fourth, and fifth grade. The system was set up so that there were supervisors for writing, music, and reading. Evidently, the young graduate, possessing the self-confidence that came from her experiences at Howard, didn't show the kind of anxiety that the others did when the supervisors came around to assess her teaching. "I remember," she said, "that one of the supervisors wanted to know why I wasn't afraid and nervous when she came by to see me. So I answered that 'Well, I'm doing the best that I can. So why should I be afraid?'"[9]

More disconcerting was the situation she had to confront outside of the classroom. Richardson had already witnessed Ku Klux Klan cross burnings in Washingtonville, New York, and during these years East St. Louis was the scene of bitter race riots. "I remember that as soon as it became dark, we would put out all of the lights in the boarding house where we lived, because we were afraid of the stone throwing through our windows. I can remember how a dentist and a physician from St. Louis would carry ammunition back and forth on a loaded hearse. They'd go across and pick it up in St. Louis and bring it back to East St. Louis. This went on for the two years that I was there," she concluded, "I never returned after the second year."[10]

By that time she had heard of another teaching position in Princeton, New Jersey. Sewell's father was a Presbyterian minister and while attending a meeting there he heard that the Princeton school system there was looking for a sixth-grade teacher. Her father gave the appropriate people her name, and Naomi promptly sent in an application. And "fortunately," she was accepted. It was there that she met Paul Robeson, who was then attending Rutgers University, and who would visit her and others who lived together in a boarding house. On the weekends, they had sing-alongs, as she called them, and Robeson would join in. Soon after that first school year was over, she met and married Clarence Richardson, before coming to New York City where she was a substitute teacher in the public schools. Both she and her husband, an Alpha, hoped that neither's funeral would clash with a fraternal function. As Richardson said, one couldn't be sure which event the other would attend.

Like Richardson, all of the founders, with the exception of Olive Jones and Eliza Shippen, married. Three wed Howard professors: Edna Brown, Frank Coleman, Omega founder, who went on to become a physics professor at Howard; Osceola Macarthy, Numa P. G.

Adams, an Alpha who was a summa cum laude graduate of the university in 1911, received his master's in chemistry from Columbia University, and would return to teach at Howard, before becoming the first Black dean of its medical school; and Vashti Turley, Carl Murphy, also an Alpha who was a graduate of Howard and Harvard, instructor of German at Howard, and later editor and publisher of his father's paper, *The Baltimore Afro-American.*

Most of the founders had children. Vashti Murphy seemed to have the most (five, all daughters and all Deltas), and Jimmie Middleton's first of two daughters had the distinction of being the first born to a founder. Catherine Brown Middleton was born in January of 1916, and Middleton's second, Amanda Belle, was born the following year.

Although many of the founders chose traditional paths taken by educated Black women of the era, an amazing number also ventured into less traditional areas—especially the arts. It was only in the late nineteenth century that Black women began publishing books in any numbers, becoming known as artists, or making national reputations on the stage. From their undergraduate days, the circle of twenty-two had shown a penchant for such activities—a quality that was characteristic of their nonconformist sensibilities. And many of them pursued their artistic expression in various ways.

Osceola Adams was the most outstanding in this regard. She had dreamed of a career on the stage and relentlessly sought its fruition. And relentless she would have to be. Upon graduation Adams, who adopted the stage name Osceola Archer, found that she could not get into the drama school of her choice. "I wanted to go to the American Academy of Dramatic Arts," she recalled, "but was refused because of my race. Finally I was accepted by the American Repertory Theater."[11] Her skin color presented another obstacle: She was too fair to fit the perceptions of directors for Black parts, so she often had to play non-Black roles, such as Miss Prism, in Oscar Wilde's *The Importance of Being Earnest.* By the thirties, she did make her debut on the Broadway stage; and also directed at such places as the American Negro Theater. It was there that she was called to be the director of a play entitled *Days of Our Youth* featuring two young men making their dramatic debuts: Harry Belafonte and Sidney Poitier.

Even when she was forced to teach between jobs, she kept her focus on drama—and breaking down racial barriers. Between 1939 and 1941 she taught dramatic arts at Bennett College in Greensboro, North Carolina, where in that short period she made a historical first for the school and Blacks. Bennett was invited to participate in the North Carolina Drama Festival, an annual event sponsored by the association of drama departments from colleges and high schools throughout the state. Adams's group were invited as guests, as there were no Black affiliates in the association, and therefore they were not an official part of the competition. But when the invitation came, she thought it an "excellent opportunity to propagandize these young white people."[12] She selected Paul Peters's *Letter to the President,* a drama about a Black sharecropper whose frustration at being unable to support his family by farming under that exploitive system violently retaliates against the White farm owner. The title of the one-act play came from a scene in which the young daughter of the sharecropper writes a letter to the President begging him to somehow stop the lynch mob that has gathered outside their cabin door. In the end, the mob succeeds in burning down the cabin, consuming the entire family within its flames.

Although the Bennett group was technically ineligible to take part in the competition, their performance was so moving that they received the winner's plaque—the first time a Black group had done so in the twenty-five years of its history.

Adams wasn't the only one to pursue the arts. Myra Hemmings, who received her master's in speech from Northwestern University, and taught in San Antonio, was also very active in amateur theater. She was a major figure in the San Antonio Negro Little Theater, where she directed many of its productions. Her husband, John "Pop" Hemmings was a dramatist and its director. Ethel Watson, in addition to her teaching career, noted that she was well remembered for her dramatic performances in Ocala, Florida, where she once presented *She Stoops to Conquer,* and in her home Parkersburg, West Virginia's, Smoot Theater. In the latter she presented two "all-colored revues—giving an exceptionally clever performance and displaying gorgeous costumes which I designed and made of satins, tricotine spangles, and tarleton," she wrote in a bio sketch. "I have been the only colored who has ever given a performance at Smoot Theater for Warner Brothers in Parkersburg, West Virginia," she noted.[13]

There were also wordsmiths in the group. To no one's surprise Madree White, who believed deeply in Kelly Miller's conviction of the power of the pen to fight injustice, became a journalist; she also wrote poetry, and gathered a number of poems in a volume titled *Reveries in a Poetic Vein.* Wertie Weaver published a novel, *Valley of the Poor,* about racism, poverty, and exploitation—"diseases" that science attempts to overcome.

Others also honed their talents in the musical arena. After briefly teaching in San Antonio, Zephyr Carter moved to California, and worked as a security officer for the state's Department of Employment—perhaps to help support her love for singing chorus background music for films and television shows. Pauline Minor taught school in Alabama, South Carolina, and Pennsylvania, and also embarked on a career as a soprano soloist and hymn writer. She became a missionary in the Apostolic Church of Philadelphia, and published a book, *Soul Echoes,* which featured forty of her own compositions, including "My Lord Is a Refuge" and "Get Off the Judgment Seat." Minor also sang selections from Handel, Black composer Harry Burleigh, and others in recital.

EXTENDING THE VISION

Throughout their lives, many would continue their deep friendships—for "we were like a family," as Richardson observed—found chapters and participate in Delta activities, and watch the organization grow to heights that even they had never dreamed. Through it all they would have the satisfaction of knowing that they had created a new women's organization, one that responded to an age to that "demanded wide-awake, constructive, concerted action for the goals of Negro womanhood . . . and all womanhood," as Vashti Murphy observed.[14] Such deep feelings in a period when national Black organizations were emerging as effective weapons against racism, sexism, and social isolation were certain to take root on other campuses. As news of the establishment spread among the growing Black college population, interest grew. Among the first to express their desire to join this burgeoning national movement were coeds attending Wilberforce University in Ohio. Wilberforce, named after an English abolitionist, William Wilberforce, was established in 1855 by the Cincinnati Conference of the Methodist Episcopal Church. Its first students, according to John Hope Franklin, were mainly the "mulatto children of Southern planters."[15] It was closed briefly at the beginning of the Civil War, then reopened under the auspices of the African Methodist Episcopal Church. (Its list of leading professors included Mary Church Terrell, who taught there early in her professional career.) Mutual interest spurred correspondence between Ruby Martin—a Wilberforce sophomore (who would graduate magna cum laude) from Germantown, Ohio—and Madree White as early as 1913. There were eight students on the Ohio campus eager to join the sorority and the time to act on it came in 1914. Ruby Martin and Howard's Frances Gunner were both slated to be delegates from their schools for a student conference in Atlanta, Georgia, that year. Alpha Chapter authorized Gunner to conduct initiation rites for Martin and to instruct her in the procedure for establishing Beta Chapter when she returned to Ohio. This was done and in that year, Annie Singleton, Margaret Glass, Bernice Sandler, Helen Ferguson, Beatrice Mason, Freddie Billings, Nakomis Boyd, Marie Ody, Iolyn Springfield, and Ruby Martin became the charter members of the second chapter of Delta Sigma Theta to be organized, on February 5, 1914.[16] Ever vigilant of the potential influence of honorary members, the establishment of Beta Chapter also gave Deltas the opportunity to induct prominent women. They would include Sarah Scarborough, wife of Wilberforce president Dr. William Scarborough, whose home was opened to the members of the chapter and became unofficially known as the Delta House; Josephine Washington, dean of women at the institution; and an instructor, Julia Gee Hunnicut. The most prominent among them however, Hallie Quinn Brown, a Wilberforce graduate in 1873, had recently been elected to its board of trustees. She was a nationally known educator, serving as dean of Allen University in Columbia, South Carolina, before teaching at Wilberforce; and a lecturer and elocutionist who traveled widely. In the 1890s, Brown had toured England—where she had been the guest of the princess of Wales— speaking and raising funds for the Ohio university, as well as speaking on behalf of the International Women's Conference and the World's Women's Christian Temperance Union. One of the forces in the national Black women's club movement, Brown was president of the Ohio State Federation of Women's Clubs, and also vice-president of the Ohio Council of Republican Women.

Both the establishment of the undergraduate chapter and the addition of these honorary members were historic events in themselves. But how Beta came about has deep implications, as Helen Edmonds points out. In order that the Wilberforce chapter be established, Alpha Chapter relinquished some of its sovereign power, and delegated authority. This tradition would be an important one, distinguishing the sorority from those organizations and institutions that were more autocratic—including the universities that most had attended. Also Beta Chapter was given an equality in the sisterhood without "a trial or probationary period," and so looked upon it as a peer. The commonality of interests was greater than the need for supremacy of the founding chapter, situated at "the Capstone of Negro Education," as Howard was known in fashionable, cosmopolitan Washington, D.C.

Beta Chapter, in turn, took its responsibilities very seriously. In fact, it went beyond the rules of Alpha Chapter to make sure that it lived up to the sorority's standards. Like Alpha, it expected the highest scholarship but went a little beyond with its unwritten law that under no circumstances were Wilberforce Deltas to "flunk" examinations. Like Alpha, it was as eager to "monopolize the best offices in the student organizations."[17] And not only did Beta Chapter follow the founding chapter's lead in selecting quality members, it even had the faculty participate in the selection. Names of future Deltas were submitted to the entire faculty for approval before they were selected to be a part of the sorority.

The entrance of America into World War I in 1917 had a disrupting effect on college campuses and the growth of Delta, but by 1918 a new chapter was founded at the University of Pennsylvania in Philadelphia. The specific motive for focusing on the Ivy League school is not clear. In fact, there is some evidence that not all Deltas were so eager to bring in the group; a feeling that seemed due to the reputation of the highly social Philadelphia women. It was Gabrielle Pelham, according to Edmonds, who convinced Alpha Chapter not to look negatively at the Philadelphia coeds, led by an outstanding student who had come there in 1915: Sadie (Tanner Mossell) Alexander. Alexander came from an extraordinary Philadelphia family on both the Mossell and Tanner sides: She was the niece of the famous artist Henry O. Tanner; her father was the first Black to graduate from the University of Pennsylvania Law School; and the seemingly ubiquitous Lewis B. Moore of Howard was married to her aunt. A friend and future national president of Delta who also attended the university, Anna (Johnson) Julian, described Alexander as a serious student and "nothing of a social butterfly. Around Philadelphia at that time was a group of women whose sole aspiration seemed to be in the public limelight, to be seen at this party or that party. This was not Sadie's thing."[18]

Members of the Alpha Chapter had written to Alexander as early as 1913, to help them establish a Delta chapter at the Ivy League school. However, the minimum requirement of five eligible members delayed things. "There were only two Black women students on the campus, and the other one beside myself had gone to normal school so that she was a junior and she would be graduating in another year," recalled the Philadelphian. Not until 1918 could U of P meet the minimum. The four young women in addition to Alexander were: Julia Polk, Esther (Butler) King, Pauline Young, and Virginia Alexander. And all were exceptional. "There wasn't one who didn't have a 'B' average," Sadie T. M. Alexander recalled, "and three had 'A' averages." Virginia Alexander would soon be Sadie T. M. Alexander's sister-in-law, and subsequently one of the few Black women physicians in the country. Described as a "progressive Black medical doctor," she also became the friend and physician of Alice Dunbar-Nelson, a writer who was married to the famous poet Paul Laurence Dunbar between 1898 and 1902 and became an honorary member of the sorority. Mrs. Alexander described Virginia as the prettiest of the Philadelphia group, with beautiful eyes and long, long, sweeping eyelashes. "Virginia," she used to tell her, "if I just had your eyelashes, I would have every boy in this campus after me."[19]

Pauline Young was the niece of Alice Dunbar-Nelson and lived with her after the latter's divorce and remarriage. Alexander remembers her working as a theater usher in Wilmington, Delaware. With books in tow, she would have to rush to the train after classes were over and study while the play was being performed. Julia Polk was from Camden, New Jersey, and was described by Alexander as dark brown with beautiful white teeth. Esther King was from Washington, D.C., and was one of the few Black students whose parents could afford for her to live on campus. Even those who, like Alexander, came from prominent families enjoyed few such luxuries—especially in this period of postwar inflation when the standard of living increased 50 percent between 1915 and 1918. "Virginia had a full scholarship, I didn't have anything at all," observed Alexander, "but my people were able to pay the tuition. I got one dollar a week and I had to buy my paper out of that—and my carfare was 10¢ a day. So you know how much I had left." In order to save some money, the students would often walk across the bridge, cutting three cents from the transportation fares. That was not an inconsiderable amount of money in those days. The savings, said Alexander, were enough to buy her future husband, Raymond Pace Alexander, (who became an outstanding judge) a briefcase when he went to Harvard Law School. As far as clothes were concerned, "I never had a dress that my mother didn't make," Alexander concluded.[20]

Alpha Chapter's Lillian Skinner was sent to the Pennsylvania campus to organize the Gamma Chapter, which held its meetings at Sadie T. M. Alexander's house at 2908 Diamond Street—the former home of Henry O. Tanner and which would become an official historical landmark. The sorors would also sponsor outstanding programs in the university's Houston Hall. The Gamma sorors would go out on Sundays and strategically cover as many churches as they could to publicize them. "We brought Dr. Du Bois there to speak and Carter Woodson to speak. We had Marian Anderson when she was just beginning to sing in Philadelphia," Alexander recalled,[21] and others included the eminent lawyer, Charles Hamilton Houston. These were heady days, observed Anna Julian, a later U of P student who would become national president. The young students admired such people, especially Du Bois, from afar, but "we never expected to lay eyes on them," she said. In addition, they inducted Alice Dunbar-Nelson as an honorary member.

Alice Ruth Moore Dunbar-Nelson (1875–1935) was at the time an organizer for the Middle Atlantic states in the woman suffrage campaign, subsequently becoming the first woman to serve on the State Republican Committee of Delaware. Born in New Orleans, she was well known in Black and Creole musical and literary circles, and had matriculated at Cornell, Columbia, and the University of Pennsylvania. The editor of her diary, Gloria T. Hull, describes her as tall, attractive, with auburn hair and an imposing appearance. She was elegant and fashionable in dress. Beyond being known in political and social circles, Dunbar-Nelson was a well regarded author of poetry and short stories, and published volumes including *Violets and Other Tales* and *The Goodness of St. Roque.* Considered the family genius, she was beautiful, talented, and temperamental, said Hull. In addition Dunbar-Nelson taught at Delaware State and Howard High School in Delaware, and with her second husband, Robert J. Nelson, coedited the *Wilmington Advocate* from 1920 to 1922. As early as 1916, she was given a tea by Alpha Chapter at Howard, which took place in Miner Hall. Tables were arranged in the triangular form of the letter delta. There were palms, flowers, and Delta pennants decorating the room. Twenty-nine members, including Eliza Shippen, Bertha Campbell, Edna Coleman, Gabrielle Pelham, Nannie Burroughs, and Mary Terrell were in attendance to hear the honoree give a talk on the suffrage movement.

The three chapters stayed in close communication, corresponding at least once every three months as an article in the constitution stipulated, and worked "enthusiastically together" as Edna Morris reported. By the fall of 1918, a fourth chapter was in the making when coeds at the University of Iowa in Iowa City communicated to sorors at Wilberforce that they were interested in joining the sorority. Prospective candidates, Helen (Dameron) Beshears, Mamie (Diggs) Robertson, Harriette (Alexander) Vines, Ola (Calhoun) Morehead, Helen (Lucas) Banks, Violetta (London) Fields, Elizabeth (Gross) Green, and Adah (Hyde) Johnson, were all duly considered, investigated, and approved to become members. Of the group, Adah Johnson stood out, becoming one of the first two Black women students to graduate from the school. Her father, Robert Hyde, a former slave in Virginia, and illiterate, was credited with inventing one of the first electric carpet sweepers sold in this country, and patented a soap and cleaning formula that was sold nationwide for many years. He also ran a real estate and employment business. His ambition also extended to his children and he was determined that they get a college education. It was that dream, Johnson has said, that spurred her on to finish work on her bachelor's degree at Iowa University. "In my time, most young people quit school around the eighth grade," she said. "The few girls who graduated from high school went right off and got married. . . ." But like so many of her peers in the sorority, she was more interested in being a teacher than in marriage, keeping house, or raising children. "People really thought I was strange when I didn't marry until I was thirty-two."[22]

Beta's Edwinna (Woodyard) Primas was dispatched to help organize Delta Chapter, and its establishment on April 4, 1919, also added a particularly prominent honorary member: Gertrude (Durden) Rush, the first and then only Black woman lawyer in the state of Iowa, the first Black woman to be admitted to the National Bar Association, and a member of the Iowa Association of the National Association of Colored Women's Clubs.

Primas, and Beta Chapter, situated in the Midwest, where a large number of accredited schools accepted Blacks, would also be instrumental in the creation of another chapter seven months later. There was great interest in the sorority by young women at Ohio State University, and Primas, along with other Beta members, including Jennie (Mustapha) Tate, who was recently assigned as secretary of the YWCA in Columbus, investigated the records and personalities of the students. All was found satisfactory; approval was granted by Alpha, Beta, Gamma, and Delta chapters; and Epsilon Chapter was born. The chapter, organized on November 19, 1919, included Phila

Ann (McGillery) White, Catherine (Thompson) Alexander, Bernice N. Copeland, Fairy Shores Burrell, and Alberta Hanley.

The establishment of the five chapters revealed some important patterns of the sorority. That the Wilberforce group initiated the chartering of two other chapters further confirmed the sense of equality among them. This idea was extended when Beta sought the approval of the other chapters in organizing the Ohio State or Epsilon chapter. Although Black campus sorors were active in recruiting new chapters, it is interesting that there was very early a trend toward growth on predominantly White campuses. It was mutually understood that if there was a need for sororities at a place like Howard or Wilberforce, there was even a greater one at non-Black schools, where coeds suffered from the all too familiar refrain of discrimination because of their gender as well as their color. Even at an institution like the University of Iowa—which in 1847 became the first state college to admit women on equal terms with men, the status of female students was tenuous. As late as 1891, members of the faculty openly questioned whether "society would be better served if the money spent for [women's] collegiate education were diverted to a school in cookery." Also there were usually many fewer women than men on coeducational campuses, making Black women a minority within a minority. As late as 1917–1918 at the University of Iowa, a Big Ten state school, there were 1,780 women compared with 3,303 men.[23]

In the case of Black students, their needs were social, emotional, political, and *very* practical. Of the latter, the need for living quarters was paramount. For, what was taken for granted by White students was a major issue for Black ones. Not only were they prohibited from campus housing but their options were fewer. Black students in all too many instances were forced to live in Black residential areas far from the campus and which offered less than ideal conditions. Sometimes the distance required hours of travel on trolley cars. Rents were often higher in Black neighborhoods, reflecting the inflated prices of the housing there. And too many found themselves in homes where there was no running water, improper lighting for study, and poor ventilation. And sharing quarters with non-students who did not require quiet study could also be a problem. So for Black students, and particularly for women, a sorority house served a much greater purpose than as a center for socializing: It could have a great impact on one's grades and quality of the college experience.

The situation at Iowa was particularly galling. The women's dorm was described as a fireproof building with its sleeping, dining, and recreation rooms, its parlors, kitchen, bakery and laundry providing a "dream home" for girls long denied any such measure of luxury. The only feature to be deplored was its limited availability; scarcely more than 150 girls could be accommodated within its comfortable walls. If it was "limited" for White coeds, it was entirely off limits to Black women, who were not allowed to live on campus.

However, by 1919, the cooperative and determined spirit of Black women of two generations would ease the housing situation. It was in that year that the Delta women received help from the Iowa State Federation of Women's Clubs that was organized in 1902 and incorporated in 1913. Through the leadership of Mrs. S. Joe Brown, a lawyer and one of its members, a home that would serve as a dormitory was purchased and maintained by the organization. She was aided by Mrs. Helen Lemme, a Delta and university staff employee who would subsequently have the distinction of having an Iowa City elementary school named after her. The Browns seemed to have an intimate connection with the state college and the civic life of the Iowa City community. S. Joe Brown had graduated from its undergraduate school in 1898, later receiving his LL.B. at the university in 1901 and the A.M. degree in 1902. After leaving that campus, he became superintendent of public instruction in Muchakinok, Iowa, and president of the Des Moines Interracial Commission. Helen Lemme and her husband Allen had maintained a private residence for Black students. In addition to the other services for the students that she provided, it was the place where a Black barber would come twice a week to cut the hair of the young men, as the local barber shops refused to accommodate them.[24]

The sorority house was described by an observer in the 1940s as "neat and attractive in appearance" and was located in a good residential area. Its location seemed to be preferable to that of the Black fraternity house that served the college (Kappa Alpha Psi had established a chapter there in 1914, and Alpha Phi Alpha later established one in 1922) said to be in "that part of the city which is a less desirable place to live." As late as the forties, however, most of the studying still had to be done in the libraries. The main reason was that meals weren't served in the sorority house and the nearest café that served them was ten blocks away, requiring much coming and going. But many of the problems associated with housing were nevertheless solved by the purchase of the sorority house. And it is interesting to note that some years later, a charter member of Delta Chapter, Helen Beshears, became president of the Iowa Federation of Colored Women's Clubs, and a member of the board of trustees to oversee the affairs of the home.

NATIONALIZING AN IDEA

By 1919, the Black fraternal movement was making its mark on the college population, both on predominantly White campuses and Black. The oldest of the Greek-letter groups, Alpha Phi Alpha, had in that year nineteen chapters. And according to Numa P. G. Adams, there were thirteen "distinct Negro fraternities in twenty-two different institutions of higher learning, of which sixteen are white and six are colored."[25] Total membership was 1,487. Among those members, in both the fraternities and sororities, were the most prominent leaders and scholars of the day. And at this point in the movement's development, one could see little but its positive qualities. As Adams noted, the members of the groups had higher grade averages. Noting that the Alphas were handling $2,500 to $3,000 annually, the groups also made the students act responsibly.

Adams also saw advantage in growing numbers of students on prestigious White campuses joining the organizations. It gave those on the Black campuses the opportunity to compare curricula and so demand that the Black schools "maintain a high and modern standard of education"—a demand that underlined the student movements of the twenties on Black campuses. The students on the interracial campuses also had a particularly "strong bond of union," he observed, because they found themselves in such hostile environments. They thus brought a new "spirit and purpose" to the interactions, "for they had problems." In turn the Black campus students got a better and firsthand understanding of those problems in integrated settings.[26]

The youngest major group in this burgeoning movement, Delta Sigma Theta, had come a long way in the six years of its existence. It had outstanding students with a strong sense of purpose, outstanding honorary members who were role models and offered guidance. The young organization had already set the tone for their equitable dealings with each other, and could now point to such important accomplishments as the sorority house in Iowa. Now the time had come for the next step in their development: creating a national organization.

"We were summoned to Washington, D.C., by Alpha Chapter," recalled Sadie Alexander, and she and Virginia Alexander prepared to take the train from Philadelphia. Despite the excited anticipation of the trip, and the meeting's great import, the first thing that had to be reckoned with was getting the funds to travel. "Of course, there was no treasury in those days," she said, "and when we were about to leave, we counted our few pennies."[27] Train fare was five dollars. When the two women counted their money, little would be left for meals. "We ate a big breakfast," said Alexander, "because we didn't know what we could get once we got there (in fact, we didn't get much)."[28] Nevertheless, the two women still couldn't fend off their hunger pains en route. They pooled their money to buy a pot of baked beans, which then, on the Pennsylvania Railroad, cost fifty cents. "We got the pot of baked beans and the brown bread." What they didn't know at the time was they could have had more. "The waiter, whom we recognized as a fellow who used to be in school with us, kept saying, 'Don't you want milk? Don't you want tea; don't you want coffee?' And we kept saying, 'Oh no, this is all!' When we asked him for the bill, he said, 'Oh, there wouldn't be any bill for you girls.' Oh, we could have kicked ourselves, as hungry as we were," she laughed.[29]

They arrived to find representatives from Alpha Chapter, who had extended the invitation, led by Carrie (Sutton) Brooks, the chapter president. Ohio State's Epsilon Chapter soror was also there. The expense from Iowa was just too steep for the Delta representative, and a sudden death in the family of the Wilberforce soror kept her from coming. Nevertheless, the missing delegates contacted those in Washington to authorize the other delegates to count them in favor of any measures voted by those in session.[30] They had planned to hold their meetings in dormitory rooms until Dean Lewis B. Moore, Sadie T. Alexander's uncle, offered them his offices. So, "it was there in the main building on the second floor at Howard University that the Grand Chapter was established," noted Alexander. "And there I was elected the president of the Grand Chapter . . . no money in the treasury—and officers by name."[31]

What they did have was tremendous enthusiasm and the spirit of a movement about to unfold. And true to their democratic leanings, every chapter was represented in the first national offices of this first national convention. From Alpha Chapter at Howard was Anne (McCary) Dingle, corresponding secretary; and Harriete Robinson, custodian. From the nominees sent by correspondence by Beta Chapter at Wilberforce, Geraldine E. Jackson was chosen vice-president; Gamma was represented by Sadie T. M. Alexander as president and Virginia M. Alexander, treasurer; Delta Chapter's officers were Mildred I. (Griffin) Dobson and Hazel (Shaw) Maynard, given the posts of chaplain and sergeant at arms, respectively. From Epsilon was Catherine E. (Thompson) Alexander and Bernice N. Copeland, recording secretary and journalist, respectively.

The young women accomplished a great deal from the time they assembled on the Howard University campus on December 27, 1919. As Morris described, the convention had "resolved itself into a committee of a whole to draw up a set of rules to regulate the immediate conference, to work out an appropriate constitution for the proposed national sisterhood, and to discuss problems in perfecting such an organization."[32] Three days later, a "national program was suggested and decided upon, uniformity of procedure was outlined. At the end of the meeting, the delegates, visitors, and the hostess chapter were imbued, says Morris, with a "renewed determination and a greater belief in the possibilities of the sisterhood." At the close of the first national convention, they "stood with bowed heads and hands joined while the benediction was said and the hymn, 'God Be With You 'Til We Meet Again' was sung, and the convention closed to meet at Wilberforce University, the seat of Beta Chapter, in 1920."[33]

CHAPTER 4

GROUNDS FOR A
MOVEMENT

Fueled by the advances and pathos of the post–World War I years, the twenties would be a heady decade for Delta Sigma Theta. There had been gains by Blacks who in the hundreds of thousands left the South for jobs in northern industries. There was also the inevitable White backlash in the ensuing competition for jobs, in the political implications of Blacks swelling northern cities, in the increasing articulation of Black pride expressed in the literature, music, and discourse of the Harlem Renaissance. In 1919, a resuscitated Ku Klux Klan boasted membership of over 100,000 and now its activities spread well past the Mason-Dixon Line where there were some half-million more Blacks as a result of the migration. The twenty major racial riots that took place between the spring and fall of that year made it known as the "red summer." The backlash and the proclamations of "the new Negro," created, in turn, a new defiance among Blacks, one no longer mitigated by the powerful conservative influences of Booker T. Washington, who died in 1915.

By the twenties, all of these developments would have a discernible impact on Black college students, and thus on the sorority movement itself. First, growing industrialization and urbanization brought on a virtual explosion in the numbers of Blacks attaining degrees in general, and in the northern schools in particular. Between 1917 and 1927, students in Black colleges increased from 2,132 to 13,580, or sixfold.[1] There was also a dramatic increase in predominantly white northern campuses. In 1914, for example, there were 60 Black graduates of northern schools; between 1920 and 1933, the *annual* number of such students increased from 156 to 439, or 181 percent.[2] And in the eleven-year period between 1926 and 1936, there were more Black graduates than in the one-hundred-year period prior to 1826.

There was also a significant gain in those earning master's degrees. Sixty-six had earned them in the nine years before 1920; between 1921 and 1930, the number rose to 493. The increase in professional degrees in medicine, law, and other fields, for the same periods was not as dramatic, but still showed an upward trajectory: from 2,984 to 3,299. Ph.D.'s rose from fourteen to thirty-one.[3] Of the latter, the twenties saw the first Ph.D.'s earned by Black women; two of the first three to earn them—Eva Dykes and Sadie Alexander—were Deltas; the third was Georgianna Ross Simpson. Their pioneering efforts symbolized the general advancement of Black women who, in the twenties, represented 20 percent of all graduates from Black colleges.

Additionally, Black women were beginning to institutionalize their educational concerns. By 1922, as previously noted, Lucy Slowe became the first dean of women at Howard University. In the following year, she became president of the newly formed National Association of College Women (the American Association of University Women did not recognize Blacks). By 1925, the Black association had branches in Washington; Baltimore; Wilmington; New York; Petersburg; St. Louis; Charleston (West Virginia); Portsmouth; Cleveland; Kansas City; and Chicago. Its purposes were to improve conditions and raise standards of Black colleges, and in particular, "to further education among Negro girls and women."[4]

The White backlash that was a result of this activity was not unexpected, but it made it no less easier to bear. Especially for college students in northern universities the isolation, and shock of a new environment compounded by racism could be devastating. Numa P. G. Adams observed that Black students, many of them from small schools "and an ancient order of discipline," found themselves attending classes that were larger than the entire enrollment of their high school. The city also offered new attractions—and distractions—all of which caused the student "to lose a great deal of time in trying to find himself."[5]

That search would be made all the more frustrating by the social ostracism, on the campuses themselves. "They have problems of discrimination to solve and stern prejudices to overcome; hence it is natural for these students to organize for their own protection and for social advantage."[6] In the twenties, "protection" was paramount. The chancellor of Ohio State University, for example, though not personally against having Blacks on that campus, observed that "the sentiment north of the Ohio River seems to be so persistent against the Negro in skilled labor that I doubt very much whether an educated Negro has a fair [opportunity] . . . in this part of the country."[7] At the University of Kansas, the interracial state institution which probably had in the postwar years more Blacks on its campus—175 out of a population of 5,000—prohibited Blacks and Whites from playing together in contact sports. As was typical at other such schools, Blacks were barred from student glee clubs, dances, and literary societies and were segregated in college cafeterias—if allowed to eat in them at all. In a number of schools they were prohibited from using the swimming pools, although one could not graduate without learning to swim.[8] At best, the prejudices shown toward Black students were passively rather than aggressively hostile, as Ohio State Chancellor Ernest H. Lindley noted: "Whenever colored girls use the restrooms considerable, the white girls make no protest, but simply abandon these rooms to the colored girls."[9] And when a Black sorority achieved the highest scholastic average at Colorado Teachers College, the Greek Council refused to award the usual cup given in recognition of the achievement. Instead they abolished the award entirely.[10]

Even at Oberlin College, long the citadel of the abolitionist tradition, the first White university to admit Blacks, and which could boast such alumnae as the artist Edmonia Lewis, the teacher and scholar Anna Julia Cooper, and Mary Church Terrell, was in open retreat of its past racial policies. As faculty members informed Kelly Miller as early as 1913, "It was impossible to uphold old Oberlin's ideals because of student prejudices."[11] Edna Coleman, who attended graduate school there, related the story of meeting a White student who would ask her, incredulously, "Are *you* smart? *I'm* smart, are you smart?"[12] Unfortunately, the discrimination at Oberlin wasn't limited to its student body. Its acting dean of women, Frances Hosford, gave support to a few White students who were trying to discourage Black girls from living in the college dormitories. Interestingly, Terrell's niece, Mary, was there at the time, and enlisted the support of NAACP's William Pickens in the conflict.[13]

The Ivy League schools were no exceptions to these assaults, which reached a new intensity in the decade. At Dartmouth, according to its president, Blacks were seen as "pariahs." At Harvard, where the future husbands of Sadie T. Mossell (Raymond Pace Alexander) and Anna Johnson (Percy Julian) were roommates, Blacks were banned from the dormitories for the first time. At the University of Pennsylvania, Anna Julian, who was a student there between 1921 and 1925, recalled, Black students faced many prejudices—both within and outside the campus. "We couldn't swim in the pool, we couldn't live in the dormitories and had to stay off-campus," she recalled. "There was no place that a Black student could get anything to eat in a restaurant. I had classes from seven in the morning to nine in the evening." She continued, "That meant that I had to go all day without food after lunchtime."[14] Still, the U of P students were more fortunate than most. An anthropology teacher who heard of their plight convinced the manager of the college cafeteria to permit the students to eat there.

Discrimination also abounded for Black medical students, who could not intern at White hospitals. Many had to leave in the second year for Howard or Meharry. Black women would be hit with a double blow. As women they were forced to get their degree in education, though they may have taken the same courses as men, Anna Julian observed. As Blacks, they could not do their practice teaching in Philadelphia as White students did. Nevertheless, there were attempts to rectify the situation. When Julian and others were notified to do their practice teaching at Washington's Dunbar High School, they got the administration there to say that they couldn't take any more and that the University of Pennsylvania should plan for the student teachers locally.[15] This, however, would be quite a task, even in the city of "Brotherly Love." Even with someone of Sadie Alexander's talents: a woman who graduated with honors in 1918, who received her master's in economics in 1919, and would, within a year, be the first Black woman in the country to receive a Ph.D., she would not be able to find work in Philadelphia. Before she passed her law boards, she was forced to work as an assistant actuary in the Black North Carolina Mutual Company.

So, if there was a need for fraternal organizations on Black campuses, it reached a point of sheer desperation on White ones where Black students were virtually under siege. Not surprisingly, northern campuses, especially, would be fertile ground upon which the sorority would grow. Between 1919 and 1929, no less than forty-five chapters (twenty-seven undergraduate and eighteen graduate) would be established, and by 1930 they would be found in every region—New England, the Middle Atlantic States, the Midwest, Far West and the Pacific Coast—a spread that necessitated the creation of regional entities in the sorority. With the notable exception of Black land-grant colleges, campus chapters would be found in every category of the nation's institutions of higher learning: private Black colleges such as Tuskegee and Fisk; Ivy League schools such as the University of Pennsylvania; large state schools such as the University of California; and Big Ten schools such as the University of Michigan. True to form, honorary members inducted in this period reflected the leading political and cultural figures of the time, among them Mary McLeod Bethune, and Jessie Fauset, the most prolific novelist of the Harlem Renaissance.

The maturing of the organization was reflected in its creation of graduate chapters and a new category of membership—associate members—older women who were influential in their own communities. At the same time, the sorors also reaffirmed the notion that their sorority was foremost a student organization by limiting the number of associate members to three per year. The seriousness—and audacity—of the young sorors was also seen in the stipulation that the associate members be subjected to a probationary period during which they could not vote, hold office, or participate in business meetings until deemed sufficiently serious about their membership. (By 1925, there was less need for the category of members, and they were given full membership privileges.)

There would be nine national conventions during the decade, each bringing some new development and programmatic thrust to the national body. There would be the establishment of scholarship funds; May Week, which emphasized education in the communities; the Jabberwock—an annual event that combined cultural expression and talent with fund-raising. The Deltas would inaugurate plans for the *Delta Bulletin,* an internal publication apprising members of Delta's problems and accomplishments, and adopt an official hymn. There would also be the first efforts toward intrafraternal cooperation. Finally, the sorority would take a public stand against the mounting prejudices against Blacks and women. And by the end of the decade, the sisterhood would be sorely tested, as the first flush of excitement ended and serious conflicts threatened to tear it asunder.

Their first year as a national organization was indeed an intense one, and exciting as well. As Edna Morris observed, "Everything was new, everyone was pioneering in the field of sorority activity, and since every project was more or less experimental, the sorors, individually and collectively seemed deeply concerned."[16] The first new chapter to be established after the national convention was Zeta, at the University of Cincinnati in October of 1920. It was the first Black Greek-letter organization to be established on that campus; and it was, again, Edwina Woodyard from Wilberforce who was dispatched to charter the seventeen undergraduates and graduates into the Delta constellation. Among its members was Ethel (LaMay) Calimese, a future national president.* President Sadie Mossell personally inducted two chapters herself, traveling that November to Syracuse and Cornell universities in upstate New York to bring the Eta and Theta chapters respectively into the fold. Alice (Lucas) Brickler headed the Syracuse chapter and Irene Trigg accepted the charter for Cornell's Theta Chapter. Grand journalist Bernice Copeland was busy with other details: A name for the official journal had to be found, and the chapters were invited to submit suggestions. Simply enough, *The Delta,* the recommendation of the Iowa sorors, was selected. The only discomforting news, as Edna Morris reported, was there was one national officer who was shirking her task: Anne (McCary) Dingle, the corresponding secretary. That fact would have subsequent significance, but in the meantime, it fell upon the president to "issue the call" for the next national convention, which would be held in Wilberforce, Ohio, on December 28, 1920.

Although the Christmas holidays were an opportune time to meet because the sorors were on vacation and dormitory meeting places were free, they were also the coldest time to meet. At Wilberforce, the house where a number of them were staying—belonging to a relative of Alexander's—was so cold that they huddled together in one bed. "And when we got up in the morning to wash the water in the pitcher was frozen," Alexander recalled, "so I went downstairs to my cousin's wife and I asked her if we could have some hot water. And she said, 'What do you want, to make some tea?' And I said, 'No, we wanted to wash.' 'Oh,' she said, 'my dear, we don't use that much electricity!'"[17]

The use of electricity wasn't the only thing carefully scrutinized at Wilberforce. Among the students, alcohol was forbidden and so was dancing, making the efforts of the Alpha fraternity to entertain the

---

*The others were Blanche (Dixon) Belsinger, Louise (Penn) Sandifer, Beatrice Morton, Ida Mae Rhodes, and Laverne (Friason) Watson, all undergraduates. Graduates were Cleo (Hall) Perry, Sarah White, Mary (Holloway) Weatherly, Edith Howard, Neola Robinson, Martha (Hall) Ross, Maude Ragan, Mary Lee Tate, Jennie (Austin) Fletcher, Marie (Belsinger) Ryder, and Camille (Friason) Hood.

visiting Deltas an intriguing challenge. "Even a little wine" was out of the question, noted Alexander, since its discovery would be cause for immediate expulsion, but they did engage in one of the prohibitions of the time: dancing in the fraternity house. To avoid being caught, "the boys stationed themselves [strategically along the route] from the president's house to the Alpha house [so that they would be able] to run each way and tell each man when the president was coming to greet this group of fine young ladies that didn't dance," Alexander recalled. When the "relay" signaled the imminent arrival of the president, "the music was to stop so he didn't know that we were dancing."[18]

Of greater preoccupation was the serious business of the convention where delegates from all of the chartered chapters were present—as well as honorary members Hallie Quinn Brown, Malvinia Mitchell, and Julia Gee, all Wilberforce faculty members. It was here that graduate chapters were first authorized, and two of them, Alpha Beta, and Beta Beta, in New York City and Washington, D.C., respectively, were approved. The introduction of graduate chapters required new regulations, as well. They could exist where all applying persons, the first five of whom had to be sorors already, were graduates. Undergraduate chapters were to include only undergraduate and honorary members, and faculty sponsors; only when there were not enough graduate or undergraduate members to institute separate chapters could a "mixed" chapter be authorized. No doubt this careful distinction was made in light of the experience of the founding chapter, where there was an inherent conflict between graduate and undergraduate members in the same organization.

Nevertheless, a mixed chapter was often necessary and at the convention, Iota Chapter in Boston was organized. Virginia Alexander was selected to charter the chapter there and initiate prospective sorors from Wellesley, Radcliffe, Smith, Mount Holyoke, Simmons, and Boston University. There was also the business of the induction of honorary members and the induction of officers. Florence Cole Talbert was favorably voted upon. Talbert, as Alice Dunbar-Nelson noted at the time, was one of the few Black vocalists who was achieving operatic roles abroad. She had graduated from the Chicago Musical College in 1916, studied in Rome, Milan, and Naples, and subsequently became a soloist with the Los Angeles and Chicago symphony orchestras. She also served as dean of music at Wiley College in Marshall, Texas. Talbert would be an active participant in Delta activities in the coming years, and write the music for the official Delta Hymn whose words would be written by Dunbar-Nelson.

As with the rest of the convention, the election of officers went smoothly. Mildred I. (Griffin) Dobson was moved to the vice-presidential spot; and Virginia Alexander changed offices to become parliamentarian. Bernice Copeland remained as journalist, and Harriet Robinson and Lena Edwards, both of Alpha Chapter were elected corresponding secretary and custodian, respectively. Beta Chapter's Rachel (Brock) Pratt became recording secretary; and the newer chapters were represented by Ida Rhodes of Zeta (University of Cincinnati) as treasurer; Alice (Lucas) Brickler of Cornell's Eta Chapter as chaplain; and Irene Trigg from the Theta Chapter at Syracuse as sergeant at arms.

The tremendous satisfaction regarding Sadie Alexander's leadership also assured her reelection—and a continuing emphasis of the sorority on education and Black pride. It was her idea to initiate one of the organization's most effective and long-lasting programs, voted upon at the Wilberforce meeting: May Week. Its objective was to raise the consciousness of young people about the importance of higher education. The slogan "Invest in Education," was adopted and each May a week was to be set aside in that month for programs that stressed academic and professional achievement. The programs would feature speakers and activities that grade-school students would participate in. In 1922, for example, Alexander's own chapter presented James Weldon Johnson, who as executive director of the NAACP was leading the fight for the Dyer anti-lynching bill. He had also served as consul to Nicaragua, and was a novelist and poet of some note. His poem "Lift Every Voice and Sing," set to music by his brother, J. Rosamond Johnson, was so popular, it was known as the Negro national anthem.

In addition to his address, Gamma Chapter also sponsored a contest among the city's eighth-grade students for the best composition on "Why I Should Like to Attend High School." Judges were local educators and the winners received a medal. Other chapters also had good programs. Ohio State's Epsilon Chapter presented a play, *Ethiopia's Day,* written and directed by sorors Alberta Henley and Anna Hughes, respectively. Other chapters engaged speakers like Mary Church Terrell, and sent Delta members around to public high schools "to carry the message of high ideals in education among our people."[19]

THE RUSH TO ORGANIZE

For Delta, as well as other Greek-letter groups, the early twenties was a critical period for its chapter growth. The fraternal idea had taken hold, and the organizations were preoccupied with establishing new chapters on college campuses throughout the country. That preoccupation became all the more urgent because of the competition among the groups to be the first to plant their fraternal flags on a campus, and/or to attract the most outstanding students to their organization. For Delta, the rush to organize forced the sorority to begin to reassess the criteria for prospective members, shore up its administrative machinery, and look toward interfraternal cooperation on broader issues that faced all of the groups.

Between the conventions of 1920 and 1921, four new Delta chapters were established. On February 21, 1921, Kappa Chapter at the University of California at Berkeley came into existence; another mixed chapter, Lambda, in Chicago was established later in the year, as were Mu Chapter at the University of Pittsburgh and Nu at the University of Michigan. Despite the rush to bring in new sorors, however, the national organization still looked toward university deans and other college administrators—in addition to the recommendations of the Deltas themselves who were on the constant lookout for outstanding students—for their approval. The college administrators were apprised of Delta's academic standards and asked to give recommendations and provide transcripts. At the University of California, for example, the dean of women, Lucy Stebbins, was contacted to forward names of those she felt were suited Delta's membership. Among those on the list who would be inducted were Onilda Taylor, Elizabeth Gordon, Louise Thompson, Creola Cook, Myrtle Price and Gladys Brown, and Vivian (Osborne) Marsh. The input of the dean at the University of California—and other schools—was probably a good strategy. It certainly legitimatized the sorority in the eyes of not only its members but, in this case, the predominantly White university community. Such sanction is essential to social movement organizations, particularly one composed of Black women.

Nevertheless, the fact that the sorority was playing by mainstream rules didn't make its recruitment efforts any less sanguine. In the face of competition from the AKAs, which were also attempting to organize the chapter there, "each prospective soror was fought over one by one," Louise Thompson recalled.[20] And there were the inevitable excesses of such intense proselytizing from the two major sororities. Thompson remembered the pressure put on the students. There was the prying into personal and family lives, and the use of "the stick" more than the "carrot" to get them to join one sorority or another. For the AKAs, those efforts were led by Ida Jackson, who would become the first Black high school teacher in the state's public education system and subsequently the AKA's national president or Supreme Basileus. For the Deltas, Ida Mae Myller from Wilberforce's Beta Chapter, who was in California on other business, was authorized to establish Kappa Chapter, with, no doubt, a sense of urgency. There was also a race to be the first Greek-letter organization established there, a race that Delta won. It thus became the first such organization, of men or women, to be established in California and perhaps on the Pacific Coast, observes Helen Edmonds. (AKA was established on the campus in 1922.)

But if the sororities needed the students, the students also needed them. Louise Thompson, for example, was drawn to sorority life for the reason that many others were: It offered a refuge from the racial isolation of the campus, and in her case, the isolation that she had experienced as a child. Born in Chicago, her experience was more harsh than that of many others. She had been shuttled by a peripatetic family to no less than twenty different grammar schools in states such as Idaho and Oregon where there were few Blacks. In California, there was more of a community, though substantial numbers of Afro-Americans did not settle there until the post–World War II years. As a student at the University of California between 1919 and 1923 she came "at last into contact with a community of striving Blacks," as Langston Hughes biographer Arnold Rampersand wrote.[21] Despite her criticism about some of its methods, that sense of belonging was enhanced, she said, by membership in Delta.

Other aspects of the growth of the sorority also offer some insight into the nature of the movement in this period. The organizing of Nu Chapter at the University of Michigan, with charter members Jessie Craig, Letty Wickcliffe (subsequently grand sergeant at arms), Thelma Chiles, Prudence (Beasley) Perry, and Marie Hackley of Beta Chapter, currently studying at Michigan's medical school—reflected the continuing interest in the Big Ten schools. And the creation of the mixed Lambda Chapter in Chicago and Mu at the University of Pittsburgh pointed out how the development of the sorority reflected the peripatetic lives of educated Black women.

More than most they moved from one city, state, and region to another, because of the fewer options they had to attend school, and find a professional job. Their children and husbands had fewer choices as well. So it was not unusual for them to be in different places, sometimes from year to year, and one of the strengths of the sorority movement was that its very structure accommodated their itineraries and search for sisterhood throughout the country. In 1921, for example, Chicago was the home of founders Osceola Adams and Marguerite Alexander, as well as Vivian Mason from Alpha Chapter; Margaret (Watkins) Hardiman, Marie (Ody) Cobb, Freddie Billings, and Ruby (Martin) Payne—who were all Wilberforce Beta members. They recommended that a chapter be formed to include students who were attending the schools in the Chicago area. The first charter members were graduate students from the University of Chicago and quite a few who were graduates of Fisk—which as yet did not have a Delta chapter. Osceola Adams became the first president of Lambda—subsequently she would also serve as grand treasurer of the national organization. Estelle (Webster) MacNeal, Tillie (Houston) White, and Sophia Boaz also were Lambda charter members. Four years later, Lambda would be reorganized with the establishment of a graduate chapter under the direction of Martha (Hall) Ross of Cincinnati.

Beta Chapter members, who were responsible for so much of the expansion of the sorority in these years, were also the initiators of the creation of Mu Chapter at the University of Pittsburgh. Edwina Primas, who had been dispatched to organize the Zeta Chapter at the University of Cincinnati, and Marie MacNeal were then living in Pittsburgh, and with another Beta member, Eileen Springfield Clark, sought permission to induct an enthusiastic group of coeds on the Pittsburgh campus. It was granted and in addition to MacNeal and Clark, Elbertha Davis, Gladys Greene, Dorothy Lewis, and Rose Willis became charter members. Woodyard transferred from the Beta Chapter to become a member of Mu and would become grand vice-president the following December when elections were held at the third national convention in Philadelphia.

THE CONVENTIONS, 1921–1924

By 1921, the year of the third national convention, the annual meeting was becoming more and more significant. It provided the forum for prominent leaders, such as Dunbar-Nelson, to educate the membership about important issues. It was a means for sorors to renew their ties to the organization. Planned social and cultural events in which all took part, cemented the sisterhood, and provided the opportunity for closer association with other Greek-letter groups who often met in the same locality. Most important, it was at these meetings that the major decisions were implemented, and the concerns that preoccupied the sorority were expressed. The third, fourth, and fifth national conventions reflected all of these elements.

"Had to get up early and rush for the train to be in Philadelphia by 10:00 for opening session of Delta Sigma Theta [convention] . . ." reads a December 1921 entry in the diary of Alice Dunbar-Nelson.[22]

> *Goodly number of delegates and visitors in attendance. Dr. Cole [Talbert] much in evidence, and irritating Sadie by her insistence on the beginning of the program. Virginia, airy as usual; lots of nice girls . . . and some girls from Cincinnati. . . . After her opening speech, Sadie introduced me. My voice was horrible, but I did my best. Made speech on the development of the club idea among our women, and the big job of the young women of the sorority inculcating race pride. Some men drifted in . . . Seemed to have put it over, the girls quite enthusiastic. Promised to be back for the reception that night.*[23]

So began the sorority's third annual convention, with its public meeting at the Christian Street branch of the YWCA in Philadelphia. Its closed sessions were held at the recently opened Bennett Club on the University of Pennsylvania campus; the Deltas were the first Black organization given permission to use it and the Howard *Record* praised their "untiring and successful efforts to secure it.[24] Demanding the use of traditionally segregated facilities, they knew, was a way to break down barriers, and a strategy to be used whenever possible. The "nice girls" whom Dunbar-Nelson spoke of included representatives from Wilberforce, Syracuse, Cornell, Chicago, and Howard universities. There were also delegates from the campus chapters at Michigan, Pittsburgh, Cincinnati, and of course Pennsylvania. Of special note for the *Record* was the attendance of several Howard graduates: Eva Dykes, Grace Coleman, Dorothy Pelham, and Dorothy Robinson.

At this convention, Dunbar-Nelson and the others continued to concentrate on authorizing new chapters: Xi, a mixed chapter in Louisville that included a coed from McGill University in Montreal; Omicron, at the University of Nebraska in Lincoln; and several graduate chapters that were city- rather than campus-based. The latter included Gamma Sigma and Delta Sigma at Cincinnati and Wilberforce, respectively, Epsilon Sigma in Baltimore, and Zeta Sigma at Tuskegee Institute in Tuskegee, Alabama. Tuskegee, of course, was the home of the famed educator, Booker T. Washington; and after his death, his third wife, Margaret Murray Washington—made an honorary member of the sorority—continued to serve as dean of women at the college. She was also active in the National Association of Colored Women where she had been president from 1912 to 1916. Upon the establishment of Delta Sigma Theta on the Tuskeegee campus, her home became the sorority's meeting place there.

One of the main forces behind Baltimore's Epsilon Sigma was Vashti Murphy, who had moved to Baltimore in 1917 with her newspaper publisher husband, Carl Murphy. Known as "Miss Vash" to students, sorority meetings were held in her Myrtle Street home. Murphy would have a chance to entertain a number of sorors who planned to come there to celebrate the holiday season—and also take care of some Delta business after the close of the 1921 convention. There had been problems in getting Boston's Iota Chapter off the ground, and it was discovered that a number of prospective members would be in Baltimore. Virginia Alexander, Edna Morris, Ida Rhodes, Ethel Calimese, Alice Lucas, Vivian Mason, and Sadie Alexander would go there to initiate two students from Radcliffe— Charlotte West and Thelma Garland—and Frances Ware of Brown University.

There were also some other important administrative decisions to be made before the meeting ended. Edna Morris's main concern centered on the scholastic standards of prospective sorors. Under the influence of Sadie Alexander, Delta, nominally at least, only accepted chapters at institutions that were rated "A" by the Association of American Universities, the North Central Association of Colleges and Secondary Schools, or the Northwest Association of Secondary and Higher Schools. Further, a young woman had to have a B average, and, as some remember, even a B + average was desirable where competition was particularly stiff. Alexander had had the responsibility of investigating and making decisions about the numerous applications coming to her office—and had rejected quite a few. In light of the fact of the tremendous paperwork involved, as well as the fact that such important decisions were concentrated in the hands of the president, a decision was made at the third convention to establish a National Representative office, headed first by Ida Rhodes, whose primary function was to sift through the applications. Later, a Committee on Standards and a Committee on Scholastic Grades would take over these duties—which would be the most fundamental and controversial throughout the sorority's history.

At the end of the convention, the election of officers in Philadelphia resulted in another term for Sadie Alexander as president; Edwina Woodyard, vice-president; Edna Morris (from Beta Chapter) recording secretary; Ethel Calimese, corresponding secretary; Virginia Alexander, treasurer; Anna Julian, journalist; Ida Rhodes, representative; Vivian Marsh, sergeant at arms; Alice Lucas, chaplain; Lillian Woodyard, custodian.

Plans began to be made for the next convention, to be held in Des Moines, Iowa, following the order of founding of the host chapters. However, the long distance so many had to travel and the few members then at Iowa made the site impractical. So, Lambda Chapter in Chicago, where many sorors were residing and where many were coming for the holidays, was selected for the fourth national convention, December 26–30, 1922.

Although there are few records regarding the deliberations of this meeting, discussions seemed to center around May Week programs and another innovation conceived by Alexander, the scholarship award and college tuition loan funds for members of the sorority. The idea behind these programs was more than just financial aid. The educational concerns of the sorority also centered around ways to inspire high school students to attend college and undergraduates to maintain high scholastic averages and continue to graduate school. Alexander, herself, of course had already earned her Ph.D. in economics, and in five years would get her LL.B. from the University of Pennsylvania.

There was also another prominent issue on the table. In April, seven months before the December convention, there had been the first meeting of the National Interfraternal Council in Washington, D.C. Later in the year, Alexander was elected chair of the council, which was made up of members from the four Black fraternities and three sororities. Its early objectives showed a common concern of all the Greek-letter organizations regarding the quality of student members, as it sought to "establish uniform qualifications for all candidates seeking membership in Greek-letter organizations; and limit the initiating of graduate members to persons holding degrees from schools on an accredited list that was to be prepared."[25] There was also a recommendation that "fraternal groups abandon underhanded competition and insidious propaganda"—a testament, no doubt, to some of the "all's fair in love, war, and competition for members" tactics used by the groups.

The first Black interfraternal council is said to have been initiated by Omega Psi Phi in 1914 at Howard University.[26] This new effort would be the first of many throughout the decades to form a cooperative association that would benefit all of the groups. During some periods interfraternal unity could be very effective as a galvanizing force of educated men and women, many of them leaders in their fields. But for the most part, this goal has been an elusive one. Nevertheless, the 1922 meeting attested to the great growth in all of the groups, and in the face of mounting pressures from the broader society and from some of their own institutions, a need to work together. And, as Helen Edmonds notes, the election of Alexander to the post of president afforded "a clear indication of the Sorority's preeminence in the eyes of the delegates."[27]

The fifth convention, hosted by Epsilon Chapter at Ohio State University, took place in Columbus in December of 1923. As at the others, the emphasis was on continued chapter growth, and five new chapters were authorized. Tau Chapter was established in Detroit, the city that would become one of the most powerful influences in the national organization. It became the home of students from the University of Detroit and Wayne State University, and was organized by Lillian Brown, formerly of Alpha Chapter; Prudence Perry, and Sara (Pelham) Speaks—daughter of Gabrielle Pelham—of Nu Chapter at the University of Michigan. Upsilon Chapter at the University of Southern California was founded on the heels of the Berkeley chapter and spearheaded by Vivian Marsh. And Eta Beta came to life in Dallas, largely due to the efforts of Frederica Dodd, who just three years before had married John H. Dodd, a Howard Medical School graduate who was well on his way to being one of the city's leading physicians and community leaders. Lillian Alexander was commissioned to establish

Rho Chapter in New York City, for undergraduates at Hunter College, Barnard, and New York University.

But many considered the real plum to be Sigma Chapter, organized at Atlanta's Clark College. The bustling city had a particular meaning for upwardly mobile Blacks. It was both the business and intellectual center of the national Black community. The southern city was the site of the Atlanta conferences, which took place between 1896 and 1914, and was directed by W.F.B. Du Bois, a professor at Atlanta University. The conferences featured discussions and scholarly analyses of educational, religious, and economic issues facing Blacks at the time, and as historian John Hope Franklin observed, they provided the "first real sociological research in the South."[28] The city was also the home of prominent Black institutions of higher education, including Spelman College, Clark College, Morehouse, Morris Brown, and Gammon Theological Seminary. And Atlanta was quickly becoming the wellspring for the Southern Negro Renaissance, as it was called, because of the important cultural figures there, such as the writer Benjamin Brawley, who was teaching at Morehouse, and scholars and educators such as James Weldon Johnson, Carolyn Bond Day, and John Hope. It was also the home of some of the most successful Black entrepreneurs in the country. At the heart of the businesses of Herman Perry, S. W. Walker, and Alonzo Herndon were Black insurance companies that became the basis for diverse enterprises including real estate, banking, construction, and other service industries. All of this activity generated a number of Atlanta first families, made up of the old bourgeoisie as well as newcomers who achieved financially and educationally.

No wonder that both the AKAs and Deltas, the two largest sororities, would focus a competitive attention there. Nevertheless, there was a traditional resistance to Greek-letter organizations: Several of the schools, including Spelman, the prestigious women's college, did not allow the establishment of sororities. As was also true at several other, notably Black schools, administrators felt that they distracted students from their studies; others were suspicious of any secret student organization (especially when Blacks began to engage in student strikes on Black campuses); and there was also the feeling that such organizations perpetuated class and even color distinctions among Blacks.

It was partly in defense against these charges that Numa P. G. Adams published the 1919 article referred to earlier. Adams had also stated that it was human nature for groups to form on one basis or another, and that at least with the Greek-letter societies there were regulation and constructive goals. Human nature was very much evident in Atlanta. In lieu of sororities and fraternities, such groups as the "Owls" and "Wolves" were present, reports Edmonds.[29] Both boasted having the most prestigious membership; however, the only clear distinction between the two groups was their skin color. The Wolves, observes Edmonds, had fair complexions, while "the receding shades were found in the Owls." Although worthy newcomers were invited into the groups, men were more readily accepted than women outsiders.

Atlanta University, and subsequently Clark College and the others, did permit the establishment of Greek-letter groups, and both the Deltas and the AKAs rushed to make inroads in the city, authorizing chapters in the same year. Delta's Edna Morris inducted the Sigma Chapter, and in the absence of sorors to supervise the first probates, Samuel Nabrit, dean of Atlanta University, an Omega man, "assumed the role of 'Worthy Superior' by self-appointment."[30]

Three other events made the fifth national convention particularly memorable. It took place at the same time as the general convention of Alpha Phi Alpha fraternity, and together all the members made a pilgrimage to Dayton, site of the home and shrine of the first nationally recognized Black poet, Paul Laurence Dunbar, who had died seventeen years before. The two groups also came together for Alpha's annual banquet, where Sadie Alexander spoke on "The Growth of Sororities."[31] The second event was the induction of Mary McLeod Bethune—upon the recommendation of her friend, Hallie Quinn Brown—as an honorary member. By 1923, Bethune was already well known as the founder of the Daytona School for Girls in Florida, which in that year, merged with Cookman College to become Bethune-Cookman College. She was also a leader of the National Association of Colored Women and in the following year would beat out Ida B. Wells-Barnett for the national presidency. In subsequent years Bethune would be founder and president of the National Council of Negro Women, a Cabinet member in the Franklin D. Roosevelt administration, and one of the most influential advocates of the rights of Blacks and women.

The third event that made the Columbus convention such a significant one was Sadie Alexander's declining the nomination to serve a fifth term. No doubt, her marriage to Raymond Pace Alexander just the month before, and her plans to attend law school, influenced her decision. Her retirement from office must have provided a moving moment for the delegates who had come to the convention. She had indeed accomplished much. Her stature alone invested the sorority, the fourth Black Greek-letter organization to be founded, with a preeminence early in its history. Her insistence on high standards made the Deltas, perhaps, the most prestigious of the organizations during this period, and her initiation of such programs as May Week and the scholarship funds, both of which were institutionalized within the Delta structure, provided a foundation and direction for the sorority. She was also instrumental in the early growth of the sorority on the nation's most highly rated campuses and was no doubt a magnet for its most prestigious honorary members. Through Sadie T. M. Alexander's leadership, Delta was not content to be the passive vessel for young women scholars, but took on an active role in the educational movement, seeking to inspire, motivate, and assist young Black women's aspirations in a period when the issue of their higher education for them was still being debated.

An era had ended when Sadie Alexander stepped down from the presidency and was voted the first honorary grand president of the sorority. The next phase of its history would see many of her ideas and programs continued, increasing numbers of chapters established, a focus on administrative efficiency, and the movement toward greater involvement in the political and racial issues that confronted them.

PART TWO

CHAPTER 5

NEW ERA, NEW CHALLENGE

The next five years of the sorority would find it at a crossroads. Growth was bringing recognition and status; it was also creating internal disorganization—and its by-product, dissension—both of which would have to be remedied. At the same time, to ensure its viability, Delta would have to meet the demands of continuing discrimination and a radicalized Black student movement. The next two national presidents, G. Dorothy (Pelham) Beckley (1923–1926) and Ethel (LaMay) Calimese (1926–1929) had a tremendous task before them.

Dorothy Beckley, daughter of the first honorary member of Delta, was a graduate of Howard University, and an English teacher at the Shaw Junior High School in Washington, D.C. She was a popular choice, and had the kind of verve that could make her jump into the line of returning World War I soldiers and march joyously with them, as Elsie (Brown) Smith recalled. She was also a good administrator, a quality desperately needed by the organization at this time. Serving in her three-year administration would be first vice-president Vivian Marsh, who by 1925 had graduated from the University of California at Berkeley and received her master's at that institution. A new office added, second vice-president, was held by Martha Hall of Cincinnati, a prominent social worker in that city. In 1924, Virginia Alexander would take her place. Corresponding secretary was Alzada (Singleton) Burford; recording secretary, Edna Morris; treasurer was founder Osceola Adams followed by Annie Dingle; and journalist, was Pauline A. Young. For the new administration, the year would be off to an exhilarating start.

That Delta was reaching new heights was evidenced at the sixth national convention in New York City, which opened on December 27, 1924. As *The Delta* described it, the two hundred official delegates, and additonal sorors, coming from twenty-two states made up "the largest group of Negro college women at any given time" assembled for an organizational gathering. The meetings took place at the Harlem YWCA on West 137th Street, which proved to "be well suited to the purpose, possessing both ample parlor and lobby spaces conducive to informal gatherings, formal conferences and committee meetings alike," the *Journal* observed. The convention was cohosted by the New York City graduate and undergraduate chapters, Alpha Sigma and Rho. The president of the former was none other than Frances Gunner—who had been instrumental in the formation of the Beta Chapter, and was the Alpha delegate to the 1913 Intercollegiate socialist society during her undergraduate years. At the time of the convention she was secretary of the Ashland Place YWCA in Brooklyn, New York. The Rho Chapter president was Constance Willis, a student at Hunter College.

The opening public program which she presided over was a notable one. Addie Waite Hunton, a clubwoman who would be president of the NACW in just two years, and who was then vice-president of the International Council of Women of the Darker Races—welcomed the Deltas to New York City. Florence Cole Talbert sang a solo, "Lo Hear the Gentle Lark," which was followed by a piano rendition of Schuman's "Allegro from Faschingwing" by Lydia Mason, holder of the Juilliard Musical Scholarship from Fisk University. "My Heart at Thy Sweet Voice" was then sung by Charlotte Wallace Murray, and a cable from soror Jessie Fauset, who was in France at the time, was read to the convention.

The evening also saw the award of Delta's first foreign scholarship, for study in France, to Gwendolyn Bennett, a poet, painter, and illustrator whose work was seen in such publications as *Opportunity, The Messenger,* and *The Crisis*. Then an art instructor at Howard University, Bennett was also a director of the Harlem Artists Guild, which exhibited leading artists such as Jacob Lawrence and Georgette Seabrook. In an impressive ceremony, the $1,000 scholarship was presented to her by Dorothy Canfield Fisher, a novelist and writer of note who, two years later, became the only woman member of the first board of selection for the Book of the Month Club. In that position she played an important role in the success of Pearl Buck, Isak Dinesen, and Richard Wright—for whom she would write an introduction for his novel *Native Son*. "I am proud to be here," declared Fisher during the presentation. "You are doing the right thing, a thing so gravely important and so different from the usual sorority life of competition in furnishing their houses with Oriental rugs, etc." Saying that "greatness is the solution to every problem," she noted her extreme pleasure to bestow the award, for the "encouragement of greatness to Gwendolyn Bennett." Bennett, as the *Journal* described, then "came forward daintily shy and overcome by this sudden news" to receive the award from Fisher, who, "in the manner of the French, kissed Soror Gwendolyn upon each cheek."[1] The display of respect and affection by Canfield, who was white, was pointedly mentioned in publication.

This was also the convention where the official Delta Hymn was selected. Beta Chapter had submitted a fine piece of music with lyrics by Isabel Askew and music by another chapter member, Anna Dorsey Wilson. Four members of the Wilberforce group, including Askew and accompanied by Wilson, performed the music for the Delta delegates. Edna Morris reported that it was well-liked by the group, but would be overshadowed by another composition. As the story has it, Alice Dunbar-Nelson and Florence Cole Talbert sequestered themselves at some point during the meeting and emerged with lyrics and music of their own. "Soror Nelson read the poetry," wrote Morris, "after which Soror Talbert followed with the words set to music which she had composed. The two honorary sorors, together, very reverently, dedicated and gave the words and music over to Delta Sigma Theta Sorority as its property."[2] Though the Beta Hymn was "delightfully inspiring," in the Delta historian's words, the response to the Cole Talbert–Nelson creation was effusive. "The convention," said Morris, "much impressed with the beauty of the sentiment so pleasingly expressed by Soror Nelson's words and thrilled to ecstacsy by the melodious strains of Soror Talbert's music, enthusiastically adopted [it] as the official hymn."[3] (Nevertheless, the Beta Hymn was not discarded. It was used by chapters on special occasions and subsequently was adopted as part of the official ritual of the sorority.)

No less impressive were the gala social events that took place at the convention. The Deltas, afterall, were meeting in Harlem at the height of the Renaissance and the galas were more festive and cosmopolitan than most. There was the Delta annual ball at the grand ballroom of the Brooklyn Academy of Music, where the "mirror-like" floor, filled "with dancing maidens in colors of every hue, sombered only by the swallow-tails of our partners" was likened to a "virtual fairyland."4 On New Year's Day, from 11:00 A.M. to 4:00 P.M., the local chapter of the Kappa Alpha Psi fraternity hosted an open house at the studio of A'Lelia Walker, daughter of Madame C. J. Walker, the millionaire hairdressing magnate and clubwoman. A'Lelia, who inherited much of her mother's wealth, hosted some of the most lavish, celebrity-studded parties of the era. The gathering at 136th Street and Lenox Avenue was in honor of the Greek-letter groups who were visiting the city at the time: the Deltas, Zeta Phi Beta, and Alpha Phi Alpha. They would also be guests of the *Pittsburgh Courier* and *The New York News* which held informal receptions at their offices. Finally, there was the reception that the AKAs hosted, in honor of the national officers, at the International House on Riverside Drive, to which the Deltas were also invited.

It would be difficult for the delegates—many of whom made special efforts to be there—to go home. It was an occasion of renewing ties and creating new ones, in a time when Black achievement and culture were being nationally celebrated. Founders Fredrica Dodd, Ethel Black, and Naomi Richardson attended. May Chinn, who would become the first Black female physician in Harlem, was there. Eslanda Robeson, writer, scholar, and wife of Paul Robeson, was present, as was future president Mae (Wright) Peck. And Sadie Alexander, fresh from her honeymoon, wouldn't have missed it for the world. Descriptions of the conference in the *The Delta* talked about it as a "source of inspiration" to work harder, and about the sense of oneness that it engendered. "Picture to yourself an appreciative audience of nearly two hundred girls, varying in size, from short to tall, in color, from the deeper browns to the palest blonds, and in dress from plainly conservative to ultra modish," Gamma Chapter's Anna Julian wrote. ". . . And what a pleasure it was to clasp the hands of sorors from as far west as California, from as far north as the Great Lakes and from as far south as Texas! It gave me that feeling of indescribable unity that after all East is West and North is South."5

The description reveals a sense of pride about the diversity of the Delta members. One of the criticisms often leveled at Black sororities is prejudice against darker-skinned women, and those who did not dress like or have the refinement of the Black elite. That there was open competition for women from long-standing and influential middle-class families, many of them part of the Black bourgeoisie, can be seen as evidence of this assertion. On the other hand, Delta's own history suggests otherwise. The founders of the organization, like the members who attended the convention, ranged from fair-skinned to dark. Myra Hemmings, the first president of Delta (and formerly president of AKA) was herself "deep brown." And scholarship and leadership qualities were unquestionably more important than family connections, or wealth, when members were considered—as is evidenced by the diverse backgrounds of the group. Questions put to founders Naomi Richardson and Bertha Campbell substantiated this view. And Sadie Alexander, in her later years also broached the subject. "One of our distinguished honorary members, I am told, stated that the reason she hadn't joined Delta when she was a young person was that she was too black," Alexander began. "Well, color didn't mean anything to us. . . . [And] we are not looking for children whose parents have the most money or have the prettiest houses where they can entertain us. . . . What did mean a great deal to us was what kind of grades you made and if you were dedicated to the causes for which we were concerned."[6]

ORGANIZATIONAL
DEVELOPMENTS

When the celebration ended, the delegates faced the tasks confronting the internal development of the sorority. New chapters had to be authorized, efficiency measures had to be enacted, and it was time to create regional divisions in order to administer the organization more effectively and stem the tide of increasing inactivity. Chapters also had to be reorganized.

In 1924, Lambda Chapter in Chicago was broken up to become two chapters: one for the undergraduates, which kept the original name; and Theta Beta which became the chapter for the older women. Graduates in Atlanta successfully petitioned for a chapter separate from that of the undergraduates. Its charter would be granted in the fall of 1925. Martha Hall was dispatched to Indianapolis to charter Chi Chapter, a mixed chapter that included students from Butler University and a group of Beta members who had found their way to that city. Among the group were Jeannette (Summers) Carey, Lucille Stokes, Frieda (Campbell) Parker, and Mary Stokes. In addition, the former grand journalist, Bernice (Copeland) Lindsey of Ohio State's Epsilon Chapter, also became a charter member. The convention also authorized Psi Chapter in June 1925; it was mixed but made up mostly of students at the University of Kansas in Lawrence. Phi Chapter, composed mainly of coeds from Drake, Iowa State, and Des Moines universities, was also inducted. Honorary member Gertrude Rush was present for the ceremony. Additional petitions for chapters were deferred by the Executive Council until the next convention. It was time to take stock, consolidate, organize themselves. One of the most important internal issues to discuss was the need for regional divisions and authorities. It was just too time-consuming and costly to focus on chapter development from one office now that its chapters crisscrossed the country, east and west, north and south. The idea came from Gamma Chapter's Alice Dunbar-Nelson, who now chaired the National Program Committee and suggested that regional conferences would also have the advantage of making the May Week educational campaigns more effective. She wanted a more extensive organization of "study-help" clubs for high school students and college freshmen. Her objective was to establish these clubs in every locale where Delta had a chapter.[7]

Dunbar-Nelson's regional idea may have also been adopted by the National Association of Colored Women, to which she also belonged. The latter would establish regional entities during the administration of Addie Waite Hunton, who was president between 1926 and 1930. For social movement organizations, especially one like Delta where social bonds were so important, regional entities had greater value than its sheer practicality. They could be a remedial measure for imbuing the zeal and enthusiasm of the national program to local chapters when their national convention representatives failed to do so.[8] And as a Delta publication noted, while "all members have the same ideals, the expression of those ideals is modified by geographical environments. Instead of regretting these differences," it continued, "we should seek to use what we can of them for our increased efficiency. Instead of withdrawing within ourselves. . . . That we are not alike is no occasion for unfriendliness."[9]

The establishment of regional entities reflects the attempt to balance the needs of the sisterhood: the importance of members getting to know each other, and making their diversity a means of coherence; and that of the effective functioning of the organization. The reasoning also indicated the understanding that an emotional commitment (zeal and enthusiasm) was necessary for the effectiveness of the national program. This is not unusual for a voluntary organization, but it indicates the particular challenge that one like Delta faced. This voluntary association was conceived through common goals, but there was no one issue that could be used as a politically galvanizing force. The sisterhood was the cohesive glue, and sisterhood was not easy to maintain when its age and geographical boundaries were becoming more and more extended.

In April of 1925, regional conferences were instituted; and at the 1925 convention, held in Des Moines that year, the reports were heard. The reviews were mixed. Four regions had been created: Eastern, Midwest, Far West, and Southern. The Midwest and Southern chapters were unable to meet. However, the Eastern meeting in Boston and the Far West Los Angeles conferences were said to be successful with "enthusiasm coupled with a spirit of good will and readiness for serious work."[10] As would be repeated often in Delta history, questionnaires, for the purpose of gathering information and establishing better understanding of its membership, were sent out regarding the regionals, whose administration was under the supervision of Anna Julian. Asked about their accomplishments, sorors mentioned the engendering of "fellowship" and of a source of information for a range of things from location of chapters to programs to the "compilation of suitable plays for May Week and the distribution of suitable Negro literature in libraries."[11]

By April of 1926, the next round of regional conferences took place. This time, Beckley, herself, presided over the Eastern regionals held on April 2 and 3 in Washington, D.C. Vivian Marsh, vice-president, took charge of the Far West meeting in Berkeley, California, on the same dates, and second vice-president Virginia Alexander directed the Midwest regional that met on April 9 and 10 in Kansas City, Missouri, where she now resided. On the same dates, southern chapters had their conference in Atlanta. As there was no sectional vice-president then elected from that region, Anna Julian presided over it. During the conference, the Advisory Committee of the Grand Chapter, made up of the national officers, voted upon the position of chair of the Southern Region for the first time, and Ruth

Wheeler was elected. (Subsequently, the regions themselves elected their own directors, who took on the duties previously given to the sectional vice-presidents.) With these regional conferences, the innovation seemed to be finally moving apace.

It was hoped that the regional conferences would help another internal matter of concern: growing inactivity among the members. It would be an issue that would plague the sorority throughout its history. Sometimes the depletion couldn't be helped. In *The Delta Journal* for example, several undergraduate chapters expressed their frustrations that were beyond their control. The reporter from Omicron Chapter at the University of Nebraska complained that their chapter had felt "discouraged this year. Two of our already small group had to teach this year; another, is at home because of illness in the family; thus our ranks are reduced to two. At the university," she continued, "there are more girls than ever before, but nearly all are registered for the two-year teacher's course, which is not a degree course. . . . We tried to interest the girls in working for a degree, but without success this far. . . . We who are left are one hundred percent loyal," the writer concluded, "Delta's welfare is ever before us, and we pray for her continued growth over the years."[12] In a similar vein, Zeta Beta Chapter of Tuskegee, though recently taking on "new life" had "suffered such a depletion of numbers at the beginning of this scholastic year that it has been difficult to effect a reorganization and get a program under way with the enthusiasm necessary for successful accomplishment."[13] Later in the year, the news of the death of Margaret Murray Washington would be another blow to the struggling chapter, whose members attended and took part in the funeral rites.

But it was the attrition of the graduate sorors that was of greater concern. It was easier to get members than keep them financially active. Older sorors, especially, became involved in careers. There was also a lull in the kind of activity that was instituted by the charismatic Alexander, and the less-exciting, nuts-and-bolts tasks were not as attractive. Finally, there may well have been the perception that invites apathy in a social movement organization. But inactivity was a virus that began to affect Delta's organizational goals. Beckley discovered that there was only $211 in the Scholarship Fund, $86 in the Student Loan Fund, and in 1925 receipts from the scholarship tax were $56. The latter figure possessed Lillian A. Alexander, chair of the Scholarship Committee, to write that although the first scholarship award was no doubt pleasing to the sorors, there was much work to be done. "Deltas!! Do you know that up to December 17 the Treasurer had received scholarship assessments from only 28 members throughout the entire sorority!"[15] The situation moved the national office to require that chapters pay the scholarship assessments as well as Grand Chapter dues before they would be considered financial. But inactivity, unfortunately, even affected the national officers. *The Delta Sigma Theta Bulletin*, a new publication, established earlier in her administration to keep sorors apprised of sorority developments Beckley announced dramatically, was edited and published by an emergency staff when the journalist (Pauline Young) "suddenly and unexpectedly abandoned the project."[16] All of which prompted Anna Julian to write "we cannot afford to rest on seen or unseen laurels. There is much work which we, and only we, can do for the Race and for Delta. But we can do little without efficiency as our guide and nothing with procrastination as our taskmaster."[17]

Pelham refused to be defeated by the situation, and confronted it squarely. She announced a campaign against inactivity and created a new category of corresponding members, which allowed graduate sorors who were frequently relocating themselves far from chapter seats to be more involved with the sorority. Under the new designation, a group of six financially active members could be represented as a unit, and elect a delegate among them who could take part and vote in national or regional conferences. "This recognition seemed to encourage the floating sorors to seek active status," observed Edna Morris.[18] "Delta units were authorized in communities where at least three corresponding members were able to get together to execute a local program" in the name of the sorority. And at the eighth national convention, held in Cincinnati—and whose host was Iowa State graduate Adah (Hyde) Johnson, president of Phi Chapter in Des Moines—inactivity was its dominant theme.

One of the problems, the president knew, was discouragement about the lack of efficiency within the organization. And during her administration much was accomplished. Consequently, she introduced the use of printed forms for reports, applications, and other formal documents. Chapter records were filed methodically, and *The Delta Sigma Theta Bulletin*, an official, for-members-only organ was published containing information of general interest as well as the business of the sorority. Beckley also attempted to clarify the role of the Executive Council in making decisions between conventions—with the exception of chartering chapters. And she urged that the treasurer, Annie Dingle, have the sole responsibility for receiving and recording Grand Chapter monies (assets had reached over $1,200) instead of sharing that responsibility with the secretary, Edna Morris. Beckley's recommendation was probably inspired by the conflict between the two officers, with Dingle complaining that Morris was withholding money and thus chapter dispensations weren't being credited. (The acceptance of that recommendation, though proper, would prove to be a fateful decision.) Finally, under her administration, a new nomenclature system for naming chapters was instituted. The Greek alphabet reached its end. Subsequent chapters would use two letters of the alphabet in descending order: for example, Alpha Alpha, Alpha Beta, Alpha Gamma, and so on. When the Alpha series was exhausted, new chapters would begin with Beta, then Gamma, and so on. Omega Omega would be used to signify sorors who had passed away. And Sigma as the last letter would replace Beta in identifying graduate chapters. Later "Alumnae," as in Detroit Alumnae Chapter, would replace Beta.

In terms of new programs Iota Chapter would contribute a major and long-sustaining one called the "Jabberwock." Conceived by Marion (Conover) Hope in 1925 as a variety show of music, skits, and dance, the monies made from it were earmarked for scholarships, and subsequently public service projects. It was perfect for Delta's inclinations toward the arts, and would be a showcase for Deltas who would become nationally known. (Three decades later, for example, Roberta Flack would be chair of the Jabberwock Committee for the Alpha Chapter program at Washington's Banneker Junior High School.) Other Greek organizations were invited to participate, and as the idea caught on it became a virtual Delta institution.

RACIAL CONCERNS

The year also marked another attempt to establish interfraternal cooperation when Alpha Kappa Alpha sorority telegrammed the Deltas to suggest that all fraternities and sororities meet in 1927 to hold a one-day session "for the purpose of pooling ideas for racial betterment."[19] They had undoubtedly been inspired by an address of Dean Kelly Miller who spoke at their boule (national convention) in Howard University's Rankin Chapel and urged that all of the Greek-letter organizations "unite in one big effort" toward that goal.[20] Action on the AKA proposal would be deferred until the next convention, but their role in the racial struggle was very much on their minds. The sorority had taken stands. At the 1924 convention, a resolution was passed criticizing the efforts, begun under the Woodrow Wilson administration, to resegregate the United States Civil Service. The new discrimination had even gotten Mary Church Terrell, who worked there, fired. The resolution was a mild one, however. It proposed that photographic identification—which had taken the place of fingerprints and was used as a means to discriminate against Blacks—be eliminated. But in 1924 and 1925, there was a need for a greater response to racial issues, which were reaching a climax in these years.

A focal point of those concerns was a pending Supreme Court decision concerning discrimination in housing. The case, *Corrigan* v. *Buckley,* was crucial in that an unfavorable decision could undermine a previous Supreme Court decision that had found segregated housing unconstitutional. (And, in fact, the case was lost by the NAACP.) The housing issue was a particularly hot one in the twenties because of the resistance to the new influx of Blacks who had migrated to the cities during the World War I years. Housing, Blacks understood, was an issue that meant much to their quality of life, the education of their children, and their fundamental right to first-class citizenship.

Another issue was the student movement on Black campuses. In 1924 and 1925, it had reached a new pitch that culminated in student strikes at Hampton, Fisk, Tuskegee, Howard, and other schools. The issues were academic freedom and/or the upgrading of curricula that in too many instances deemphasized liberal arts in favor of training courses. As W.E.B. Du Bois, an advocate, and sometimes a catalyst, for the movement wrote, "We are going ahead to full-fledged colleges of 'A' grade and no longer pretend that we are simply educating farm hands and servants."[21] One of the colleges he was most critical of was Hampton, from where he received an anonymous letter describing the paternalistic system there in some detail. The letter precipitated his personal involvement, which resulted in a student strike at the school and was written by none other than Berkeley charter member, Louise Thompson, then teaching on the Virginia campus. She would subsequently be fired.

At Fisk, DuBois's alma mater, the issue was academic and social freedoms. In addition to student demands to have a student government association and revise some of the rules and regulations, according to Raymond Wolters, who wrote about the movement, one of their most ardent student demands was the *right to have fraternities and sororities on the campus!*

From available evidence, the Delta organization never took a public stand on the struggles of Black students in this period. Probably, its need for sanction from college administrators prevented them from being overtly critical of them. Incurring their wrath, after all, would do little to help the Delta cause at a time when they were still attempting to make inroads on the campus. And as a social movement organization, it was important that they be seen as a legitimate entity in the eyes of those administrators. The Deltas believed, evidently, that it was more important to reiterate the wholesome attitudes that were a by-product of sorority life. For example, in the same year, 1925, that Howard students struck over academic freedom, the Deltas, who had just acquired a sorority house, stressed its role in the development of the women students. The sorority house engendered cooperation between sorors of "several temperaments," who were in close contact with each other, soror Cathryn Robinson wrote in the *Howard University Record*. This eliminated selfishness and inculcated "respect for the rights of others." Having a sorority house, she continued, meant responsibility, and responsibility was "one of the ways by which the ideals of the organization will be truly tested."[22]

Interestingly, the sorority was more interested in expressing its views on the broader issue of women's roles than the student concerns that were bubbling on the campus. "The women of today have a broader field into which to enter than the women of a few decades ago," noted Robinson. "Their duties are not restricted to the maintaining of home life. The women of today play a vital part in the affairs of the world. Much is expected of them. Their advantages are greater, so their responsibilities increase correspondingly. Freely they receive; freely they must give." And, although the concept of public service had yet to be specifically articulated as an organizing principle (as it would be in later years), Robinson's conviction that "service is the price the world asks in return for the advantages offered"[23] was one of the philosophical underpinnings of the group.

Deltas would respond to the student struggle in their own way. By 1925, Fisk students had won many of their demands, and in the following year Delta would organize the Alpha Beta Chapter on its campus. But the organization was also anxious to exercise a broader racial role. Their mentor, Mary Church Terrell, had also responded to the student movement, writing: "Students in our universities and colleges can do much to eradicate prejudice by starting a crusade which shall have as its slogan, 'Down with discrimination against human beings on account of race, color, sex or creed.'"[24]

The perspective resulted in delegates at the seventh national convention in Iowa drawing up a statement that would be their first public pronouncement against racism. And it pulled no punches. "We feel deeply the need for protest against the growing prejudice of all kinds in the United States of America," it began. "The time has come when we feel called upon to give voice for the first time to the strong feelings which have possessed us." They stated that their claims to justice and equality were based on the contributions of the race to the country, including its "free shedding of blood" in the last war, its loyalty, and its refusal to become embittered despite continuing prejudice. It was a prejudice, the Deltas noted, perhaps thinking of Oberlin College, that was spreading "even into strongholds of the Abolitionists." The result was a growing segregation that was "becoming organized. Americans are organizing with the avowed purpose of preventing other Americans from purchasing and occupying property except in specially segregated localities.

"We commend all who have taken a stand against unjust discrimination of any sort. . . ," the pronouncement continued. "On the other hand we condemn those who have proved to be Januses in times of racial stress. . . . We do most solemnly condemn, and call upon all fair-minded men and women to condemn, the attempts at property rights discrimination that are at present being made. We see in these attempts the agencies for the destruction of the very fabric of our democracy."[25]

In December 1926, at the sorority's eighth national convention held in Cincinnati, Ohio, Dorothy Beckley, who had married earlier that year, refused the nomination for a third term. Ethel Calimese, who had been elected grand secretary at the 1921 convention as a member of Cincinnati's Zeta Chapter, was elected to take her place. Her cohorts would be Anna Julian, first vice-president; Vivian Marsh, second vice-president; Beatrice Morton, secretary; Annie Dingle, treasurer; and founder Madree White, journalist.

Ethel Calimese would preside over an organization in which many elements were in place. There were the programs established by Sadie Alexander; under Beckley's administration, the first scholarship fund awards were granted—with Ida Redmond of Syracuse University's Eta Chapter, and Louise Drake of the University of Pennsylvania's Gamma Chapter, being the first recipients. New chapters were still being organized with regularity. Under Beckley, Kappa Sigma in Houston, Lambda Sigma in St. Louis (where founder Madree White had had a hand in its establishment), Alpha Delta at West Virginia State College, Alpha Gamma at Morgan College in Baltimore (which had recently attained an "A" rating, and was aided by founder Vashti Murphy), Omega Chapter in Cleveland, and Alpha Alpha of Kansas City had all come into the fold. And though there were still some administrative problems to iron out, Beckley had made a Herculean effort to further the sorority's operational efficiency. Calimese, then, had a pretty strong foundation upon which to work. Nevertheless, a number of events would occur under her presidency, which would threaten to tear the organization apart, and thus test the new organization in its first major crisis.

THE ETHEL CALIMESE
ADMINISTRATION

The first year of her administration, 1927, was uneventful with the exception of the establishment of several chapters. Alpha Epsilon, in Pittsburgh, was made up of graduates, as well as undergraduates from such campuses as Duquesne, Carnegie Tech, and others who did not belong to the University of Pittsburgh Mu Chapter. Another predominantly Black school, Talladega College in Alabama, was added to the roster. Established in 1867, it only accepted students from the top percentiles of their high schools. In addition, three graduate chapters were given life: Mu Sigma in Norfolk, Virginia; Nu Sigma at Los Angeles, of which founder Wertie (Blackwell) Weaver would become a member; and Xi Sigma in Philadelphia.

Though there were other changes—Jeannette (Triplett) Jones from Chicago was elected second vice-president; Howard graduate

Jennie (Baer) Shief became secretary; and Dorothy Beckley was elected journalist—Ethel Calimese, Anna Julian, and Annie M. Dingle were elected for a second term at the 1927 convention in Washington, D.C. It had been decided that annual conventions were both too grueling and costly to sustain, and another was not scheduled until 1929, which would be the first biennial session. The two years separating the national meetings would be the most contentious in the sorority's young history. No new chapters were established in these years, and though historian Morris emphasized the advantage of this lull in activity "to study the history, ideals, and principles of the organization which enhanced fellowship and allowed time for correspondence,"[26] there well may have been other more causal reasons. Morris did note that during the second year of her term Calimese became ill, and thus inactive. But she recovered in time for the 1929 national convention to take place in the Pythian Building of Pittsburgh, where twenty-five chapters were seated.

The convention started on less than a harmonious note when the Credentials Committee—appointed by Calimese—challenged the seating of two delegates. The first was from a corresponding member who was teaching at Lincoln University in Kansas City, Missouri, but who had been a charter member of Los Angeles's Nu Sigma Chapter. She was denied delegate status from Nu Sigma because it was felt that she would be unable to give a firsthand report of the convention to her home chapter. Nevertheless, it was moved and accepted that she be seated with Nu Sigma, but that the action not be taken as a precedent. A similar motion prevailed when Beatrice Penman (a future national treasurer) was denied a seat because her Alpha Alpha Chapter (Kansas City) had not paid its dues for 1929 until just a few minutes before the meeting of the Credentials Committee. But the committee relented with the same caveat about setting a precedent.

This fortunately was soon followed by the highlight of the convention, which was the report from the chapters. "They were so illuminating as to the achievements of Deltas all over the country," stated the recorder of the proceedings, that the reading of them was interrupted by a motion that Sarah (Pelham) Speaks (sister of Dorothy Pelham) be permitted to publish them. Those reports and the lecture given by Alice Dunbar-Nelson at the Fellowship Tea that took place at the YWCA seemed to be the only uplifting events in 1929. Dunbar-Nelson, however, had gotten a preview of the kind of tension that could be involved even in Delta chapter meetings as an excerpt from her diary attests. "Hurry to dress and get ready to go to a Philadelphia Gamma Delta meeting," the entry began.

> *Pauline [Young] balky about going.*
>
> *We drive to Virginia's [Alexander] new house and office. Everyone is late but eventually the Delta members arrive, about fifteen of them.*
>
> *We have a three-hour session—the first part devoted to me and AIPC [American Friends Inter-Racial Peace Committee]—valuable for me and my project. Then the fateful elections. It were [sic] best to draw a veil over the harrowing scenes—the passionate appeal of me in the chair, the fateful blackballs, Wilma the Proud, the tears of Clementine. Well, all five candidates were lost, Clementine's hysterics and Wilma's passion—well, we came out at nearly 7:00, and I've seldom had such a splitting headache.[27]*

At the national convention, Gamma Chapter soror Anna Julian displayed some justified passion of her own. As acting regional director of the Southwest Region, she reported its general inactivity and the fact that the situation could have been remedied if the Budget Committee had given her the monies to travel and deal with the situation, as was authorized at the last convention. There were some problems in Tulsa, Oklahoma, where there had been a request to establish a mixed chapter that allegedly included some illegal initiates. But the refusal to release the monies for Julian to travel there had left the situation in the air. "The Tulsa girls are very much discouraged over our apparent lack of interest and neglect of what to them is a very vital problem," she wrote in her report. "Soror Smith writes me that many of the Sorors there have lost interest in Delta and instead are lending their efforts toward other community activities. I learn through her that they have two girls away on scholarship," Julian continued "one at Tuskegee and the other at Kansas State University. I wonder if we can afford to lose the interest of such energetic girls?"[28]

"After much correspondence," Julian did manage to establish the Mu Sigma Norfolk chapter, but there were problems with additional chapters because of the bad communication between the officers. She was frustrated by efforts to establish a chapter in Raleigh, North Carolina, a frustration that was shared by founder Jimmie Middleton. As early as 1925, when there were four Deltas already living in that city, there had been numerous attempts by coeds at Shaw University as well as some graduate members to establish a chapter. According to Middleton, who was living there at the time, after several attempts to get Grand Chapter's attention failed, she was asked to personally attend the Washington, D.C., convention and press their case. "I did," she recalled, "but due to some dirty politics I was refused a mixed chapter but was promised a graduate chapter." However, she was then struck by arthritis, soon after which she went to Howard's graduate school. The North Carolinians continued pushing through their regional director, but to no avail. Alpha Zeta Sigma graduate chapter wouldn't be established until 1938. And in the meantime, several of the women pursuing the chapter charter abandoned their efforts to become, in Middleton's words, "leading AKAs."

One of the worst situations existed at the newly established Fisk chapter. Several students had reported to Julian that a number of girls were about to be initiated who met neither "the scholastic requirements nor did they have certain other desirable Delta qualities." She wired the chapter's president to suspend preparations for the initiations until an investigation could be made. In the meantime Julian contacted the regional director who informed her that she had refused to okay some of the girls. One had low grades (meaning too many Cs), one received an unfavorable recommendation from Atlanta, where she had been a Pyramid (Delta pledgee), and another had begun pledging Alpha Kappa Alpha in Atlanta, and it had yet to be determined if she was now free to join Delta.

To add to the confusion, despite the regional director's questions, the national president seemed to grant permission for the young woman with the questionable grades to pledge, upon the approval of the dean of students and she was initiated into the sorority. Julian was incensed by the fact that a student with such a poor scholastic record was permitted into the sorority. At the same time, another inquiry to Atlanta, some time later, received a favorable recommendation for the young women who had been previously denied—after they graduated! To add insult to injury, the Fisk chapter didn't pay their dues or send a delegate to the regional conference. "I cannot blame the Fisk girls," concluded Anna Julian, "for they are young and inexperienced and theirs is a blunder of blind and uninstructed youth. The blame must fall on the Grand Chapter. We have failed to publish a handbook; we have failed to instruct them; we have failed to maintain a close contact and sisterly supervision with them." Such mistakes of any chapter, she wrote, "must be borne by the whole organization."[29]

The responsibility of the whole organization notwithstanding, most of the criticism was leveled at President Calimese. And it was so severe that it is doubtful that illness, or illness alone—which would have mitigated the tone—was perceived to be responsible. Regarding the Fisk situation, Beckley noted in her report that "if it is true that the President of the Grand Chapter based her authorization . . . on the approval of the Dean of Women—who is not a Delta—and thus overruled both the regional director and the first vice-president, who is the chairman of the Regional Conference Committee, the situation is one which calls for drastic action."[30]

The situation further deteriorated when it was realized that "the president of the Grand Chapter had prepared no program," though requested to do so. A motion was made that she do it forthwith. There was complaint that the president hadn't acknowledged, accepted, or rejected a report from the Committee on Accrediting Schools and Colleges, though it had been submitted to her in July of 1928. The report, described as "an exhaustive piece of scientific research," was nevertheless accepted by the convention. Calimese's inaction on this issue was particularly frustrating. A decision had to be made regarding students in Black public colleges and other institutions of lesser rating but which had good students. This was especially true of schools in the South. By 1928, the Association of Colleges and Secondary Schools of the Southern States, a group less empathetic to Black educational goals than the sorority, had recommended the consideration of Black institutions.

There was also some bad feeling about Calimese's actions in removing the director of the Far West but not the Midwest director who had been inactive. Past president Dorothy Beckley, who took on the office of journalist, also had a scathing report. She had been unable to execute her duties, and charged that "this inactivity was enforced by the policy of silence and non-communication adopted by [President Calimese and was] more shameful than any but those who have given years of untiring effort to Delta Sigma Theta can realize. And it will require the exercise of almost superhuman self control," she continued, "to prevent the deep resentment which the Journalist individually feels toward the negligence and dereliction of the President from finding expression in this report."[31] The *Bulletin* was to be planned and determined by the chief executive, as the lack of response had made it impossible to publish the information needed in it. As a result, two instead of the scheduled eight issues had been published.

Of course, Calimese also had her day in "court." But the "President's Report" was hardly convincing. The report itself was not included in the minutes because Calimese had not filed it with the secretary despite repeated requests. The discussion of it, however, is recorded and the points raised included the following assertions. Calimese had not removed the inactive director of the Midwest because she felt that she didn't have the authority to do so. (However, this still left the question of where she obtained the authority to remove the director of the Far West.) The president also complained that she didn't get reimbursed for her expenses, but it was counterclaimed that she had not made any such requests. Calimese said that she did not reply to correspondence because she never received most of the letters in question. Those that she did admit to receiving were answered. However, these replies must "have miscarried." Finally, Calimese charged that she could not carry on as president because she felt that she "did not have the cooperation of the other officers of the Grand Chapter."[32]

The miscommunications and conflicts had a particularly negative impact on the scholarship and loan fund situation. A loan and a scholarship award had been promised to a student attending Radcliffe and one attending the University of Pennsylvania. However, the treasurer, Annie Dingle, had withheld the monies because she had not received warrants from Calimese authorizing the release of funds. The reasons the president gave concerned the question of granting a loan to a graduate, instead of an undergraduate, student, and, in the case of the scholarship, the Budget Committee's not having approved it and her fear of repeating "the embarrassments and delays incident to the scholarship award of 1928–9." When it was belatedly discovered that the funds were not coming from the Grand Chapter, steps were taken to advance half of the promised amount to the students: Boston's Iota Chapter loaned the Radcliffe student $150 for that school's first semester tuition; and Jennie (Shief) Baer who subsequently became a national officer of the sorority, advanced the U of P student $200 for her first semester's tuition. Not only was it voted that those who gave the money be reimbursed by the Grand

Chapter, but that they be repaid with 6 percent interest. And the convention also clarified the extent of power of the president in this regard. Her "signature to the warrant should not be misinterpreted as the President's approval of the award," it was said. The awarding of scholarships and loans were to be left entirely to the discretion of the committee.[33]

Despite the anger expressed at the convention, it is interesting to note that the delegates took the path of offering motions to attempt to rectify the situation instead of issuing ultimatums to the president. And in fact this was done very consciously. The motions were preceded by the statement that they were offered "inasmuch as the convention was of the opinion that it did not want to be recorded as having forced a President to perform her lawful duty."[34]

The most destructive problem that the contentiousness and the confusion created was with the treasurer's office. Dingle was conspicuously absent from the proceedings. A telegram he sent to her instructing that all financial records, bankbooks, bank statements, warrants, vouchers, and other Grand Chapter property in her possession be sent by registered mail, special delivery. Secretary Jennie Baer in her report complained that she had never received receipts, which she had requested from Dingle, for the money that she had sent to her. As a result, she refused to continue forwarding the monies to the treasurer, and informed the president of same. In the absence of an audit committee at the 1927 convention, Baer requested that Calimese ascertain the status of the sorority's account.[35] In Dingle's absence, Baer was authorized to disperse the funds that she had in her possession to take care of the incurred expenses of the sorority. Of course, tie-ups on the financial side affected everything, and the Deltas would lose ground in the implementation of their programs and administrative operations. How severe the damage was would be discovered in short shrift.

But what was most painful, perhaps, was the unavoidable impact all of this had on the morale of the chapters. In Anna Julian's report, she informed the group that she had become so discouraged by these events that she wrote letters to all of the chapters and officers asking for their views of the sorority. Her actions underlined the respect that was accorded the younger members of the sorority, and the perspective of the national leadership. This was not an organization that would be run by decree from the top, even in crisis. In any case, fourteen chapters replied to her letter and there was no lack of criticism—showing that they also understood their own power and responsibility. Thirteen out of the fourteen cited the inaction of the president. Twelve noted the infrequent publication of the *Journal* and other official publications; ten stated the lack of cooperation among the national officers; eight added the lack of local enthusiasm because of the Grand Chapter inaction. There were constructive suggestions too: that the first vice-president be empowered to act when the president fails to do so; that there be an official calendar and a Delta directory; that there be no letting down of the standards; and that, where C is construed as 80 percent, a B average be required.[36]

In light of the deep feelings, fractious—if dignified—arguments, the failure of the chief executive, and the low morale that must have been an inevitable by-product, it was remarkable that the conference did not bog down and come apart. But it didn't. Committee members raised important questions that were discussed by the convention. Lillian Alexander noted that every young woman who applied for a scholarship and supplied the necessary information received one. Yet there had been a very small outlay in the previous five years out of the total sum available for that purpose. Many requests for applications had been made, she said, but were followed by "silence, indicating that the applicant could not meet the conditions. Are our requirements too rigid?" she asked. The nature of the issue she raised was a difficult one for Delta, for it was attempting to reconcile its existence as a scholarly organization whose members would be viewed not unlike those in an honor society with its social obligations. The very essence of its May Week program showed the sorors' social inclinations, and their desire not only to be a motivating force for students predisposed to achievement, but to encourage those who were not.

Another question that Alexander presented to the group was whether scholarships should indeed be given to graduate students, an idea that was criticized by President Calimese. This was an important one to consider. A graduate student, after all, was already ahead of the game; yet she was probably already motivated and could well be on her way to "great things" as a result of help from the sorority. But would those resources be better served to aid someone to climb the first step of the higher educational ladder? These were questions that the sorors would grapple with over many years.

In a related issue, more thought had to be applied to the scholarship standards. As that committee noted in its report, provisions had to be made for accepting candidates from such highly rated schools as Oberlin, which did not furnish certified grades. Even more important was the discrepancy among grading systems in the wide variety of colleges that Black women attended. The committee furnished an example:

University of Chicago	At Wilberforce	At Los Angeles
A = 92.5–100	A = 95–100	A = 95–100
B = 85–92.5	B = 85–90	B = 88–95
C = 77.5–85	C = 75–80	C = 80–88

It was suggested that the local chapter's interpretation be accepted by the Executive Council, and an adequate substitute for grade certificates be approved. There were also well thought out and good suggestions for the better running of the regional conferences, which had gone reasonably well in light of the glitches that occurred. In addition to her complaints about the president, Beckley provided detailed suggestions on how to improve the conferences. And the scholarship and tuition loan program continued, with new names nominated as recipients. There were many new and creative ideas presented about initiation, increasing activity, legislation that would clarify the roles of the officers, and new objectives: such as that proposed by Anna Julian to establish a housing fund toward the purchase of a building for the national headquarters.

The most important recommendation in regard to the external activities of the sorority was made by Layle Lane to establish a committee "that would keep in touch with the political activities of the country as they affected our group." Sarah Speaks suggested that the functions of the committee be extended "to activities other than political and that it be named a Vigilance Committee." (Ironically, Speaks was on the verge of becoming very much involved with politics. In 1933, she was secretary of the County Committee of her district; and she subsequently ran unsuccessfully for the New York State Assembly and was the Republican candidate for Congress from New York's Twenty-second Congressional District. (Her opponent and the victor in the latter race was Adam Clayton Powell, Jr.) Jeannette Jones said that such a committee could "also be alert as to educational restrictions of the group."[37] Lane was appointed the committee's first chair and selected its first members.

The convention ended with an election of officers. Anna Julian "was the unanimous choice of the house" for president. Jeannette

Jones, a future national president, was also the recipient of a unanimous vote, moved up to first vice-president. Jennie Baer, who understandably declined renomination for secretary, won the election for second vice-president; the new treasurer was Marian (Palmer) Capps from Norfolk's Mu Chapter; and secretary was Grace Woodson.

No doubt there was a sigh of relief when the final session came to an end. Nevertheless, despite the very real problems that emerged during the convention, Delta probably left that meeting a stronger organization. It had continued to go forward in the face of a crisis of confidence in the president, and that was important. Perhaps that Pittsburgh convention laid the groundwork for Delta's lack of dependence on the chief executive and for a wide delegation of powers. In fact, as the failure of Jimmie Middleton to get her chapter, and perhaps the short tenure of Madree White as journalist, indicated, even founders would not have unquestioned influence on the group. Also evident were the continued stress on equitable relationship between chapters and the national officers, and an inclination toward their smooth succession. Finally, amidst all of the confusion, it established the flagship Vigilance Committee that would enlarge their sphere and have a profound impact on the organization.

CHAPTER 6

STRENGTHENING
WITHIN—LOOKING
WITHOUT

After the 1929 convention, President-elect Anna Julian was looking forward to a well-deserved rest. She had been back at her Washington, D.C., home for two days when Dorothy Beckley dropped by to see her. "I think that there are some things that I need to tell you about the sorority,"[1] said a somber Beckley. The organization, it seems, was flat broke, and the sorority would be forced to look into initiating legal proceedings against national treasurer Annie Dingle—a realtor whose troubles can only be speculated about in the same year as the stock market crash. Although what had happened is not entirely clear, its consequences were: President Julian would have to start from scratch. The good news was that there couldn't have been a better executive to guide the sorority through the crisis. Born in Baltimore, the fifth daughter in a family of seven girls, Julian was a graduate of the University of Pennsylvania. After graduation she attained her master's at that institution and by 1935 would receive its Moore Fellowship—the highest award given to women students—to pursue her Ph.D. in sociology. Subsequently she became the first Black woman to receive a Phi Beta Kappa key from the university. Her husband, Percy

Julian, received his Ph.D. from the University of Vienna and became one of the nation's foremost scientists. He is credited with having made cortisone, a drug used chiefly for the treatment of arthritis and certain allergies, available to consumers at an affordable cost.

The new president had already held a number of important posts on both local and national levels. She had been Gamma Chapter president, grand journalist, national vice-president, and chair of the regional conferences. Proceedings of the convention in that year show her taking leadership in resolving many of the problems that arose. Julian was not only knowledgeable but exceedingly clear-headed, and understood how to move the sorority in a methodical way to the place where it needed to be.

One of the first things to be done was to have the offices of grand secretary and grand treasurer bonded to ensure against any financial losses due to their activities. Second, she moved to incorporate the national entity of Delta Sigma Theta in Washington, D.C. (Previously, Alpha Chapter of the sorority had been incorporated.) The immediate need for the action became apparent when a group of young White men at a midwestern university attempted to name their new fraternity Delta Sigma Theta. The new charter, implemented less than a month after the 1929 convention, had broader implications of course. Now the sorority had the legal power not only to carry on its business in the District of Columbia, but throughout the United States, its dependencies, and elsewhere. The new charter, whose official birth date was January 20, 1930, denoted a coming of age of the organization and the expansion of its mission. Whereas the 1913 charter stipulated that the "particular purpose and object of [Delta Sigma Theta] shall be to establish and maintain a high standard of morality and scholarship among women generally," twenty-seven years later the new charter read:

> *The principal purposes and aims of this organization shall be cultural and educational; to establish, maintain and encourage high cultural, intellectual, and moral standards among its members and the members of its subordinate chapters, and to promote and encourage achievement in education by granting scholarships, and other assistance . . . to worthy and deserving members of its*

*grand and subordinate chapters, [and] to
other individuals at its discretion.*[2]

There was no more appropriate time to initiate the "Jubilee
Year" of the sorority, a period when Deltas would take the opportunity to reevaluate their program, and according to Edna Morris,
"determine the physical and spiritual assets" of the organization.[3]
Despite the difficulties and frustrations, the sense of sisterhood remained very much intact. Julian recalled how the members were
"consumed with a burning desire to succeed; to help make Delta a
vital, viable and dynamic organization in the service of Black people.
What we lacked in material things," she continued, "was compen-
sated for in the richness of creative ideas, in idealism and a certain
spirituality, which, when combined [motivated] us to create a Delta
image of which we could be proud."[4] That spirit also helped to meet
another important goal of the Jubilee Year: to reinstate sorors who
had become inactive. Many, according to Edna Morris, returned to
the fold that year.

THE VIGILANCE COMMITTEE

They would return to find a vigorous Vig-
ilance Committee that was determined to make Delta's voice heard
on a wide range of issues. In 1930 a questionnaire was sent throughout the Delta organization to obtain the views of its members about
a federal anti-lynch law, the advisability of reorganizing the state and
federal courts (foreshadowing Franklin Roosevelt's unsuccessful attempts to do so in 1937), how education funds should be appropriated and distributed, military expenditures, and the need for laws
providing unemployment insurance and pensions among others. Like
the survey of chapters instituted by Julian in 1929, the responses
were utilized as an underpinning for Delta policy. Like other Black
groups in the period, Delta was galvinizing its organization to go
beyond criticizing racism in the broader society to demand that the
federal government abandon its own discriminatory policies as well
as use its powers to redress racial injustice. Both were at issue during
Herbert Hoover's administration that lasted from 1929 to 1933.

During that period more than fifty lynchings took place, yet Hoover remained silent on the issue. A particularly brutal one took place in Sherman, Texas, in 1930, where mob violence prevailed not only to take Black life, but destroy Black property, leaving many homeless in its wake. The incident led the Vigilance Committee to write to the mayor of the city. Describing the lynching as the most "brutal in the long list of inhumanities against the American Negro," the letter urged (rather naïvely) that the city council "appropriate sufficient money for the restoration of Negro homes and to make a public appeal for gifts and funds for the homeless." The sorority also urged, "through the Commission to Investigate Lynching, that a Federal Anti-Lynch Law be passed in the Congress."[5]

Adding insult to injury—and to the growing impatience of Blacks toward the Republican party—Hoover nominated Judge John J. Parker, of Charlotte, North Carolina, for the Supreme Court. Ten years before, Parker had remarked that the participation of Blacks in politics was a "source of evil and danger to both races."[6] To Blacks, Parker seemed to be the dangerous one. Along with other groups, Delta's voice of opposition was loud enough to be heard in the halls of the Senate—which withheld confirmation.

In the same year, Hoover angered Blacks once again, and again Delta protested. In the administration's arrangements to send mothers of slain soldiers to France in order to see the white crosses in Flanders Field that marked their graves, Black mothers would be segregated and given inferior accommodations. In the Vigilance Committee files is a letter to Secretary of War Patrick Hurley, which said that "Negro soldiers fought and died the same as whites. Both alike have returned to the earth again." Urging that the department ban any discriminatory treatment on the trip, Delta criticized "the use of public funds which in any way caters to the prejudices of white citizens against those of color."[7] Delta attacked the administration again on similar grounds in the fall of 1930, when it was discovered that a Black football player on Ohio State's team would not be allowed to play in a game with the United States Naval Academy. Letters from the committee as well as Deltas throughout the country protested that such racism, allowed to flourish, sanctioned race discrimination by the United States government. "This is a policy upon which the government has no right to ask any of its tax-payers to uphold through their maintenance of Annapolis. It is a policy which causes bitter antagonism on the part of Negroes to the government."[8]

Such words as "bitter antagonism" aimed at the government were not given—or taken—lightly. Such criticism was rising in a time of growing economic uncertainty, racial betrayal, and the attraction of ideologies that focused on class analysis and the exploitation of workers. In this pivotal year of 1930, President Mordecai Johnson, Howard University's first Black president, was criticized by the chair of the House Committee on Appropriations, for allowing communism to be taught in the school. The criticism was a thinly veiled threat to cut off federal monies from Howard, whose budget was so dependent on the Congress. "Those who are in charge of these funds have a right to inquire whether this money is being expended for the betterment of a rising generation, or whether it is being used to poison their minds against the long-established policy of our government," charged the House Appropriation chairman.[9] The words prompted a top-level meeting of Delta grand officers, who debated, according to Helen Edmonds, "throwing down the gauntlet." Although there was a statement issued supporting "academic freedom" at Howard, prudence once again, on an academic matter in a Black university, prevailed. "In the interest of not prejudicing Howard University's financial future or running the risk of decreasing future opportunities for Negro boys and girls," it was decided, "that the matter be dropped."[10]

Delta was more direct, however, when it came to having its voice heard on economic issues. Since the end of World War I, unemployment and underemployment for Blacks had been reaching crisis proportions long before the stock market crash of 1929. The situation prompted the sorority to request the secretary of labor in 1930, to create a long-range public works program.[11] They also formally urged Oscar DePriest, congressman from Illinois and the first northern Black elected to Congress, to cooperate with any federal program that "would accord economic security" for Blacks.[12]

Another communication to the administration endorsed the Norris Bill on Muscle Shoals, which would continue government, rather than private, operation of the dams on the Tennessee River built to create electric power for making nitrate for munitions and fertilizer. Public administration of the dams, it was believed, eliminated the potential for abuses by vested interests. Significantly, these requests foreshadowed the New Deal legislation that provided the Works Progress Administration and the Tennessee Valley Authority some years, and another administration, later.

An issue closer to home was the discriminatory policies of major insurance companies toward Blacks. The sorority targeted one of the worst offenders, the Metropolitan Life Insurance Company of New York, for issuing higher insurance rates to Blacks, regardless of their health histories or economic status. "As a national organization of Negro college women we urge you to abandon the program of insulting and humiliating Negro patrons," they wrote. "Dollars from Negroes have the same market value as dollars from whites. Those who spend the dollars should therefore have the same consideration granted to them as to whites."[13]

But in this important year, the sorority's concerns also went beyond the pale of domestic, and even singularly racial, concerns. Delta supported disarmament by urging President Hoover, by letter, to cooperate with other powers at the London Naval Conference, to maintain only those naval forces necessary for police purposes.[14] Also within the purview of Delta concerns were trade issues, which were having a discernible impact on the economic well-being of the country. In 1930, the sorority joined others in beseeching Republicans not to enact the Hawley-Smoot Tariff Act—proposing the highest protective tariff in United States history. Hawley-Smoot, as was feared, caused retaliatory tarriffs from other countries, resulting in a precipitous decline in trade and the economy.

Finally, Delta took a leading role in lobbying for the United States to end its proprietary role in the affairs of Haiti, fifteen years after its military intervention on the Caribbean island. President Woodrow Wilson had ordered troops there after its president, Guillaume Sam, who had ordered the execution of 167 political prisoners, was assassinated. In addition to the troops, Wilson had imposed a twenty-year treaty on the government, which gave the United States absolute power over its financial and other internal affairs. Delta joined others in urging Hoover to withdraw the military and return control of the island to the Haitians. When it was learned that the President was going to appoint a fact-finding commission in 1930, the sorority lobbied for two Afro-Americans to be a part of it: Mary Church Terrell, who among her other achievements had broad international experience and could speak French fluently; and Rayford Logan, historian and student of French culture, international affairs, and, specifically, Haitian problems. Delta president Anna Julian placed her signature on a letter to both Hoover and Senator William Borah of Idaho; the latter was asked to use his influence in the matter, both as to the appointment and the policy question. Hoover appointed no Blacks to the commission, but did engage the president of Tuskegee Institute, Dr. Robert Russa Moton, in an advisory role. The United States finally withdrew from Haiti in 1934.

Under Anna Julian's administration, Delta was taking a larger and larger role in political issues, especially those directly affecting Black Americans. In the future, that role would be vital to not only the public identity of the organization, but its internal search for stronger bonds of sisterhood. But, for now, it was its administrative machinery that needed the most attention, and it was the president's extraordinary accomplishments in this regard that averted an impending crisis.

INTERNAL DEVELOPMENTS

After 1929, a number of committees were restructured so that they could deal more autonomously with the day-to-day needs of the sorority. The informal Advisory Committee evolved into a more formalized Executive Committee, consisting of all elected national officers, including regional directors. But it was soon discovered that the committee was not adequate to deal with issues that required the consensus of chapters between conventions—now two years apart. Out of that need came an Executive Council—consisting of chapter presidents, the national president, and the national Secretary.[15] Later, even the Executive Council was deemed too burdensome, as the secretary had to poll all of the members by mail, between conventions, concerning such matters as chartering prospective chapters, in which a majority vote prevailed. So the council gave way to an Executive Board, which by 1941 was made up of national officers, regional directors, the legal advisor, board and project chairmen, and an undergraduate representative.

In 1929, a Constitution Committee (later the Constitution Board) of elected members was created. They had the increasingly burdensome task of clarifying proposed amendments, incorporating these bylaws and regulations into the constitution, interpreting legislation already on the books. It was also the reservoir for records regarding membership, the establishment of chapters, elections, and so on. The scope of their work can be better understood by the fact that, as Helen Edmonds points out, "hardly any biennial report of the Board carried less than fifty items in the wave of new proposals, revisions, and their clarification.[16] All of these items demanded the vote of the entire body, and so this was easily the most time-consuming and thankless task of every convention.

The preceding convention had also taught them that there was a need for a body to arbitrate disputes between national officers as well as between those officers and chapters. Between 1919 and 1929, it was the Grand Chapter executives who interpreted the constitution when a legal conflict arose between them and local officers or members. Such disputes were time-consuming, and required precise knowledge of the constitution and objective judgment. Experience showed that there was a need to have a committee that could both adjudicate these matters, and have the power of impeachment and/or suspension. In 1929, those responsibilities became the domain of a newly established Judiciary Board.

Three other new boards were also created in this period as a direct response to the tremendous growth of the sorority and the difficulties that emerged at the last convention. A Scholarship Board replaced the National Scholarship Committee, as voted upon by the 1933 convention in Chicago. The former more clearly defined the role and powers of the group in providing loans and scholarships. A Standards Board, replacing the Committee on Standards, expanded its responsibilities to include not only assessing the eligibility of universities and colleges to be a part of Delta, but also honorary members and chapter irregularities. Their role would become increasingly important as the eligibility of Black land-grant institutions would be debated in the early thirties. Of greatest immediate concern was the organizing of the sorority's finances. In the past, as Edmonds observed, a Finance Committee working in conjunction with the grand treasurer was adequate in dealing with the monies that flowed in from fees and dues. Even through the twenties, the budget was a matter of simple arithmetic. But as the organization became both larger and more complex, it was obvious that there was a need to restructure the committee into a Budget Board that would consider the financial needs of the sorority for the ensuing year, make budget recommendations for the Grand Chapter, and work with the grand secretary and treasurer to determine the financial policy of the organization. That there was such a need became painfully apparent in the wake of the 1929 convention.

Julian also did not let the financial difficulties of the national chapter get in the way of establishing new chapters. Although forty-one chapters had been established between 1920 and 1929, the South and Southwest were still poorly represented, prompting Julian to make an inspection tour of those regions during the first year of her administration: The result was the authorization of five new chapters: four in the Southwest and one in the South. Added to the growing list of graduate chapters would be Rho Sigma in Shreveport, Louisiana; Sigma Sigma in Austin, Texas; and Tau Sigma in Birmingham, Alabama. Undergraduate chapters were Alpha Iota and Alpha Kappa in Marshall and Austin, Texas, respectively. In addition, Iowa's Delta Chapter, which had had so much difficulty in the past, was reestablished.[17] All in all eleven chapters were added to the roster in Julian's administration.

And at the 1931 convention, further steps were taken to consolidate and enhance the machinery of the organization. It was agreed that a national officer or regional director would be authorized to visit each chapter at least once a year; a committee was also appointed to discuss the ways and means of providing for an executive secretary, who would be a paid staff member; a new office was authorized, namely that of grand historian, which would be responsible for documenting the progress of the sisterhood. Finally, the chair of the Scholarship Committee, Jeannette Jones reported that the committee had established a system whereby scholarship keys—in the manner of the Phi Beta Kappa key—would be awarded to students with outstanding academic achievement.

Although nominated for a second term, Anna Julian declined to run again. Under her leadership the sorority had not only grown, but was put on a firmer financial footing and strengthened in terms of its lobbying ability. Elected in 1931 was Gladys (Byram) Shepperd, who also brought broad experiences to the post. She had been a director of the Eastern Region and chair of the regional conferences—positions that were clearly becoming stepping stones to the presidency.

Shepperd was born in Memphis and was a graduate of Wilberforce University. She did postgraduate work at the University of Southern California and the University of Chicago—where she was initiated into Lambda Chapter in 1926. Subsequently, Shepperd taught at Coppin Normal School in Baltimore and, establishing permanent residence there, became a member of Epsilon Sigma Chapter. In her later career, she would author several books including a biographical sketch of Mary Church Terrell. Elected with her were first vice-president Naomi R. Cherot, who was initiated at Wilberforce's Beta Chapter, did her graduate work at Columbia University, and taught in Kansas City, Kansas; second vice-president Es Cobeda (Sarreals) Posey, an undergraduate of Fisk University who in two years would become an executive secretary of the YWCA in Denver; reelected secretary, Edna B. Morris, Wilberforce graduate who pursued her studies at the State University of Iowa, and then a high school teacher in Gary, Indiana; incumbent treasurer, Marian Capps, an honors graduate of Howard University and then a teacher in Norfolk, Virginia; and journalist Edna B. Kinchion.

The most important development of the next two years was the establishment of the Central Region, which included those chapters in Oklahoma, Kansas, Nebraska, Iowa, and Missouri. Naomi Cherot "perfected" the organization of the region, according to Edna Morris, and the first conference, held on May 14, 1932, in Kansas City, Kansas, "marked an enthusiastic and inspirational beginning. Accompanying Cherot to the western city was Edna Kinchion who was already reputed to "know more about rules and procedures than almost anyone."[18] (As journalist, she also knew a great deal about how to get Delta's publications out on time. Under her guidance they were released regularly.) Naturally, it fell to her to reiterate the rules that governed the regions. Before the nineteen delegates from Kansas City, Lawrence, St. Louis, and Tulsa, Kinchion reiterated the fact that the Grand Chapter makes no contribution toward the financing of any region. She also stated that each region "must map out its own yearly program that was suitable for its chapters." They were to make recommendations for consideration by the Grand Chapter and "to deal with any other business of a local nature in fostering internal development."[19]

Naomi Cherot then appointed Nominating, Recommendations, Program, and Constitution committees. The chair of the latter was a woman who would have a significant impact as long-standing grand treasurer: Beatrice E. Penman. Reports from the delegates showed a variety of activities. Educational guidance programs, lectures, a card party held for the Deltas by an AKA chapter, awarding of scholarships, observance of May Educational Week, and a variety of fundraising activities. Two cabarets raised $185 for scholarships.

There was also a great deal of activity in authorizing and establishing new chapters during Shepperd's biennial. Alpha Mu, in Greensboro, North Carolina, which had been authorized at the previous convention, was established by Lorraine Heathcock, who was the Eastern regional director. Heathcock's Midwest counterpart, Bonnie (Osborne) Smith, who had previously reestablished Delta

Chapter, also reorganized Omega Chapter, a mixed chapter in Cleveland. In the same month of May in 1932, Shepperd, herself, established Phi Sigma, a graduate chapter in Charleston, West Virginia. Bonnie Smith also brought Alpha Nu, at the University of Illinois, into the fold. The establishment of that chapter was particularly satisfying, as there had been many obstacles thrown in the way.

Forming chapters on some campuses could be a difficult struggle. Administrators were often wary of Black students forming associations, especially if there was the prospect of more than one such organization on campus. Additional problems arose if the other Black fraternal groups did not support the request. Faculty advisors, who were often the first to assess applications, to Pan-Hellenic Councils, especially in predominantly White schools, could be a problem. Often they were the first line of resistance in rejecting an application, and were not always sympathetic to Black Greek-letter organizations. On predominantly White campuses, advisors, at the least, did not understand their distinct nature and mission of Black groups or why they were necessary. For example, efforts to reestablish Mu Chapter, which had become inactive, at the University of Pittsburgh, were stymied by that school's Women's Fraternity Committee, which believed it unwise "to encourage the establishment of a second fraternity among Negro women when the total enrollment of undergraduate Negro women at the present time is only fifteen."[20] Only through the persistence of the national president, of Pittsburgh's mixed Alpha Epsilon Chapter—and of the students, who despite being unable to affiliate with a campus chapter for several years sustained their interest—did the school finally relent. And the decision had come more than two years after the first request. Some of the concerns of administrators were legitimate, others were laced with prejudicial attitudes.

This was evident in the case of Indiana University, as a Delta soror, Mary (Johnson) Yancey, pointed out. Writing years after the incident, she recalled:

> *In 1939 Indiana had a population of approximately 105 Negro students. The housing conditions provided for Negro students consisted of dilapidated shacks owned by a senile person named Samuel Dargon, a Negro who was associated with the Law Library of Indiana University. Girls who liked the bet-*

*ter things of life sought and lived in resi-
dences in the city of Bloomington. It was
during our residency in the city that eight of
us saved our money and transported Soror
Hortense Young, regional director to meet
with Dean [Kate H.] Mueller to request a
charter for a chapter of Delta Sigma Theta
Sorority. Having promised us one on completion of acceptable grades and a quota for
membership, we looked forward to a chapter
that year. . . . In the meantime, an incident
occurred which brought attention to the fact
that I.U. students should be housed in I.U.
supervised quarters. Dargon House did not
meet these qualifications and because of exis-
tent prejudeices in the I.U. operated dormitories and fear of unfavorable publicity we
were forced to move to Dargon House during the mid-semester by said Dean Mueller.
Upon her order to move us to Dargon House
which furnished no bedding and for a move
that we were entirely unprepared to make,
the girls were advised by fair-thinking professors not to move. Dean Mueller came in
our residence without knocking and ordered
one girl to Dargon House. The girl was on a
Seagram's scholarship and forfeited her education at Indiana University and went home.
The rest of us conceded and went to Dargon
House. This incident with the housing situation was so acute that two former alumni of
color who had daughters involved came to
Indiana to talk with one Kate Mueller. Upon
being introduced by me, she shook hands
with them and immediately wiped her hands
on her dress. . . . In the meantime those of
us who had chosen to become Deltas and
had successfully completed our work again
made application for a charter. This was denied or ignored, I don't remember which.*

> *Consequently, we went to Indianapolis and were made by Chi Chapter.*[21]

As Kate Mueller and others like her understood, the presence of a strong Greek-letter organization could provide a lobbying force to challenge such discriminatory practices. This was certainly true in the case of the University of Michigan, at Ann Arbor, and Ohio State University in Columbus, where Delta's Vigilance Committee pressed the schools to eliminate their discriminatory activities. Midwest director Bonnie Smith reported that the former was still attempting to keep Blacks out of its dormitories—though by the thirties other schools had begun to change such policies. At Ohio State, the home economics department sought to keep one of its students, Doris Weaver, from living in its Home Management House, though it was required of majors like herself. Although Delta wasn't the only group that intervened in these issues, its efforts no doubt were influential in the ending of such practices.[22]

As in a number of cases, the attempt to establish a chapter at the University of Illinois required persistence and tenacity. From available correspondence, it seems as if the first attempts to form a Delta chapter on an Illinois campus ran into problems as early as 1927. Frustrated by efforts to establish a chapter there, Chicago's Lambda Chapter took it upon itself to attempt to induct a University of Illinois student without securing approval of the university. This, in turn, had incited negative reactions from members of the school's administration. In response, then-President Calimese wrote a letter to Cora K. Miller, assistant dean of women, suggesting to the dean that the "true conditions [of the situation were] not mutually understood and that an explanation of Lambda's actions can be made clear and satisfactory to you."[23] Calimese had previously requested a meeting with Miller while she was in Chicago, but getting no reply, was forced to leave the city without doing so. She asked if she could see her on the campus the following week. Miller complied.

A memo summarizing the meeting was written by Miller. "Re: Delta Sigma Theta—(Colored Sorority)," it began. "Have 34 chapters, including many city chapters. Absolutely proved to her that the best way for her [Calimese] to ever get a chapter here was through the local methods. Took two interviews to do this, but she finally conceded I was right."[24] A petition for a chapter was sent along to the dean of women, a Miss Leonard, who received a letter from Calimese revealing the means by which Delta attempted to convince administrations to allow them on their campuses. "We feel certain that you will do whatever you can to help us secure a chapter, sure that you will be gratified with the benefits to our racial group at the University, and hence to the welfare of the student body of which it is a part," the president wrote. "I assure you that we shall maintain a superior standard for scholarship ('B' average) and for character, and do all in our power to promote amiable relations with the other fraternal organizations on your campus." The last phrase was in response to the argument that more than one Black group could engender counterproductive feuding—the university already had an AKA chapter. To the contrary, Calimese argued, "I believe, in the light of my knowledge of their relations in other places [the establishment of a Delta chapter], will result in a friendly competition between Alpha Kappa Alpha and Delta Sigma Theta which will promote higher scholarship, finer womanhood and more whole hearted school spirit in both groups. To this opinion I'm confident the representative members of Alpha Kappa Alpha would also subscribe." Calimese closed the letter saying that she had learned that "so few as five girls will be able to meet the university requirements of maintaining a Sorority House. This would improve greatly the living conditions of these students, which you remember we agreed were far from desirable."[25]

Nevertheless, it seems that Dean Leonard did not acquiesce so easily—to establishing a chapter or clearing the way for a sorority house. Not until 1932 were the Deltas successful in getting their chapter (and it took them another twenty years to get the sorority house!). A letter from one of the initiates to Edna Kinchion took note of the victory, and the difficulties that they had had in attaining it. "For some years now Delta has been trying to set up a chapter on this campus," the letter read in part,

> *but until this time nothing has been accomplished, due to the strong opposition from Dean Leonard, the townspeople, and the Alpha Kappa Alpha Sorority. However, Delta Sorors on the campus kept plugging away at the problem and finally succeeded in getting the Dean and her Council to pass favorably on the petition. . . . We began corresponding with the Grand Secretary immediately upon the granting of permission to organize. She*

*instructed us in the proper steps to take in
getting the chapter inaugurated here. We very
faithfully carried out her instructions, and as
a result, Alpha Nu was given birth May 14,
on the Illinois campus. . . . Five young
women knelt before three tall white candles
and solemnly took the oath of immortal
fidelity to Delta Sigma Theta.*[26]

Fortunately, not every campus was so resistant to the sorority. A
number of administrators even took the initiative in inviting its active
participation. "I can recall the president of Bishop College [in
Dallas] coming to my house to ask, 'Won't you please set up a chapter on my campus?'" noted Anna Julian. "Because the word was
getting around that we had a little more on our minds in the way of
serious business than just frivolity and social things."[27]

CHAPTER 7

"ONE BLOOD, ONE TRADITION"

By 1933, America had a new President who was called upon to stem the deepening crisis. By that year, the economic uncertainty signaled by the 1929 crash, had bottomed out to become a full-fledged Depression. Within a year, 17 percent of Whites would be regarded as "incapable of self-support in any occupation," as John Hope Franklin wrote.[1] For Blacks, of course, the numbers were even worse. Thirty-eight percent could not support themselves in any occupation—not even those of last resort. By 1935, approximately one fourth of the one and a half million domestic workers were on relief. In many cities, the Blacks on relief were three or four times the number of their White counterparts. Sixty-five percent of Black employables in Atlanta needed public assistance in 1935; in Norfolk, Virginia, the figure was 80 percent.

Whereas, the masses of Blacks had been suffering for some time, the heavy hand of the full economic collapse also delivered a blow to the professional class. Many experienced the prospect of joblessness for the first time. "Has the depression gotten you too?" wrote a Delta who had taught at Fisk to Claude Barnett, founder of the Associated Negro Press.

God but it is killing me. It has become an annual duty of mine it seems, to go in search of a job from year to year. I am beginning again, now [1933]. . . . I want you to be on the lookout again this year. I just wrote Mr. [William] Pickens [of the NAACP] . . . If you have any drag with old man [Carter G.] Woodson [of the Association of Negro Life and History] in Washington, write him about me. I wrote him asking for a job on his research staff. I have almost gotten desperate in this search for work.[2]

Even those who maintained jobs did not have a guarantee of the kind of compensation that could keep them afloat. "Salaries could not be met," recalled Anna Julian, "teachers were given IOUs, which oft times could not be used as collateral for their rent." And the failure of banks and other financial institutions left even the most thrifty with nothing. "Even I lost every cent that I had saved during my first year of teaching," Julian recalled.[3]

The Depression and its myriad social, economic, and political consequences would have a tremendous impact on Black organizations, as it would on individuals. As was true with the national government, new circumstances demanded new responses, both in kind and degree. For many, it marked a turning point. Past assumptions were challenged, new coalitions were formed, internal debates threatened, anachronistic notions assured weakening influence, if not extinction.

What made the Black organizational response so complex was that the economic crisis set two distinct racial forces in motion. On the one hand, the consequences of racism deepened. Its crudest expression emerged in the Scottsboro case in which nine Black teenagers were accused of raping two White women while on a freight train in Alabama on March 25, 1931. Two weeks later, eight of the young men were sentenced to the electric chair. The case became a national symbol of southern injustice. It also became a contest for Black loyalties. Who could better defend Blacks, traditional organizations such as the NAACP or the Communist party, which was attempting to make inroads into the Black community? (Finally, a coalition of the NAACP, the communist International Labor Defense Committee, and others who supported the young men—including the Deltas—worked together and secured their release.)

Even "milder" expressions of racial discrimination had dire consequences in these years. Relief allotments were unequal; John Hope Franklin reported that there was sometimes up to a six-dollar differential in the monthly aid given to White and Black families.[4] That differential was significant enough in the thirties to make Franklin comment that for Blacks, "added to the denials of freedom and democracy was the specter of starvation."[5]

But there was also another racial dynamic at work. It was becoming increasingly clear to an element of the White population that the economy would never recover if racial violence and such blatant inequality persisted. Such a conviction moved President Roosevelt to comment that the South was the "nation's number one economic problem." So the thirties also saw new efforts to lessen racial gaps in education, civil rights, and income. Racial violence was excoriated by White intellectuals and White women's organizations such as the Association of Southern Women for the Prevention of Lynching. And so, there was more than one approach to improve the welfare of Blacks. Some organizations turned inward to organize the masses of Blacks, which for the first time were in large enough numbers in northern cities to become an economic and political force. Others sought to exploit the conciliatory attitudes of Whites who believed that Blacks would have to be *more* equal in order to help the nation out of its economic pit. That window had been opened in the Roosevelt administration, which, though never supporting integration or absolute equality, opened the way for greater empowerment of Blacks and other groups who were not a part of the power elite.

By 1935, the philosophical differences between the two most influential figures in the NAACP, Walter White, its executive director, and *Crisis* editor W.E.B. Du Bois, over the future direction of the movement split the organization apart. Du Bois believed that the lesson of the economic crisis was that Blacks should focus their energies on strengthening their own institutions rather than attempting to integrate White ones. White, on the other hand, chose to throw the resources of the NAACP behind interracial efforts, such as the passage of the Costigan-Wagner anti-lynching bill which indicated a rising tide of liberalism. The conflict resulted in Du Bois's resignation from the organization.

That year also marked the founding of the National Council of Negro Women by Mary McLeod Bethune, who concluded that a coalition of Black women's organizations—including the sororities, with their constituency of educated youth—under the umbrella of the council was needed if Black women were to go forward. The idea had met resistance from a number of leaders, including Mary Church Terrell and others who questioned the necessity of a new organization, and/or the prudence of forming an all-Black group at this juncture in history. But the heretofore leading Black women's organization, the National Association of Colored Women, had been weakened in recent years. Organizations like the NAACP and the Urban League had civil rights and social welfare programs similar to those of the NACW, but with better financing that allowed them to implement their programs more effectively. Consequently, by 1930, the NACW had reduced its thirty-eight departments, which administered their programs, to two. And, still focusing on the role of women as that of the moral gatekeepers of the home and the race, the NACW had failed to understand the implications of more and more women becoming the sole support of their families, or to realize that the great majority of Black women, in all economic classes, would have to work throughout their lives. Jobs would no longer be thought of as temporary necessities to be held only until their husbands were able to support them. Moreover, this new idea was rooted not just in the Depression times, but in an analysis of the American economy as a whole. In an increasingly industrialized society where the work of the housewife was being seen as "valueless consumption," Sadie T. M. Alexander wrote in 1930, women had to "place themselves again among the producers of the world" and be involved in work "that resulted in the production of goods that have a price value."[6] Being a producer, she believed, also made a woman feel better about herself. All of this added up to the fact that Black women, already job-oriented, should become career-oriented, and aspire in their occupations, accordingly. The NACW was unable to respond to these changes and never again enjoyed the influence that they had had in earlier years.

The extreme circumstances of the Depression years also exposed the Greek-letter organizations to intense criticism—both from those in the organizations and from without. The *Norfolk Journal and Guide,* for example, carried a story that quoted the assistant chaplain of Hampton Institute, Rev. William King, as criticizing the groups for their "easy-going optimism" that put too great a value upon "frivolity." It was this attitude of "simple complacency," he complained, that "enveloped the country prior to the Depression," and helped to create "the conditions existing today."[7] No one was more aware of these criticisms than those within the organizations themselves. Hilda A. Davis, who had been president of Alpha Chapter in 1924–1925, had acquired a master's degree from Radcliffe in the thirties, and was dean of women at Shaw University in Raleigh, North Carolina, wrote about the mounting charges against the Greek-letter groups. "The financial depression from which the country has been struggling to rise since 1929 has given impetus to the demand that sororities justify their existence or give way to more beneficial activities," she observed. Listing the objections, she included the accusations that sororities tended to destroy the democratic spirit on the campus and that the selection for membership was made on the basis of social and financial status, and/or physical appearance. That those selected often possessed an unwarranted feeling of superiority, while those who were not chosen were crushed with a sense of inferiority, was also a common complaint. And of course the extravagance and social orientation of the groups were also cited. Among the critics were the National Association of the Deans of Women and the national organizations of the sororities themselves, Davis wrote.[8] Davis noted that the positive side of sorority life was not always given its due—its sisterhood of women of "one blood and one tradition"; its opportunities for the development of leadership and for forming lasting friendships; and its material help in loans and scholarships. But she also believed that some of the criticisms were justified. The exclusiveness of the organizations and their tendency to dominate campus elections and activities, their secrecy and interfraternal competition, she believed, were real shortcomings.

As far as the complacency issue was concerned, however, sororities and fraternities did, of course, support the important civil rights issues of the day. And by the thirties, much of the resources which had been expended for "frivolities" was redirected in other ways. "Gone were the days of the gilded, glittering tinseled 1920s," observed Helen Edmonds. "Hardly any local chapter of Delta Sigma Theta in the 1930s emptied the contents of its treasury into a big dance with an expensive 'name' band, nor would any local treasury pour its all into a sumptuous banquet to be enjoyed solely by its own members, nor did Delta's social affairs become fashionable extravaganzas at which women vied for top honors in the most recent feminine creations."[9] It was true that the local chapters were much more sensitive about having "extravagant" affairs and more focused on direct contributions to local community needs. In 1933, Zeta Chapter in Cincinnati, for example, reported that "instead of giving a public entertainment this year, the scholarship fund was raised through a contribution from each member of the sorority."[10] Their effort was successful, raising $2,089.25 to be given to twenty-five girls in amounts ranging from $100.00 to $261.25.[11] Additionally, observing that "this has been a difficult year financially and that many people have lacked even the bare necessities, Zeta and Gamma Sigma chapters did their bit by presenting to the Cincinnati Board of Education, a gift of money to be used for the needs of undernourished children."[12] Other chapters provided food baskets, aided the elderly, donated clothes, purchased equipment for playgrounds, and paid the salaries of nursery workers. A few chapters even established nursery schools. A favorite chapter project of the sorority in this period was supplying Black hospitals with beds, linen, and hospital machinery. Sometimes entire rooms would be taken care of: Chapters would provide the means for walls to be painted, curtains and shades installed, and so on.

Not all chapters, of course, heeded the exigencies of the times. Dances, parties, and fashion shows still dominated their activities, regardless of the desires of the national leadership. "Having paid their dues to Grand Chapter, they felt themselves free to do as they pleased," Delta historian Mary Elizabeth Vroman observed of such chapters. It was true that those in this category decreased greatly during the thirties. But as in the twenties, though "Grand Chapter was diligent in carrying out the sorority's program of social and political action, [there were] local chapters [who] devoted little effort to these areas . . . much more money was spent . . . on local entertainment than in promoting the goals of the national program."[13] As Hilda Davis suggested, the fault lay "not in sororities as they were set up, but in the way in which the members have been permitted to deviate from the fulfillment of these aims expressed in the charters."[14] And it was the local chapter, particularly the college chapter that was relatively insulated from the outside world, through which most people assessed the organization as a whole. There was also the fact that the social activities, not the other kinds of projects, were the most publicized and visible.

But there were also deeper problems with this question of image. As one of the very few closed-membership organizations in the Black community, and the only ones that required a college education, sororities were particularly vulnerable to the stereotypes of a less than serious bourgeoisie class that was insensitive to the needs of the less fortunate. This was deemed an even greater sin in times of great stress and when writers such as Carter G. Woodson were criticizing educated Blacks. "One of the most striking evidences of the failure of higher educations among Negroes," he observed in the 1933 edition of *The Mis-Education of the Negro,* "is their estrangement from the masses, the very people upon whom they must eventually count for carrying out a program of progress."[15]

Although Black fraternal groups were interested in progress, they were never conceived to be agents of change, and to expect them to be so made members and nonmembers alike terribly frustrated. The activities of Delta, as one national president put it, were construed to expose and educate individuals to the great issues, help them grow, and, in turn, to contribute to society as a whole. This made the role of honorary members, many of whom could be described as change agents, all the more important. "The awareness of the Depression was always there," recalled Anna Julian, "but it was not until a Nannie Burroughs or a Mary Church Terrell or a Mary McLeod Bethune, or others got up and told what exactly the situation was . . . did we fully understand what was happening."[16] It also should be remembered that although these years had dire consequences for many, they did not deeply affect the numbers in the college population. At Howard University, for example, Rayford Logan observed that "the Great Depression and the early years of the New Deal had little effect in the undergraduate colleges. The highest numbers were during the Depression years: 46 BA's in 1930; 40 in 1931 and 1932; and 38 in 1933. BS degrees numbered 40 in 1929 and 1930; 50 in 1931 and 54 in 1932."[17] Nationally, there was a similar trend. From 1930 to 1933, the number of academic degrees awarded to Blacks increased every year: 1,776; 1,784; 2,386; and 2,756, respectively. Between 1926 and 1930, the total of undergraduate and graduate degrees was 7,369; between 1931 and 1935, the number was 10,801.[18]

At Howard, the proportion of degrees given to women also increased. Between 1927 and 1934, of the 229 bachelor of arts degrees, 119 were earned by women. And as more Black colleges and universities in the South were demanding master's degrees for their faculties, the numbers of these postgraduate degrees were rising as well. Between 1927 and 1935, of the 95 master's degrees awarded, 51 were given to female students.[19] In Charles S. Johnson's sample of 5,512 graduates from both Black schools and northern schools, 36.2 percent were women, a figure that denoted "the rapid equalization of sex ratios over this present period [1930s]."[20]

The Delta membership had women with various degrees of political awareness, and if the sisterhood dynamic was to stay intact it was important that the organization not go too far beyond the level of its critical mass. And that dynamic was also highly dependent on social activities and even gala affairs. Black women led stressful lives, often felt devalued despite their education, and commonly experienced feelings of isolation and alienation. Social gatherings ameliorated all of these circumstances, and those that flaunted extravagant clothes and settings gave Black women what may have been a false sense of worth, but it was a sense of worth, nonetheless. So the sorority had to be a two-headed animal: one of which sought to have a political impact on the society, and the other to cater to the socioemotional needs of its members. The double identity was no more evident than at the twelfth national convention, held in Chicago in 1933.

Convening at the height of the Depression, the convention saw many important issues on the table, which were discussed, voted upon, and implemented with all of the urgency that the times demanded. But there was also that other part, and this convention, despite all that was happening outside of it, was probably the most extravagant in Delta's history. There was from the beginning a particularly festive air; unlike previous conventions, it took place in August so that sorors could also enjoy the ironically named, "World's Fair Century of Progress" exposition held in Chicago. The national convention had an auspicious beginning. A representative of the city's mayor, Edward J. Kelley, gave President Gladys Byram Shepperd a key to the city. Mayor Kelley also gave the sorority a fifty-dollar check for the scholarship fund. On the first afternoon, Alice Dunbar-Nelson gave an address. And during the course of the convention, there was an artists' recital at the Art Institute, featuring Florence Cole Talbert and Shirley Graham, composer of the opera *Tom-Tom,* which had premiered in Cleveland, in 1932. Graham, who later became a writer of some note and the second wife of W.E.B. Du Bois, had studied abroad and received a master's from Oberlin. She had also been the director of music at Morgan State College, where she joined the Alpha Gamma Chapter. Subsequently, Mary Church Terrell led the group in a solemn reading of the Delta Oath, and founder Osceola Adams gave a short history of the sorority.

The social activities kept sorors—and no doubt critics—buzzing for a long time after the Deltas left the Windy City. There was a Kappa Alpha Psi boat ride, and a banquet that revived the opulence of another era. The convention took place in the city's Civil Opera Building, where, "from the lofty heights of the thirty-ninth floor . . . Delta acclaimed her majestic power to the city of Chicago," wrote Elsie (Evans) Harris, social chairman of the convention, who had studied design in Paris and was working in the graduate school at

Northwestern University.[21] "Everything was perfect from the punch all the way to the liveried doorman who deftly opened cab doors," she continued. "Never was there a more beautiful or more classic finale to any event than the banquet in the Electric Club Rooms." The setting was so dazzling, another Delta who reported on the convention noted, that she forgot the menu. "Won't you be content to know that it was just any of those high-sounding things that you don't know until it is put before you," she pleaded.[22] The women, 222 of them, were attired in long-flowing evening gowns; "women of the same spirit and ideals broke bread together . . . and again pledged allegiance to that ideal which has kept them of one mind and faith 'through the bond of devotion,'" the writer observed. The dinner was served to small groups of the Deltas and their guests at tables that had gold menu cards, "exquisite yellow and red roses, and the bright glow of red tapers." But, the writer cautioned, those "will be only incidental in memory when one thinks of the miniature frozen Buckingham Fountain out of which had been carved those Greek letters which exemplify our being. The DELTA SIGMA THETA carved in ice, standing some four feet in height, and flooded with colored lights was like an image before whom one would bow in reverence," she humbly concluded.[23]

Despite all of the glamour, there was some very serious work to be done, and after the opening session of the convention on August 27, the women got down to work. The most important issue before them was the accreditation question, which had been broached at earlier conventions and which would have to be resolved at this one. On December 1, 1932, at the annual meeting of the Association of Colleges and Secondary Schools of the Southern States, the association's Executive Committee voted to grant ratings to many Black institutions. Among the institutions that received the standard four-year-college class B rating were Black land-grant colleges in Florida, Kentucky, Louisiana, North Carolina, Texas, and Virginia. Already, Black land-grant schools in Missouri and West Virginia were recognized as such by the North Central Association of Colleges. Thus by 1933, eight Black land-grant institutions, in the words of educator and scholar John W. Davis, "qualify for positions of honor among the better institutions situated in their areas of academic accreditation."[24]

Of course, in the past, the sorority only accepted "A"-rated colleges, but there was considerable pressure building to widen its academic net and include other schools—especially those Black land-grant colleges that had become accredited. Several factors made the ensuing debate come to a head. First, of course, the Depression had challenged the idea that a selected few were to speak for—without speaking to—the masses of Blacks who had become an electoral force in the cities. This was the issue behind Carter G. Woodson's criticism of the continuing, self-imposed gulf among the different classes of Blacks. Among the educated group, there was increasing sensitivity about the stratification of those who attended the highly rated northern and private Black schools and those in the lesser-rated institutions. Of the latter, the largest group of colleges were the Black land-grant institutions that were beginning to come into their own, and were the subject of books and journal articles in new publications like *Journal of Negro Education*.

Before the thirties the reputation of the Black land-grant schools—with the exception of West Virginia State—was not very high. Their origins were in the Morrill Act of 1862, which set aside thirty thousand acres of land for the support of the agricultural and mechanical arts in each state. Both private colleges, such as Cornell and the Massachusetts Institute of Technology, and public institutions, such as Michigan State, owed their early support to this law. In 1890, a second Morrill Act was passed that provided further funds for institutions to teach the "various branches of mathematical, physical, natural and economic science."[25] It also prohibited monies being sent to any school that made distinctions of race or color—but at the same time provided for the establishment of separate colleges for Blacks and Whites. As a result there were seventeen Black land-grant colleges established. Some states like Mississippi created schools such as Alcorn University out of whole cloth. This was also true in Georgia, Delaware, North Carolina, West Virginia, Texas, and Oklahoma. Others, such as South Carolina and Virginia, used already existing schools—Claflin University and Hampton Institute, respectively—as their land-grant institutions. Kentucky and five other states designated their state normal schools to receive federal funds; Maryland and Tennessee arranged for the congressional monies to be assigned to private schools, Morgan College and Knoxville College, respectively. (In 1912, Tennessee altered this arrangement and established a Black land-grant institution at Nashville.)

Predictably, the course of the Black schools was not the same as that of their White counterparts in states like Michigan and Wisconsin. Unlike the White land-grant schools, funds for research were negligible. "Not one of the states that supports a separate land-grant college for Negroes has established in connection with the institution for Negroes an experiment station," commented Davis,[26] who became a president of West Virginia State. Although curricula were conceived in the same liberal arts tradition as they were for other schools, the fact that many southerners were generally hostile to Black education, or saw Blacks as uneducable, meant that the course studies of the Black schools did not even attempt to meet those of the White. This was compounded by the fact that there were few Black high schools. As late as 1916, only twelve students of college grade were enrolled in all seventeen colleges.[27]

Nevertheless, by the end of the twenties, a number of circumstances converged to raise the level of the Black land-grant institutions. The rapid industrialization of the South and the need for more highly skilled workers forced the issue of raising their educational standards. Consequently, philanthropies and other private sources such as the General Education Board, the Rosenwald Fund, and the Phelps-Stokes Fund began pouring substantial funds into Black schools—especially in the South where 97 percent of the 38,000 Blacks receiving collegiate instruction in 1933 were attending school.[28] In addition, legislation such as the Smith-Bankhead Act, passed in 1920, had been providing supplementary federal appropriations for paying the salaries of teachers of agricultural, trade, and home economics subjects. And the vast improvement in the high school situation began to have an impact on the college population. By 1930–1931, there were 5,679 Black students enrolled for collegiate-level instruction at the land-grants, making up more than one fourth of the total of Black students in all colleges. This marked the first year in which the number surpassed that of the high school enrollment in these schools.[29]

Such progress despite overwhelming odds, and the fact that the schools were still receiving smaller proportions of state funds each year, catalyzed many activists to lobby intensely on their behalf. Studies showed that in 1930, the difference in expenditures between Black and White schools was 252 percent, compared to 48 percent thirty years before. Even in a state like North Carolina, where there was greater attention focused on Black education than in more hostile states, more money was spent for *school trucks* for White children than was spent on new schools for Blacks. The salaries of Black and White teachers was appallingly unequal, a disparity that was also reflected in physical plants and new services such as visual aids. And by the mid-thirties, at the depth of the Depression, there was decreasing support from the philanthropic institutions, forcing schools like Virginia Union and Shaw universities to curtail their training of lawyers and phyisicians.

It was exceedingly clear that for many of the schools, and especially the land-grant institutions, it was primarily the lack of resources that kept them from being competitive. Among those agitating on behalf of the Black land-grant schools were the Deltas, who, in 1930, petitioned the federal government to increase its aid to these institutions. For Delta to then not permit the schools to be a part of their organization put the sorority in an awkward position, to say the least.

Refusing to accept these campuses also put Delta at odds with its own revised statement of purpose, which proclaimed that it no longer confined membership to liberal arts women, and which stressed helping a wide range of Black college-women. Additionally, by the early thirties, there was a growing intellectual elite in the South, including many of Delta's own members—and founders— who were teaching in the land-grant schools and others that didn't have "A" ratings. Additionally, the sorority had already made exceptions in schools such as Wilberforce, and Clark College in Atlanta whose social prestige outweighed its academic rating. And as was commonly known, in its desire to establish chapters on campuses where there were few Black students, or where some particularly desirable student was sought for membership, requirements weren't always strictly adhered to. Finally, there were pragmatic considerations. Undoubtedly, the shadow of AKA, Delta's main competitor, whose national convention, or boule, was meeting in the same city that summer, played a part. Although the AKAs wouldn't resolve the ratings issue until 1937, AKA chapters were already established at Virginia State, North Carolina A and T, and Tennessee State, among others. Anna Julian recalled that AKA didn't require the same standards as Delta. At least partly as a consequence, the AKAs had many more chapters by 1933: 104 compared to Delta's 62. Delta's opening of the gates would greatly increase the membership, and by extension, the influence and treasury of the sorority.

There was also another sensibility operating in the sorority in the 1930s. The new generation of women had different attitudes about education and status than the older women. As Johnson noted in his 1936 study of graduates in the early thirties, "The older students came, more often, from homes of meager education and income, but with aspirations definitely fixed above their status. Where education was sought at all it appears to have been sought passionately and with an almost blind faith in the mystic values of such an experience.

The drive was the elevation of social status, which was, in effect, an attempt at social emancipation." But the present generation had motives that were somewhat different, he observed. More of their parents were high school and college educated, had a more sober assessment of the value of education, and so, education in and of itself, was no longer "a highly exceptional achievement." Both parents and their children believed college education important, Johnson continued, but for a different reason. "The dominant drive is now more immediately utilitarian than social" on the part of both parents and their children. "The urge to social elevation is somewhat changed in character, from a question of a lowly group status to that of competition for social prestige among these various emerging groups."30

So, achieving high grades and honors in college was no longer as important as it had been in the past; the burden of proof that Blacks could succeed did not weigh as heavily on the present generation. This would seem to smooth the path for the acceptance of the "B" schools in the sorority. On the other hand, if the social prestige associated with college was of greater importance, that could present a roadblock. For although the present generation was not unsympathetic or unfamiliar with the experience of aspiring above one's present status, the students from the lesser-rated schools could affect the *social* prestige of the sorority as a whole. The prospect of many young women coming into the sorority who were from poorer households, from the rural South, were first-generation college educated, or were less cosmopolitan in their experience and outlook was not looked upon with the traditional class bias of other groups, but with a social bias. A social bias that was repugnant if logical in light of a racial experience that blocked so many other avenues of social prestige.

And then, of course, there were those with the unadulterated conviction that permitting the "B" schools within the sorority would lower the academic standards of the sorority. The debate about standards, which would reemerge in different forms throughout the history of the sorority, went to the heart of how members viewed the role of the organization. Should its organizing principle be more in line with Greek-letter societies such as Phi Beta Kappa—with its more objective and quantifiable criteria? Or should Delta's social and political objectives outweigh such criteria, which, after all, were established by a dominant majority whose interests were often pursued at the expense of Blacks? The issue came into sharp focus after the 1932 decision of the Association of Colleges and Secondary

Schools of the Southern States. That it would be a hotly debated one became immediately evident at the Chicago convention.

At the fifth session, held on the morning of August 30, the report of the Committee on Standards began on a contentious note: "Because the problem of standards [is of] increasing importance and because demands are constantly being made to lower Delta standards, it is felt that some definite settlement of the questions should be arrived at during this convention."[31] The committee recommended that college chapters rated "B" by the Southern Association, or not accredited at all, should suspend all initiations until they come up to standard. It then suggested that those schools be given a four- or five-year probation period at the end of which those still not accredited should be "permanently dropped from the Delta list." Also recommended was the rejection of those schools accredited only by the American Teachers Association, because the committee felt "that the acceptance of these two groups would lower present Delta standards too much." The committee, chaired by Miriam Mathews of Nu Sigma in Los Angeles, then presented a status report of the fifty-two colleges and universities that were on the present Delta list. All but eleven were rated "A" by various accrediting agencies.* Of the eleven, six were rated "B" by the Southern Association, including Clark College, North Carolina A and T University, Virginia Union University, Virginia State University, Wiley College, and Bishop College. The remaining five were not accredited at all: Bates College, Duquesne University, Framingham State College at Framingham, Massachusetts, Samuel Huston College, and Wilberforce University. A heated discussion immediately ensued. The report was biased against the South and Southwest, many felt. And it was in those regions that a dual system of education was practiced. For a decade, it was argued, those schools had met the requirements of their regional rating associations but "the spirit of racial intolerance and prejudice had prevented their accreditation, and . . . the Grand Chapter should take this factor into consideration."[32] At that session, the Standards Committee report was tabled because of "the controversial points involved."[33]

It was brought up again, the next day, at the ninth session, during the Committee on Recommendations report. Mary Smith Buford of Omicron Sigma in Tulsa, made a minority report recommending that

---

*The Association of American Universities, the Association of Colleges and Secondary Schools of the Southern States, the Middle States Association of Colleges and Secondary Schools, the North Central Association of Colleges and Secondary Schools, and the Northwest Association of Secondary and Higher Schools.

the "B" schools be accepted as chapter seats of the sorority. But voting was deferred until the completed Standards Committee report was made. The latter was again interrupted over the "B" school question. It looked as if there was going to be another logjam regarding the issue until Buford took the initiative. She made her recommendation into a motion, which forced a vote on the issue. Buford's bold gamble paid off: The motion carried, narrowly, 20 to 17. Following the vote, there was a suggestion from the floor that a supplement to the Southern Association's criteria be presented. Although no more details were given, the supplement seems to have taken into account—as earlier requested—the prejudicial aspects of the rating systems, while at the same time maintaining some of the standards of the agencies. So a compromise was struck. The "B" colleges and universities as rated by the Southern Association and the others were accepted provided that they fulfilled all the standard requirements *except* those pertaining to salaries and training of faculty.[34] Later, the standards for libraries—which said that a college library should have no less than eight thousand volumes, exclusive of public documents and should have a definite annual appropriation for the purchase of books—were also exempted. (The need for better libraries was subsequently an issue in which both the sorority and Mary McLeod Bethune, as director of the Negro Division of the National Youth Administration, would become actively engaged. Both initiated library projects. Bethune's, in 1937, was to train and make one hundred librarians available to Black institutions that needed such library personnel in order to be accredited. Delta would think the issue of enough import to make it its first national project.)

The compromise supplement also gave the "B" schools seven years to become "A" institutions, or lose their right to initiate.[35] The sorority's decision was important in several respects. In sheer numbers, Delta would expand rapidly. In 1934, thirteen more chapters were added to its roll; and as Helen Edmonds observed, the succeeding conventions of 1934, 1937, 1939, and 1941 set up undergraduate and graduate chapters in almost every state, especially in the South.*

*In 1938, founder Jimmie Middleton, then living in Washington, D.C., saw her beloved Alpha Zeta Sigma Chapter established, finally, in Raleigh, North Carolina after years of effort; by 1941, Delta chapters were founded at Alabama State Teachers College; Bluefield State Teachers College (West Virginia); Dillard University (Louisiana); Florida A and M University; Langston University (Oklahoma); LeMoyne College (Tennessee); Miner Teachers College (Washington, D.C.); North Carolina A and T; Philander Smith College (Arkansas); San Diego Teachers College (California); Shaw University (North Carolina); South Carolina State College; Southern University (Louisiana); Tennesse A and T; Virginia Union University; Tuskegee Institute (Alabama); and Virginia State University; among others.

That, in turn, set the stage for the institution of major, long-term national projects that were created in response to the particular needs of Blacks below the Mason-Dixon Line. By the late forties and fifties, the implementation of those projects would transform the structure of the organization and the type of executive needed to lead it.

Delta would also become more identified with its role as a "public service sorority." The projects, which will be discussed later, played an important part in that perception, as well as did the fact that the sorority had consciously deviated from its more "exclusive" beginnings. It also could become a more legitimate lobbyist for broader issues affecting all Blacks—and this it would do with great vigor in succeeding years.

Other business of the convention included legislation that increased the amount of scholarship aid. Now the minimum given would be $100, the maximum $500. One hundred dollars was donated to the Scottsboro Fund and another $100 to the Association for the Study of Negro Life and History. The hiring of an executive secretary came a bit closer with the appointment of a search committee that would investigate women to fill the post. And, at the last session, there was the all-important vote for national officers. As was true with her immediate predecessors, Gladys Byram Shepperd declined renomination for president, leaving Jeannette Triplett Jones, Lorraine Heathcock, and Naomi Cherot in the field. Three ballots were required for the presidential election, as none of the candidates had received a majority of the votes from the thirty-seven delegates present. On the third ballot, Jones was elected. Founder Myra Hemmings was elected vice-president, and other officers included: Edna Morris (who also declined the presidential nomination), secretary; Marian Capps, treasurer; and Edna M. Kinchion, journalist.

The group must have been heartened to have resolved the pressing matter of the "B" schools, as well as the fact that their treasury had a gross of $10,060.00. About a third of their budget would be spent for their scholarship funds ($2,911.75) and another $1,303.95 was targeted for a housing fund to purchase a headquarters building. Their improved financial situation reflected not only the increase in numbers but their successful campaigns against inactivity and inefficient collection of monies. Of the sixty-two chapters chartered by the time of the 1933 convention, fifty-seven were fully functioning and fifty-two were financial.[36] That roster would also include Alpha

Omicron Chapter in Seattle, the first Black Greek-letter organization in the Northwest. It was established in 1933 by seven Deltas, including founder Bertha Campbell, who had been living in Seattle for the last ten years, and also served on the YWCA Board of Management, and the Woman's Auxiliary of the Seattle Urban League.

Indeed, Jeannette Triplett Jones would preside over an organization that had ironed out many of its internal problems, was on the cusp of unprecedented growth—both in numbers and the breadth of its programs—and which would engage actively in racial, economic, and legislative issues. Jones, a graduate of the University of Chicago with a Ph.D. degree and a teacher at Phillips High School in that city, seemed to be the right president at the right time. She had held important positions in the sorority: president of Lambda Chapter, director of the Midwest Region, first and second vice-president of the national organization, and chair of the National Scholarship Board. And, as evidenced by her leadership in the sorority and subsequent civic activities, she also had a heightened political awareness.

In terms of the sorority itself, it was not long before she challenged its priorities and spending habits. Of the latter, Jones questioned the cost benefits of the most sacred of activities: national conventions. Those attending the upcoming national meeting in Los Angeles, would spend about $200 for transportation, room, and board, she calculated. And this sum would not include what one would spend for clothes and other "aids to beauty"—which, she sardonically observed, "were considered as indispensable as the railroad ticket."[37] Ten years and five conventions later, that would add up to $200,000 for each soror—not to mention the expenditure of friends and relatives who came along; and the less quantifiable cost in terms of time and energy—both physical and spiritual. "Could the money be put to better use?" Jones asked. But the president understood that the question had socioemotional implications. Psychoanalysts, she noted, observed that women were such great convention enthusiasts because they "were used for a means of escape . . . or in the absence of many-sided interests, searching for a substitute for that which is lacking." Educated Black women, she knew, had their own kind of frustration. Imbued with the same training as men and White women, their world was often smaller, more isolated, and laden with roles of middle-class convention. This sometimes also narrowed their vision. People who attended conventions should "begin increasingly *to think* and not *to reflect* thought and accept predigested opinions," Jones opined. "They must begin to stop thinking in terms of pennies concerning the program and other essential features of their organization and to stop spending thousands on inconsequentials. If they attend conventions because of sincere interest in the welfare of the organization and not because they have acquired a pleasant habit," she continued, "they will be willing to hold their conventions away from the city . . . in some secluded and appropriate location where the high cost of conventioning may be properly reduced." Not only would conventions then become less costly, but the women would be free from "unnecessary distractions," allowing "a better esprit de corps" as a result of "the closer association and cooperation" in such a setting. Then the convention "habit" can become an "asset," Jones concluded.[38]

Such observations underlined the sorority's attempts to strike a balance between the social needs of the sisterhood and those of the organization. The latter had to be particularly clear because the times demanded coalitions between groups, forcing them to become accountable to other constituencies as well as their own. The first coalition which had to be established was among the Greek-letter groups themselves.

In May of 1930 the first meeting of the National Pan-Hellenic Council (NPHC) had taken place at Howard University. The NPHC evolved out of the earlier National Interfraternal Council, in a new effort toward coalition to strengthen the influence of the Black Greek-letter organizations. Evidence of their renewed determination prompted then-Delta president Anna Julian, elected treasurer of the NPHC, to observe that the coming together of these organizations was a "significant step in the history of Greek-Letter Societies"—a step that had been "thwarted" in the past. Its purpose was to arrive at a "unanimity of thought and action as far as possible in the conduct of Greek-letter collegiate fraternities and sororities, and consideration of problems of mutual interest to the member organizations."[39] Those interests were dual in nature. There was concern about collegiate matters: scholastic standards, securing Black representation in White interfraternal organizations, and discrimination against Black students in dormitories on predominantly White campuses. The NPHC was particularly active concerning the last issue, documenting exclusionary practices as well as sending letters of protest and requesting conferences with university administrators.

But there were also broader issues and so broader coalitions to be realized. The most prominent of these was the Joint Committee of the National Recovery Association. The twenty-four-member organization was formed in response to the National Recovery Act of 1933, which authorized labor codes that regulated minimum wages and the length of the work week for various industries. As important as such questions were to Blacks, they found themselves with little lobbying power in Washington in the early days of the New Deal. The thirties found even the major civil rights organizations such as the NAACP and Urban League practically bankrupt. Consequently, as historian Harvard Sitkoff noted: "Afro-Americans could do nothing to counter the control over the early New Deal exercised by Southern Congressmen in alliance with well-financed industrial associations, local unions, and farm lobbies. . . . Not a single Negro organization sent a spokesman to testify at the congressional hearings considering farm and industrial legislation."[40]

There was a dire need for a cooperative effort and by October of 1933, organizations that promoted the rights of Afro-Americans did come together under the umbrella of the Joint Committee. Formally established on September 15 of the same year, its purpose was to "secure the combined efforts of racial and interracial organizations and agencies in the protection and promotion of the welfare of Negroes, both wage-earners and consumers."[41] In addition to the Greek-letter groups, and the major civil rights organizations, other members included the AME Church, the National Association of Colored Women's Clubs, the National Bar and Medical associations, the National Catholic Interracial Foundation, the Women's Auxiliary of the National Baptist Foundation, and the YWCA, among others. The officers of the organization included executive secretary John P. Davis, who would subsequently organize the National Negro Congress; chairman George E. Haynes, sociologist and one of the first executive officers of the National Urban League; technical advisor Robert C. Weaver, who would be appointed as a race relations officer in the Department of the Interior under Roosevelt; and treasurer Nannie Burroughs. The representatives included such notables as the historian and educator Charles W. Wesley, attorney William H. Hastie, and Mary Church Terrell. Representing Delta was the chair of the Vigilance Committee, Esther (Popel) Shaw, who was a Phi Beta Kappa graduate of Dickinson College, a modern language teacher in Washington, D.C., and a writer and poet whose work appeared in *Opportunity, The Crisis,* and the *New York Herald Tribune.* All in all, the Black member organizations represented some four million Afro-Americans through their various branches.

The Joint Committee immediately began filling the void of Black interest group representation. It prepared briefs, wrote letters, conducted interviews with those in charge of establishing codes, and appeared at some seventy code hearings, with the strength that its numbers represented. It kept its members informed of activities as typified by grand secretary Edna Morris alerting the sorority on February 27, 1933, of upcoming code hearings on March 5 in Washington, where all of the code authorities were to meet. She recommended that "every chapter register protests against the treatment of Negro workers under the codes; that all urge in their communications the abolition of the Southern differential in wages and hours, retained in the codes; that they seek the appointment of a Negro representative on the Labor Advisory Board and the Consumers Board";[42] and that they mail these communications to the President and other authorities over the codes. Unfortunately, however, the committee's impact was stymied by lack of funds. Its budget, derived from the contributions of the various member-organizations, was never able to exceed $5,000.

Nevertheless, there were some successes. In the fall of 1934, for example, Esther Shaw reported the favorable resolution of the Maidwell Garment Factory case that came about largely through the efforts of the committee. In that year a Black woman employee in the Arkansas factory registered a complaint to the committee that Maid-well was not living up to the wage codes, which should have paid the 194 Black women workers at Maid-well at least $12 a week. Instead they were earning only half of that. The committee investigated the matter, got affidavits from the women, and filed a complaint with the National Recovery Agency, which administered the program. The NRA was slow to act, but finally ruled in favor of the women, who received more than $4,000 in back wages. The Joint Committee's efforts also helped to incorporate Black workers who were excluded from the code regulations, such as farm workers and domestics, into the recovery legislation. And the committee did help to secure a ruling that workers in cotton gins—the vast majority of them Black—should be categorized as industrial workers and thus were entitled to minimum wage and other labor benefits provided for in the National Recovery Act. The committee also helped to ameliorate conditions and wages for tobacco workers in North Carolina and Virginia, and mine workers in Alabama, among others. And finally, it successfully proselytized for Black appointments to various agencies. Although the victories may have been minor ones compared to the inequities that continued to exist, the findings of the Joint Committee provided valuable documentation of the "Raw Deal," as some put it, and raised the political consciousness of Black organizations, which would thus be better prepared to engage in the long struggle for equal rights. This was certainly true for the Delta organization, which was willing to now support not only individuals in need, but causes critical to the masses of Blacks—even the more radical ones. This was evident in their public support of Louise Thompson, an organizer of the left-wing International Workers Order (IWO).

Thompson, the charter member of Kappa Chapter, who was fired from Hampton, subsequently moved to Chicago where she and Jeannette Jones became friends. Eventually, she moved to Harlem, where she came to know many of the Black cultural and political figures there; she had a short-lived marriage to the writer Wallace Thurman, and was a secretary for the writers Langston Hughes and Zora Neale Hurston. In the early thirties, Thompson traveled to the Soviet Union with Hughes and a number of other writers, and upon her return became involved with the Scottsboro Boys case—and one of its most important Communist lawyers, William Patterson, whom she would marry in 1940. In 1934, Thompson became involved with the IWO, which organized and secured work benefits for its ten thousand members. In May of that year, while she was working among the striking mill and mine workers in Birmingham, Alabama, the police raided the apartment where she and six other organizers were meeting, confiscated the Communist literature that they found there, and arrested the group. When Thompson insisted that she was merely a maid in the house, she was freed—but only for a short time. When her true identity was discovered, she was rearrested. Notices about the incident were published in newspapers throughout the country, and when Jeannette Jones heard about it, she had to make a decision. Black groups were being constantly smeared with charges of communism, which were used to justify either ignoring them, cutting off support, or worse, arresting their members. Just three years before, Howard University's appropriations were threatened and a federal investigation ensued when it was discovered that the curriculum included analyses of left-wing politics and that its president, Mordecai Johnson, had praised the success of the Soviet Union in ameliorating the plight of the poor in that country. Nevertheless, though there was little that the sorority could actually *do* about Thompson's plight, it was decided that their open support of the activist was important not only as a statement of racial solidarity but one that evoked the Delta sisterhood. "Dear

Louise," the letter on official stationery from the Delta president
began:

> *This message comes to you from your hun-*
> *dreds of sorors who want to stretch out their*
> *hands to you across the distance and silence*
> *that separates, to say that your welfare, your*
> *comfort and your safety is our heartfelt con-*
> *cern. Thoughts of love and cheer and conso-*
> *lation go out from us to you, for are you not*
> *one with us . . . ? Doubtless ere this reaches*
> *you by way of some circuitous route, all will*
> *be well. We feel that it can be but a matter of*
> *time before this incident will be a part of the*
> *inglorious past of the southern section of our*
> *country. Some of us are expecting soon to be*
> *able to grasp your hand and say to you the*
> *many other things that are deep down in our*
> *hearts. Praying that this message reaches*
> *you, we are,*
>
> *Yours in Delta,*
> *Jeannette [Triplett Jones]*[43]

Thompson was subsequently released, and promoted to national
secretary of the English branches of the IWO. Now living in California, Thompson, though critical of much of sorority life, nevertheless
remembered the above correspondence—which she has kept all
these years—with appreciation and a special fondness for Jeannette
Jones.

In the meantime, the Vigilance Committee
led by Esther Shaw and later Anna Julian lent its support to educational, employment, and civil rights issues throughout the thirties. In
an "Open Letter" published in the 1935 *Bulletin,* Shaw noted that
the Vigilance Committee had been able to keep "an ear to the
ground" and, whenever possible, "voice a protest in the name of our
sorority against injustice of various kinds where our racial group has
been concerned."[44] Delta had lent its name and support to federal
antilynching bills, protests against the firing of soror Mabel Byrd
from the National Recovery Act Advisory Board, and the curtail-
ment of the women's educational program at Harvard "as a so-called

economy measure." It was very active in the coalition of groups that sought amendments to ensure that Blacks got their fair share from the proposed Harrison-Fletcher Bill, which asked for increased federal aid to education. They supported two bills proposed by Black Illinois congressman Arthur W. Mitchell, which would prohibit segregation in interstate facilities and assure that the highest scorer on the civil service test would be appointed. (As it stood, a selection was made from the three highest scorers, a method that virtually assured that Blacks would be overlooked.) On the other side of the civil service coin, Delta also supported the Ramspeck Bill, which provided for the extension of the Civil Service Act. Under the bill, many unclassified workers, a large number of whom were Black, would be granted security, tenure, and grade classification. In the racial discrimination fight, the Deltas worked with the Citizens Committee, a coalition, which led the fight for Marian Anderson to sing in Constitution Hall after the Daughters of the American Revolution denied the request. (The issue became a cause when First Lady Eleanor Roosevelt resigned from the DAR in protest and Anderson sung instead, by invitation of Secretary of the Interior Harold Ickes, from the steps of the Lincoln Memorial. Her triumphant recital was attended by over seventy-five thousand people, and thereafter Constitution Hall, as well as many major American opera companies, opened their doors to Blacks.)

From the beginning, the Vigilance Committee was conceived to work not only through the national office but through local chapters as well. Although the quality of the local committees varied, a number of chapters were able to have an impact on their communities. In the thirties, for example, Omega Sigma, a graduate chapter in Berkeley, was able to get conessions from the school board in South Berkeley after it threatened to close down schools in the district.

During these years, the sorority also worked in league with, supported, and/or contributed to civil rights organizations such as the National Urban League and the NAACP. It gave annual donations to the Association for the Study of Negro Life and History, worked closely with Mary McLeod Bethune in the National Youth Administration, and cooperated with the National Negro Congress, a progressive coalition of over five hundred Black organizations. By the end of the tumultuous decade, Delta had become an integral part of the movement to secure equal political, educational, and economic rights for Blacks. The sorority had evolved from a narrow purpose to embrace a broader one. As Mary McLeod Bethune would observe:

> *[the] Delta girl . . . is one who has been given the opportunity of education and broad development: she is one who has enjoyed the privileges of culture and selected environment. . . . It is pleasing to a heartfelt depth to see her not as self-centered, not desirous of selfish power, not wanting the plaudits of people, not wanting glory—but with a purpose which directs her activities and all that she may control toward lifting somebody else.* [45]

Founders of Delta Sigma Theta in 1913. Bottom row (left to right): Winona Cargile Alexander, Madree Penn White, Wertie Blackwell Weaver, Vashti Turley Murphy, Ethel Cuff Black, Frederica Chase Dodd. Middle row: Pauline Oberdorfer Minor, Edna Brown Coleman, Edith Motte Young, Marguerite Young Alexander, Naomi Sewell Richardson. Top row: Myra Davis Hemmings, Mamie Reddy Rose, Bertha Pitts Campbell, Florence Letcher Toms, Olive Jones, Jessie McGuire Dent, Jimmie Bugg Middleton, Ethel Carr Watson

Deltas at the 1924 national convention in New York City

At the height of fashion—
founder Florence Letcher
Toms

Soror Mary Church
Terrell (at right)
being honored

Soror Barbara Jordan and past national president Lillian Benbow

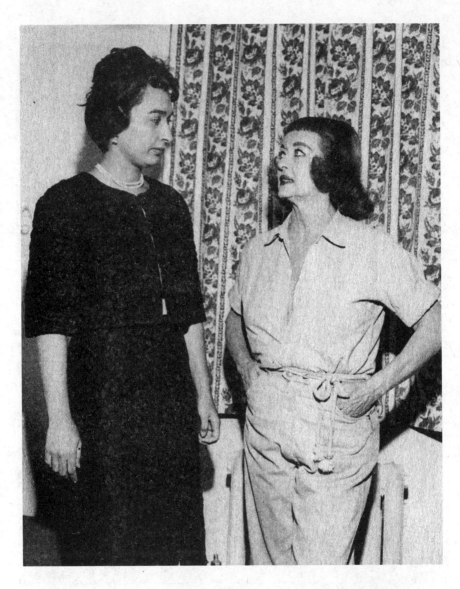

Past president Jeanne L. Noble and actress Bette Davis discuss latter's appearance and acceptance of award for having encouraged the casting of Blacks in non-stereotypical movie roles.

The Bookmobile in Carrollton, Georgia

Presidential candidate Jesse Jackson and immediate past president Hortense G. Canady

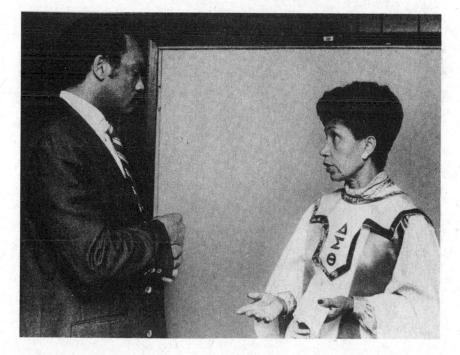

Past national presidents (far right to left) Geraldine P. Woods and Frankie M. Freeman and Deltas discuss legislation with former President Lyndon B. Johnson.

An important gathering—Mamie Eisenhower (left center), Soror Mary McLeod Bethune (right center), and past president Dorothy I. Height (top row, second from left) at a Delta meeting

Past executive director Lynnette Taylor with
former President Gerald Ford

Past national presidents. Front row (left to right): Gladys Byram Shepperd (1931–33), Anna Johnson Julian (1929–31), Sadie T. M. Alexander (1919–23), the first national president of Delta, Thelma T. Daley (1975–79), and Vivian Marsh (1935–39). Back row: Mae Wright Allen Peck (1944–47), Dorothy P. Harrison (1956–58), Jeanne L. Noble (1958–63), Geraldine P. Woods (1963–67), Frankie M. Freeman (1967–71), and national president Mona H. Bailey (1979–   )

From the Howard University archives

ETHEL L. CUFF, ΔΣΘ
Wilmington, Del.

Howard Academy '11

"Her life is but a sleep and a forgetting."

University Choral Society. Chairman Inter-collegiate Committee Y. W. C. A., 1911–12. Vice-President of T. C. C. C., 1912–13. Vice-President of the ΔΣΘ Sorority.

Lena Horne (second from left) with sorors

Former President John F. Kennedy at the Delta Golden Jubilee Anniversary, past president Jeanne L. Noble, presiding

Founders Winona Cargile Alexander and
Osceola Macarthy Adams (seated left to
right) and past national president Thelma T.
Daley, Soror Alexis Herman, and immediate
past national first vice-president Yvonne
Kennedy who was elected national president
in August 1988 (standing left to right)

Founder Naomi Sewell Richardson (center)
and the Mid-Hudson Valley Alumnae
Chapter's Jean Sharon Porter (left) and Anna
Bell Kane (right)

"Miss Vash"—Vashti Turley
Murphy

Florence Letcher Toms and
her husband, Charles

Florence Cole Talbert, who wrote
the music for the official Delta
Hymn. Alice Dunbar-Nelson wrote
the lyrics.

Meetings, meetings, meetings—past
presidents Geraldine P. Woods and Hortense
G. Canady (left to right) and chair of the
national finance committee, Marcia Fudge

Founder Bertha Pitts
Campbell (in her nineties)
kicking up her heels

Founders (left to right) Winona Cargile
Alexander, Bertha Pitts Campbell, Zephyr
Chisom Carter, and Osceola Macarthy Adams

Founders (left to right) Ethel Cuff Black, Wertie Blackwell Weaver, and Madree Penn White being presented violets by soror Allie Miller Holley

The Legacy Continues—founder Bertha Pitts
Campbell and Delta sorors

CHAPTER 8

FROM COALITION TO AUTONOMY

The next three presidents—Vivian Marsh (1935–1939), Elsie Austin (1939–1944), and Mae (Wright) Downs (1944–1947)—would find a Delta organization that was experienced in public affairs: well known and respected by other organizations, and which had penetrated every region of the country. Its numbers surpassed two thousand by 1939, and the sorority was prepared to be both a partner with other organizations in their efforts to realize specific objectives and to launch its own national projects.

At the close of the 1935 convention, Jeannette Jones, citing personal illness and illness in her family, declined a second nomination for the presidency. Among the most progressive of Delta's national presidents, Jones had no doubt raised the political consciousness of the organization. Elected to lead the sorority through its next phase were Vivian Marsh to head the organization; Mary Lou (Davis) Robertson of Shreveport, Louisiana, vice-president; Edna M. Kinchion of Belton, Texas, secretary; Marian Capps of Norfolk, Virginia, treasurer; the journalist position would be filled by Faye Jackson of Los Angeles. The significant contribution of Edna Morris, including ten years as grand secretary, was recognized by conferring upon her the title of secretary emeritus; the first time that other than a national president was given that distinction.

Vivian Marsh had been the force behind the establishment of Berkeley's Kappa Chapter in 1921, and since then had been responsible for five additional chapters on the West Coast. The most recent was Omega Sigma, a graduate chapter, organized in 1934, of which she was president. Marsh had also served as national first and second vice-president, as Far West regional director, chair of the National Program Committee, and a member of the Vigilance Committee. During her four years in office, the sorority would begin to move toward initiating its own projects in addition to supporting other groups. In a period when Blacks were very conscious about pooling their efforts, Delta continued to lend aid to the NAACP, the National Urban League, and the National Negro Congress. During the mid and late thirties, Alpha Kappa Alpha had two major programmatic initiatives: the Mississippi Health Project, which provided for general care clinics and the immunization of thousands of children and residents in rural areas of the state; and the National Non-Partisan Council, a lobby that worked in conjunction with the NAACP. Delta, along with other Greek-letter groups, was invited to participate in these projects, and did, especially in the council—though the AKAs continued to "carry the ball" in these notable efforts.

The highlight of Delta's cooperative efforts in this period was when Marsh was asked by the NAACP's executive secretary, Walter White, to serve as a lobbyist in January and February of 1938 for the passage of the Costigan-Wagner federal anti-lynching bill. It was a critical period in the more than decade-long struggle to win such legislation. Since the bill was first introduced in 1935, White had mounted an effective campaign for its passage in the House and mobilized the support of other organizations, both Black and White, to get it passed in the recalcitrant Senate. After two particularly violent lynchings in this period, Gallup polls showed that the majority of Americans—both North and South—wanted the bill passed. After the Delta national convention held in Cleveland in 1937, White asked Marsh to come to Washington to personally lobby for the legislation. For two weeks, Marsh recalled, she stumped the country, talking about and urging the passage of the bill. Though the bill failed to become law, the campaign not only decreased the number of lynchings, but revealed the potential power of the liberal coalition and was further evidence, as New Deal historian Harvard Sitkoff noted, that the Black struggle had been professionalized. This fact would have an impact on Delta's vision as well.

But in order to realize an organizational vision which extended beyond merely supporting other initiatives to creating its own national projects, a number of things had to happen. There would have to be a greater sense of coherence among the rapidly expanding membership, a broad consensus about the initiative itself, and a lessening of tensions among the leadership. The administration of Vivian Marsh began to move Delta in that direction. With the 1937 and 1939 conventions taking place in Cleveland and New York City, respectively, and Marsh being based on the West Coast, the president took advantage of the long distances to visit a great many chapters personally during her administration. More than any president before her, she spoke frequently on college campuses and to Delta graduate chapters across the country. Approaching the ideal that a national officer should have one-to-one contact with sorors throughout all of the regions, Marsh went a long way, as future president Mae Wright Peck noted, toward, lifting the morale of the sorority, which had been dampened by the Dingle affair, the Calimese administration, and the Depression.

Even more important to the development of the sorority in this period was the president's appointment as state supervisor in the Negro Affairs Division of the National Youth Administration (NYA), one of the programs created under Franklin D. Roosevelt's New Deal. The NYA, directed at finding employment work-relief, or vocational training for young people between the ages of sixteen and twenty-four, was of special interest to the sorority. There had been numerous conferences between Delta representatives and Mary McLeod Bethune, the director of NYA's Negro Affairs Division, in an effort to aid Black youth. Of particular interest to both the agency and the sorority were those issues concerning Black educational institutions and students. Under Bethune's stewardship, federal expenditures for Black students attending college rose from $75,060 in 1936–1937 to $111,105 in 1940–1941. During the seven years that the student aid fund was in existence, 4,118 students received a total of $609,930.[1]

Related programs of the NYA included the training of high school teachers for Black rural schools in Mississippi, where so few high schools admitted Blacks that scarcely any youths were able to take advantage of the NYA student aid funds; and the aforementioned project to make one hundred librarians available to Black colleges and universities that needed library science personnel to become accredited. Undoubtedly the thrust of the NYA influenced that of the two largest Black sororities. It is no coincidence that the first AKA national project centered on training teachers for rural Mississippi schools, a project that later paved the way for their health clinics in that state; and that Delta's first nationwide effort was providing library services in the rural South.

THE NATIONAL LIBRARY PROJECT

It was the 1937 national convention in Cleveland that authorized the National Library Project. The plan was to establish a traveling library in areas of the South where such services were not available to Blacks. Two years later at the 1939 convention held in New York City with its theme, Broader Horizons for Youth of Tomorrow, $2,500 was advanced to get the project going under Anne Duncan, its chair from 1937 to 1950. The complexity of planning required, the domestic exigencies of World War II, and internal problems kept the project from actually being implemented until 1945. The determination of the sorority to keep it alive all those years was the tremendous need for library services in the South.

The new focus in the thirties on education in general and Black education in particular, dramatically revealed the need for library services especially among the rural Black population. The Progressive education movement led by John Dewey was espousing child-centered education that stressed teaching through motivation and the student's own life experiences rather than rote and autocratic methods. At the same time, Black scholars such as Charles S. Johnson talked about the need of Blacks who were not only physically segregated but culturally isolated. "Where many other instrumentalities fail," he said, "books may, when available serve as an open sesame to the world outside. The ability to read can be developed to only a limited extent unless there are reading materials at hand."[2] Not only were books provided by segregated school systems inadequate in both quantity and quality, there were also few resources available outside of the system. In his book *Patterns of Negro Segregation,* Johnson wrote that "public libraries represent an area of extreme racial distinction, since these publicly supported institutions sometimes make no provisions for Negroes."

In addition to the obvious need, the special place of the librarian in the Black community was another factor. Like the teacher, the librarian was role model, primary purveyor of information, and agent for passing on culture and history. As Spelman College president Johnnetta Cole, a Delta and a Floridian who grew up in the segregated South of the forties noted in a recent interview, librarians along with teachers made up the intellectual tradition in those communities.

Although there had been more efforts in the past to extend these publicly supported institutions to the Black community, Johnson's views were an understatement. Out of nearly nine million Blacks in the thirteen southern states in 1930, over six million were without public library service. By 1939, things had improved somewhat, but not much. In that year there were 774 libraries throughout the South and of that number, 99 served Blacks.[3] One fifth of the southern Black population as a whole had access to public institutions; but only 5 percent of the rural population did. Heroic efforts had been made by local PTA groups, community groups, churches, and similar organizations to raise funds and find competent personnel to support the inadequately financed, and usually small, public library branches designated for Blacks. But they had made only a dent. It was increasingly clear that the hard-won struggles to increase aid to Black education would be virtually meaningless if reading material remained so unavailable.

The next step for the sorority was to plan how it would fill the vacuum. It was important that chapters be an integral part of the process (eventually individual chapters would carry the responsibility of sustaining the project) and each, it was decided, would be assessed the cost of ten books, at an estimated $2.50 apiece. Each book would bear the name of the contributing chapter. Grand Chapter would then purchase twenty-five book baskets with lock and key to facilitate the transportation of the books.

Need, the potential of local chapter involvement, as well as Delta professionals who could help administer the project, all had an impact on the site selection of the first traveling library: Franklin County, North Carolina. Franklin, the most needy of the counties in the state, had seventeen one-teacher schools, eleven two-teacher schools, seven three-teacher schools, and three schools that had five or more teachers. The county seat of Franklinton had only two one-teacher schools and five two-teacher schools for Blacks, operating for grades one through twelve.[4]

Also important to the site selection was the presence of a Delta who was willing, and more than able, to assist the project. Her name was Mollie Houston Lee, and she had taught library science at Atlanta University and North Carolina College, and served as city supervisor of school libraries in Raleigh. Lee was also an activist in her field. She had founded the Richard B. Harrison Library, organized the North Carolina Library Association, and served on a number of interracial city, county, and state library boards. Lee asked another Delta, Dr. Virginia Lacy Jones, who was the director of library science at Atlanta University, to permit graduating students majoring in the field to help formulate plans for the project. Their recommendations, many of them suggesting criteria (i.e., that a town Delta served have no less than a thousand residents, and that local teachers and principals be asked to accept responsibility for the distribution of the books) as well as methods of registration and other administrative details to be worked out.

The numerous obstacles which had to be overcome—including the fact that orders for the book baskets took two years to fulfill because of the manufacturer's obligations to its government war contracts—made the official launching of the project all the more satisfying. There was much enthusiasm and fanfare surrounding the project's opening, which was attended by founder Jimmie Middleton, the county superintendent, officials of the county school board, and other leading officials and dignitaries. The operation worked by allowing each school in the county to borrow one basket—containing books on a variety of subjects and Black history—for a one-month period. One teacher from each of the schools took responsibility for the basket. The response was as much as one could hope. After only one year, a teacher wrote to the sorority: "I wish to say that the books were a God-sent Blessing. . . . [the library project] has developed a wider reading interest, comprehension of deeper meanings and better study habits in my grade. . . . It created a desire to read a book during some of his or her leisure time."[5] The teacher went on to say that interest had been so stimulated that her seventh grade took it upon themselves to add some thirty-five more books to their class shelves. Its success can be attested to by the letters of commendation received by the sorority, especially from teachers, but particularly the activities that the attention to the region had inspired. Four years after the project had been initiated, the citizens of Louisburg in Franklin County expressed their willingness to finance a new library center and building that would be furnished by modern equipment through fund-raising efforts of the Louisburg teachers. Dedicated April 11, 1949, the building bore the name of Delta Sigma Theta Public Library, and in a formal ceremony the library keys were presented to its librarian, Mildred McCullers, by the mayor of the city. Delta, in turn, gave their namesake $500 to be spent solely on books.

The sorority did not rest on the laurels of the one success, however. Other sites were chosen in Harolson, Heard, and Carroll counties, situated in western Georgia. These were the most bereft areas in a state that had only ninety-three libraries for the entire population, with only four that served Blacks! This meant that about 48 percent of Whites, compared to under 16 percent of Blacks, had access to such service.[6] Additionally, there were other motives for coming into this particular area. First of all, there had already been a great deal of chapter activity, through Iota Sigma at the Atlanta University graduate school. In 1947, they had already supported efforts to improve the facilities of a Black regional branch in Carrollton. Iota had contributed $500 to the project, which, in turn, had stimulated interest on the part of local Black leaders, who offered a matching donation for the program. The evidence of Black participation spurred the state library authorities to allocate more money, and in fact trebled the Delta grant. Within a year, then, over $11,000 was available to the King Street branch for the purchase of new books. By 1950, there had been enough commitment and interest in the Carrollton program to push the state government to provide a war surplus building to house the library, which now had a collection of over two thousand books.

The Carrollton Library still needed library materials, furniture, a film projector, and more trained personnel. It was at this point that the national chapter stepped in to fill these needs—and another one as well. Service to rural schools and families was still problematic. Needed was a bookmobile that could go to the more isolated areas of the state. The national chapter had already purchased one, with the idea of it going to North Carolina. But before these plans could be realized, the state legislature allocated funds for its own bookmobiles. Plans were made to send the bookmobile to Carroll County. For its part, Delta had provided the bookmobile for sharing books with Blacks in Georgia, had filled it with $3,000 worth of books, and found an outstanding librarian to drive it, Leroy Childs. Childs, in turn, became a popular figure who encouraged and guided children and their parents in the use of the service. He became symbolic, as an observer noted, of all of the understanding and all of the books within his truck.[7] Delta's contributions to library services in western Georgia earned the sorority the American Library Association's American Library Letter Award, in 1954, given for the outstanding contribution of the year. In appreciation for Child's contribution to this recognition, the sorority gave him a scholarship grant that enabled him to finish his graduate studies at Atlanta University. The last demonstration project that Delta engaged in was one along the lines of the North Carolina book-basket operation, at St. Helena Island in South Carolina. By 1956, nine "library outposts" had been created to serve that island community. In that year, the Grand Chapter also voted to end the model programs on the national level. "Having pointed the way," Delta historian Mary Elizabeth Vroman observed, "Delta now decided that in the future its Library Program would operate only on the chapter level."[8]

ORGANIZATIONAL DEVELOPMENTS

The new confidence of the sorority in the late thirties did not mean an absence of internal dissension largely caused by new administrative problems coming as a result of Delta's explosive growth. Between the conventions of 1935 and 1937, some twenty-one new chapters were established, and in her biennial report, grand secretary Edna Kinchion complained that too many chapters failed to carry out national program directives and recommendations. The confusion was reflected at the Cleveland convention, held in December of 1937, where sessions were in such disarray that much of the convention's business remained unfinished. This included the all-important Recommendations Report, which was never read. Attempts to compile, distribute, and get the recommendations voted upon through the mails was, according to Kinchion, an exercise in frustration. She also noted conflicts with President Marsh over the interpretation and acceptance of the accreditation rating of Bluefield State College in West Virginia, and Langston University in Oklahoma. And there were conflicts between the treasurer, Marian (Palmer) Capps and the Audit Committee over the collection of monies and the timeliness of financial reports. The

report revealed not only some personality conflicts, particularly between Kinchion and Marsh, but remaining structural problems. The
office of the grand secretary was burdened with a great deal of responsibility without corresponding authority or resources to execute
her duties efficiently. She was expected to fulfill orders for sorority
pins, membership certificates, rituals, constitutions, and similar materials for an organization that now numbered in excess of 1,300 paid
members, 729 new initiates, and nearly a hundred chapters. The office was also the repository for collected monies and the final arbiter
that determined if the financial reports accurately reflected the
amounts received in her office. Finally, the secretary was, of course,
responsible for all correspondence and this alone was a Herculean
task. Kinchion reported that between January of 1938 and August of
1939, she had written 1,417 personal letters, and if form letters were
included, the number was 2,060.[9] All of this was done in the hours
that were not filled by her six-day-a-week work schedule, in an office
at home that contained several files (two of which were described as
crowded beyond capacity and broken), a Royal long-carriage type-
writer, a stapler, a hole puncher, and some stamp pads. Little wonder that she would complain, "Many times I have taxed and
overtaxed myself almost to the point of breaking." And responding
to those who suggested that she step down, she cited her eleven
years of service to the sorority as Southwest regional director, grand
journalist, and grand secretary, and concluded: "It is my hope that
you will not be too harsh in your decision of negligence. In some
instances I plead guilty to your accusations . . . but I say again . . . I
have done the best under the circumstances."[10]

An executive secretary who would be a paid staff person to handle much of the business was never needed more. Previous conventions had authorized such a position, and a deadline of March 15,
1938, for filling it had been approved. But, probably largely because
of the problems of the 1937 convention, the date was postponed; and
one thing after another prevented the hiring of an executive secretary as well as the purchasing of a national headquarters for another
decade. Barring the realization of those two remedies, combined
with natural personality conflicts, it was inevitable that tensions
would rise. The result could be bickering, often over petty disputes
that were not the real cause but the result of frustrations. This, of
course, discouraged even the most dedicated Deltas. One of these
was Osceola Adams, who hadn't been active in sorority affairs for
some years. That she was occupied with her career, an upcoming
teaching assignment at Bennett College, and a son ready to enter

Dartmouth, was not the only reason for her not remaining active. In a letter to Vivian Marsh in April of 1937, Adams expressed regrets about the "trials" that Marsh had had to endure for the last year and a half. She continued:

> *I have been so disgusted with the endless bickering, the pettiness, selfish motives, and lack of cooperation which continue to persist in Delta to the detriment of any constructive program which might be undertaken, that I have all but despaired. I can only wonder at your having the heart to carry on in the face of these discouraging conditions. Of course, someone must carry if we are to justify our existence and live up to our high purpose, but does it not follow that in all these years we would have learned the elemental lesson of cooperation? Will we never grow up as an organization? Think of the precious years and energy and money we waste in fighting over the trivial things, the little petty personal differences which should be lost sight of in the united effort to put over some truly worthwhile program . . . which will be a credit to us. What have we as an organization to show for the years?* [11]

The penetrating question was answered in the following decade with the library project, among others, as well as scholarship aid. And the organization had given much support and energy to other organizations and civil rights coalitions. Nevertheless, it could not be denied that Delta's potential had yet to be reached and that there was little concrete that one could point to in the years before the national projects or even the hiring of a staff worker or executive secretary.

Edna Kinchion had thoughts on this matter, too. In her biennial report she noted that Delta's greatest contribution was that it had been a "great teacher." It has "made friendship an art," she said; "by means of its comprehensive oaths and obligations it has instilled into the lives of hundreds, a principle and a devotion to cause and purpose." But, she went on to say, these things came not by chance, but because of "the persistence and stern determination" on the part of the few who "love Delta enough to work and sacrifice and be crucified and abused and misunderstood. Every Delta's energy has not been directed along productive lines." Kinchion ended with a challenge to the group: "to enact laws and institute changes to meet the need of our ever increasing sisterhood. . . . I charge each," she said, "to rededicate her life, to reread the vows and obligations taken at the time of initiation. I charge you to determine that now is the time for all good Deltas to come to the aid of the party. I charge you to decide the kind of Delta you are and be governed accordingly."[12] And, as evidenced by much that went on at the 1939 convention in New York City, the sorority did.

That year yet another World's Fair was celebrated, this time in New York, making the August 28–31 conclave held at the St. James Presbyterian Church an especially exciting one. Among the over 350 Deltas present were those not regularly seen at the national meetings. A number of founders had come, who by 1939 were middle-aged. Frederica Dodd was there. After marrying John Dodd, a physician, she went to the Atlanta University graduate school and left teaching to work with the Texas Relief Commission during the Depression years and subsequently became one of the state's earliest Black social workers for United Charities, later known as the Family Bureau. Naomi Richardson, who was still living and teaching in the New York City school system and active with the Alpha Sigma Chapter there also attended. Ethel Black, who had remained close to Richardson, and was teaching at P.S. 108 in Richmond Hill, Queens, was also in attendance. She also was married in that year, to David Horton Black, a real estate agent. Florence Toms, known to her friends as "Flossie," made one of her few appearances at a national convention in New York, as well. She had been married to Charles H. Toms, an attorney, for fifteen years, was assistant principal at Garnet-Patterson Junior High School in Washington, D.C., and would soon come to New York to earn a master's degree from New York University. Eliza Shippen, teaching at Miner Teachers College in Washington, D.C., would, in five years, get a Ph.D. degree from the University of Pennsylvania. And the irrepressible Jimmie Middleton, now the proud holder of a master's degree from Howard and charter member of Raleigh Alumnae Chapter, rounded out the list. All were honored guests and speakers at the formal Delta banquet, as was Mary Church Terrell, who also took an active part in the deliberations and was the designated parliamentarian for some of the sessions. Sadie T. M. Alexander, the second woman attorney to hold the office of assistant solicitor general of Philadelphia, was also in attendance and addressed the public meeting session. She had recently left the city position to enter private practice with her husband, Raymond Pace Alexander. Along with the first grand president, the first grand secretary, Catherine Alexander, was also in attendance. Florence Cole Talbert was there, along with other concert artists, pianist Ethel Ramos-Harris (who was also a member of Anna Julian's Vigilance Committee) and Muriel Rahn.

Unlike the previous convention, much was able to be accomplished—including the incorporation, along with the recorded vote, on the unfinished Recommendations Report from two years before. Many of those recommendations centered around scholarship awards and loans. By 1939, Helen Edmonds reports, the scholarship aid program had grown to the extent that tuition grants to high school graduates were increased from $50 to $150; individual undergraduate scholarship grants to Delta women were increased from $50 to $250; and special grants to graduate women were increasd to $500 and beyond, often to $1,000.[13] Awards for foreign study would be for $250; awards for chapters with the highest grade average would be $25. Loans were to be limited to $250, in the belief that a higher sum would be too much of a burden to pay back. Another recommendation was that instead of the $250 scholarship for graduate sorors, an annual $100 award would be given to a Delta who was still attending an accredited college or university. The latter, it was decided, was more in need of the funds.

A good deal of legislation was passed to ease the administrative burdens of the national officers, including more expenses for the grand president and secretary. The convention also heard a substantive report from the Vigilance Committee, headed by Anna Julian, which covered the lobbying efforts of the sorority, noted earlier. And there was movement on the headquarters issue, even if it would not yet be resolved. A six-room brick house with two baths and two kitchens, located near Howard University and facing the reservoir, was found by the committee. However, they were advised by Charles H. Houston, the well-known attorney, that the asking price was too high. The owner wanted $7,000; the Deltas, on the advice of counsel, were willing to pay $6,200.

There were also uplifting reports about chapter activities, and the usual fare about scholarship achievements of individuals and chapters. Beta Omicron Chapter of Knoxville won the chapter award for the highest average, and the regional award went to the East. Dorothy Maynor, a Delta who had been recently acclaimed by the famed conductor, Serge Koussevitsky, was given $1,000 for study abroad.

In this year, Delta would also help support a foreign exchange student, Kumari Paul, whom a soror got to know while studying in India. Additionally, an award of $500 apiece was given to two graduates of Lincoln and Virginia Union universities to pursue their studies.

A draft of the Delta history had been written and presented to the group by Edna Morris, furthering the sense of legacy that the presence of the founders and former officers brought to the convention. And the election results were met with a good deal of enthusiasm. Back on the scene was Sara Speaks, who was then practicing law after being defeated in a 1937 race for the New York State Assembly. Speaks, who would be the Republican candidate to challenge Adam Clayton Powell, Jr., to represent the state's Twenty-second Congressional District in 1944, was unanimously elected to the Constitution Committee. Founder Jimmie Middleton was appointed to the Scholarship Board. Most were also pleased by the election of national officers. The next grand president would be Elsie Austin, described by Morris as a "brilliant scholar and attorney, and legal advisor to the Recorder of Deeds in Washington, D.C." Vice-president was Mae Peck from Baltimore; Beatrice Penman of Kansas City, Kansas, was elected treasurer (Marian Capps had decided to retire after ten years of service); Frances Griffin of Houston, journalist; Edna Morris, historian; and, by the largest margin of all the candidates—37 delegate votes to her rival's 7—Edna Kinchion was reelected secretary.

They would preside over 100 chapters: 26 in the Midwest, 16 in the Central Region, 13 in the Southwest, 8 in the Far West, 21 in the East, and 16 in the South. The number of financial sorors, 2,000, now surpassed that of the AKAs, which was 1,057 according to Marjorie Parker—despite the fact that their membership also doubled between 1933 and 1938, by accepting the "B"-rated schools.[14] The Delta budget had grown to $11,062.

The sorority was especially proud of Elsie Austin. She was the first Black woman to graduate from the University of Cincinnati's College of Law, and had contributed to that school's *Law Review* and the University of Colorado's *Rocky Mountain Law Review*. Like so many others, she had succeeded against the odds and discouraging words about her aspirations. Austin's father, she recalled, told her that "law was not a thing for a woman to do,"[15] an admonition that may have brought on, while in school, an asthma condition that was so severe, she sometimes blacked out.

And of course there was the all too familiar racism she encountered. Even after she had become a member of the Cincinnati Bar, Austin remembered, she was not allowed to use the university's law library. Nevertheless, Austin went on to become the first Black woman to serve as assistant attorney general of the state of Ohio, and advisor in the General Counsel's Department of the National Labor Relations Board.

It did not take the new president long to analyze what had to be done to further the goals of the sorority. Again, there had to be a focus on administrative efficiency, and Austin declared that the reorganization of records, bookkeeping, and filing systems would be of the highest priority. In addition, she inaugurated a procedure whereby the treasurer would now receive payment of fees and other monies directly. By June of 1940, Austin called an Executive Committee meeting in Washington, D.C., where plans were discussed to further the National Library Project; and provide for an executive secretary and a national headquarters. Another idea for a national project was also brought to the fore at the Washington meeting, by a soror who was then executive secretary of the YWCA in Washington. Her name was Dorothy I. Height and her position had made her keenly aware of the issue of job opportunities for Black women. She proposed that Delta undertake a job analysis program as a national project. The Executive Committee approved the idea and appointed Height as chair of the project, and plans were made to set up experimental centers in each of Delta's six regions.

The plan was an ambitious one. It would include investigations of new opportunities that were opened to women in general but were still closed to Black women; the securing of greater numbers of positions for Black women in those occupations that were available to them; and their greater representation on those boards and commissions that controlled labor policy. Finally, the study was to seek ways in which working conditions for Black women in "unskilled" occupations, such as domestic work, could be improved. A progress report was expected by the 1941 national convention that was to take place in Detroit. At that time the delegates would vote their rejection or acceptance of the program as a long-term national project.

As Height no doubt understood, job opportunities for women, and especially Black women, was an issue whose time had come. By 1940 there were significant changes in women's employment. By that year six out of seven married women worked. For Blacks, one in three over the age of fourteen was in the labor force. Yet they held the most marginal positions of all classes of labor, as sociologist

Charles S. Johnson noted. Some 60 percent were in service and domestic occupations and appeals to the Women's Bureau, headed at the time by Mary Anderson, to take an active role in improving the status of Black women workers, fell on hostile ears. Instead of looking at discriminatory practices, the conditions that many were forced to work under, and the many kinds of disadvantages that they faced, Anderson and others responded that the onus was on Black women themselves to improve their status. They had "to prove themselves capable of developing skills and ready work habits," the Women's Bureau chief was quoted as saying; they had to show that they were worthy of advancement.[16] Black women would have to look out for themselves in the foreseeable future—a future that would have a new sense of urgency with the attack on Pearl Harbor on December 7, 1941.

C H A P T E R   9

COMING OF AGE

T hat day of "infamy,"
as President Roosevelt called it, came less than three weeks before the
sixteenth national convention was held on December 26–30 in Detroit.
It was there where many of the sorors first heard that grand secretary
Edna Kinchion had passed away suddenly—a death that was
mourned by the entire organization. The two unforeseen events
forced the carefully laid plans of Austin to be put on hold.
Kinchion's massive files had to be transferred to the president's
home in Washington, D.C., until an acting secretary could be found;
and the exigencies of the war altered many plans, schedules, and
projects—most notably those of the library service. At the same
time, however, the war made the proposed jobs project all the more
important.

THE NATIONAL JOBS PROJECT

When the Second World War erupted in
Europe in 1939, the United States began gearing up for the manufacturing of war materials: By 1940, Congress had appropriated almost

$18 billion for armament production. Now that America was to be directly involved in the war, there could be unprecedented opportunities for Black workers, much as there was during the last global conflict. Unlike in the past, however, there were now some five million Whites who were unemployed, and employers, saying Blacks lacked the necessary skills, hired Whites first, and often exclusively. Blacks increased their pressure on the federal government and received some encouraging signs. As early as August of 1940, the National Defense Advisory Committee issued a statement against discrimination in the hiring of Blacks in defense plants. The United States Office of Education subsequently stated that there should be no discrimination where their funds were used for defense training programs. And the Office of Production Management established a Negro Employment and Training Branch in its Labor Division to facilitate the employment of Blacks in the defense industries. Even Roosevelt made public statements against racism in hiring policies.

Nevertheless, all of the thunder produced little rain—until A. Philip Randolph, president of the Brotherhood of Sleeping Car Porters, started making threats. In January of 1941, he promised that 50,000 to 100,000 Blacks would march on Washington if something wasn't done. By June 25, something was. Responding to the pressure, Roosevelt issued Executive Order 8802, which said: "There shall be no discrimination in the employment of workers in defense industries or Government because of race, creed, color, or national origin. . . . And it is the duty of employers and of labor organizations . . . to provide for the full and equitable participation of all workers in defense industries." The order also established the Federal Employment Practices Commission (FEPC) to act as a watchdog over its implementation. Of course, the executive order did not magically solve the problem. But a door had been opened, and the racial climate of both government and private industry had been made more temperate.

So, there was no better time to introduce what was first called the Jobs Analysis and Opportunities Project before the Detroit Convention in 1941. Elsie Austin presented the report which emphasized "equitable exposure of Negro women to job opportunities," utilizing "the wealth of leadership in Delta Sigma Theta in order to give direction, aid and advice in the economic problems of Negro women."[1] The four-point approach to the project included fact-finding; ensuring that workers understood the problems facing them; giving guidance and encouragement, especially to younger women; and working to create intelligent public opinion about the need to improve the status of Black working women.

The implementation of the project would come from local chapters, which would be in a good position to understand the special needs of their particular communities, the local organizations that could have an impact on employment, and the local political structure. It was also urged that tangible results be publicized as soon as they might be achieved.

The convention was also impressed by the fact that experimental models of the project had already begun. According to Edmonds, it was the Baltimore center's report that was the most convincing. The Baltimore center, with the support of that city's Epsilon Sigma Chapter, conducted an Occupational Conference for Women in Industry on May 18, 1941. Two sorors, Maude William and Hilda Orr, served as area cochairmen, and past president Gladys Shepperd presided.[2] The Baltimore model had several phases. There was the analysis of new opportunities for Black women—in this case these centered around the new defense plants there—as well as their status and working conditions in the jobs that they already held: in the cleaning, laundry, metal, and clothing industries. A detailed questionnaire was sent out to those employed asking about wages, numbers employed, benefits, opportunities for advancement, availability of training, and whether women workers were organized, among other things. There were also extensive interviews conducted.

The responses showed that only one plant was unionized—and that one by the progressive Congress of Industrial Organizations (CIO). It was also gleaned that Black women, on the whole, were distrustful of unions. Not surprisingly it was also discovered that Black women earned less in wages than White women for the same kind and amount of work. Concerning numbers employed, it was found that Black women were in a ratio of one to five in the clothing industries; food packing companies employed a relatively high number (about one hundred) of Black women; and the metal companies hired Black women exclusively. All of the employees reported little chance for advancement or salary raises, no paid sick days or vacations, and segregation in lunchrooms where Blacks were forced to eat at different times than Whites—if there weren't separate facilities. If there was more than one facility, that used by Blacks was inferior—and the same was true for restrooms. Although the more than one hundred women interviewed had had from twelve to fifteen years' experience on their jobs, none of their employers offered training programs. And the workers were unaware of the government courses that would prepare them for defense work and better job opportunities in this period.

The last phases of the jobs project included a panel discussion and recommendations. Industrial secretary of the Baltimore Urban League, Furman L. Templeton was brought in, as was an executive in the Social Security Division of the Department of Interior, H. Norman Milburn, Jr. All of the information gathered made the tasks and the objectives of the Baltimore project clear. Black women should be urged to enter defense classes and seek to rise from un-skilled to skilled classifications; attention had to be paid to the issues of unionization and to help domestic workers and other service workers to secure higher salaries and better working conditions; and there should be efforts to effectively collaborate with such organizations as the Urban League, the YWCA, the Council of Negro Organizations, and other groups dealing with employment issues. As a follow-up, employers were contacted to let them know that the sorority was aware of the problems of Black women workers, and they were asked to pledge their cooperation. Special attention was focused on such businesses as the Glenn L. Martin Company, which had defense contracts and were legally bound not to discriminate in their hiring practices.[3]

Embracing the jobs project as a national one had broad implications for the sorority. With the exception of the scholarship grants, it would be the first major undertaking that focused specifically on Black women. It would also be a national program that was truly chapter-driven; and it would virtually assure more intimate, meaningful relationships between the chapters, local institutions and organizations, and communities. The Deltas would also be tackling an issue that had equal significance for all Black women in various walks of life. As stated in the report, the idea was to win job opportunities and improved working conditions for Black women in all kinds and levels of employment, both in the public and private sector.

Nevertheless, there were many questions raised after the presentation of the report—many of which, one sensed, were really challenges to the concept of involving the sorority in an activity which took it far afield of its traditional concerns and constituency. There was, for example, discussion of the name: Should the initiative be called a "project" or a "program"? was the question from one soror. She was told that the words were interchangeable.[4] Some maintained that other agencies and organizations that specialized in employment were better equipped to handle such an operation. Austin replied that the idea was to work in league with these groups, and that there were aspects to this project other than job seeking.[5] Still others believed that Deltas should expend their energies by lobbying for legislation, such as that which would allow domestic workers to share in the social security program. Another soror skeptically asked how the sorority could financially support yet another national project when the library project "had been creeping at a snail's pace for the last two years." That comment evoked a particularly sharp response from the president who riposted that no great expenditures would be required in the initial phases of the program, and that, in any case, its potential impact was invaluable. Elsie Austin received "hearty applause," noted Helen Edmonds, when she suggested that since "Deltas had so fruitful a way of getting money for their parties and formal dances, it was high time they appropriated money for worthwhile projects in their communities."[6] Another soror, Elizabeth Gordon from Oklahoma City, went to the heart of the matter. "I think it is a worthwhile project," she said, "and that it is necessary for all of us . . . to recognize that we have a certain obligation in belonging to a national organization, and that only through supporting such a project as this, can we make good this obligation. . . . At one of the other conventions, we discussed the question of the justification of the existence of Greek-letter organizations, and even though we don't have to question the justification of our organizations, we at least have to prove [their worth].[7] Her view held sway; the report was adopted and the Jobs Analysis and Opportunities Project became a national project.

THE WARTIME EMERGENCY

Of course, at this sixteenth convention, there was great preoccupation with the attack on Pearl Harbor and United States involvement in the war. For the Afro-American community, the call to arms both heightened the contradictions of defending a country that practiced racism at home, on the one hand and, on the other, provided the opportunity for proving their worth and patriotism in a society that believed Blacks had neither. The presence of Mary McLeod Bethune as the keynote speaker for the meeting personified both ideas. The Black Cabinet member was still seething over the failure of the War Department to invite the National Council of Negro Women (NCNW) to a conference on organizing women for the war effort. Bethune had established the NCNW in 1935 to represent the interests of Black women and their organizations for just such a purpose. She expressed her displeasure to Secretary of War Henry L. Stimson, writing that Blacks insisted "upon being considered a part of our American democracy" and that their interests "are too often neglected, ignored or scuttled unless we have effective representation in the formative stages of these projects and proposals. We are not blind to what is happening. We are not humiliated," Bethune concluded. "We are incensed."[8]

Addressing the Delta convention some months later, she nevertheless observed that "our intelligence, our abilities, and our strength must now be used in a supreme effort of giving maximum service to the nation and in preserving those values which make democracy worth fighting for." That effort, went the thinking of the time, would be evidence that Blacks were willing—and able—to make worthwhile contributions during the present crisis, and by extension to mainstream society in war and peace.[9] Delta responded in kind—and quickly. Adopting as its slogan "Delta Dynamic for Defense," the convention resolved to pledge its support to the government and the President of the United States, cooperate with the National Defense Program, invest in Defense Savings Bonds and encourage others to do likewise, lend its support to USOs—especially those serving Black servicemen—and support all organizations that sought further progress for Blacks and the nation.[10]

One of the sorority's first acts was to purchase $5,000 worth of United States Defense Bonds, winning praise from Jesse O. Thomas—a Black representative from the U.S. Treasury Department—for being the first national organization of Black women to make such a large purchase.[11] Follow-up consisted of planning to invest systematically in War Bonds throughout the emergency. To much fanfare, the 1944 convention pledged $10,000 worth of bonds, and the news was covered extensively in the Black press. A photograph in the Chicago *Bee,* for instance, showed William Pickens, the outstanding leader of the NAACP and, since 1942, the director of the interracial section of the Treasury's Savings Bond Divison, receiving the check from Beatrice Penman, Delta's grand treasurer. Pickens had flown from Washington to Kansas City, Kansas, for the event. Delta's national office also urged individuals and local chapters to do their part. The effort yielded much fruit. Regions and chapters responded with their own bond drives, and a number had dramatic results. Alpha Gamma Sigma of Memphis, sold $98,000 worth of War Bonds during one drive; Omicron Sigma at Tulsa and Alpha Phi at Wichita reached $20,000. The Central Region bought over $54,000 worth of bonds.[12]

A Victory Book Drive was also launched in 1942 under the direction of grand jouranlist Victoria McCall, whose objective was to collect books for servicemen's use in military camps throughout the country. This and other projects focused on military facilities. Books were donated by the Southwest Region to Camp Swift in Texas; chapters furnished lounges for servicemen and rooms for the WACs, taught defense classes, and donated Red Cross kits. In 1945, Delta launched a successful campaign, in cooperation with the Seventh War Loan Drive, to purchase an ambulance. Out of these activities, individual Deltas emerged who showed the ability to galvanize sorors for the various wartime projects: One of them was Gwendolyn H. Higginbotham, regional director of the South, who would be an important figure in years to come.

Austin proved to be an effective galvanizer herself. She saw to it that Delta was on the mailing list of all important government initiatives concerning the war, resulting in many Deltas—as Edmonds observed—receiving mail directly from the federal government for the first time. She appeared on the famous *Wings over Jordan* radio program, reporting Delta's efforts and accomplishments in the war effort.

At the Detroit convention, Bethune talked about Black women using their "talents and abilities" to serve the national interest, so that they would never place themselves "in a position where our patriotism can be doubted." But this did not mean that they were to be passive. It was also necessary to "preserve those values which make democracy worth fighting for." For Black women that meant that they were duty-bound to "become a part of every endeavor in which American women engage."[13] This included, of course, becoming a part of the women's forces, such as the WAVEs, the WACs, and the WAFs, all representing various branches of the armed services. And insisting that, once accepted, they be integrated into the mainstream of military life and services.

However, even the opportunity to serve was not granted easily. It required agitation on the part of interested groups, and even after the principle was won, long meetings about how Black women were to "fit" in the armed service. Elsie Austin related, for example, a 1943 meeting between a Lieutenant Commander McAfee of the WAVEs and Black women leaders, including representatives of the AKA-led Non-Partisan Council, the NCNW, Dorothy Height of the YWCA, and Austin herself. Under discussion was a "proposed program for admitting Negro women to the WAVEs."[14] The group was advised, wrote Austin, that "the Navy had under consideration a plan whereby a segregated unit of Negro WAVEs was to be formed and trained at one of the Southern Negro colleges."

The Black representatives balked. They pointed out the "evils of segregation," noted Austin, and the advisability of a plan that included complete integration. "We felt," she said "that we could assure the success of such a plan since we would try to obtain the highest type of women for the service, if it was to be fully integrated." Of course, it was not to be. Black women continued to protest only to be told at a subsequent meeting in 1944 that "while the Navy desired a non-discriminatory policy, it could not add to its war responsibilities with a program of race assimilations or adjustments." The Black servicewomen would be assigned where they were needed and/or accepted—and those assignments would probably be racially motivated, the representatives were told. "Some commanders, for instance," Austin wrote, reporting on the results of the meeting, "had said they would like WAVEs for the effect of raising the morale of the Negro men in the Navy."[15] That may not have been exactly the primary role envisioned by the women, and there was no question that they were sorely disappointed by the Navy's attitude. Nevertheless, their persistence did gain them some small victories. The Navy consented to provide officer training at Smith College for six women who would then be assigned on an integrated basis. Others would follow, the Navy assured. It was a small opening in the solidly segregated walls surrounding the arsenals of democracy. But it was an opening, nonetheless.

By August of 1944, the second wartime national meeting of the sorority drew some three hundred delegates from thirty-nine states to Wilberforce, anxious to hear about the results of the bond drives and the status of Black women in the armed services—a number of whom were Deltas—as well as other issues that compelled attention.

One of the latter was the movement to abolish the poll tax, which had gained much momentum since 1942 when the House voted to do away with it. As usual, southern senators—with the notable exception of Claude Pepper from Florida—stood as a solid bloc against its passage. Although the tax would not be abolished in both state and federal elections until the sixties, the senators south of the Mason-Dixon Line found themselves virtually alone in attempting to uphold the tax. This alone showed progress from the days of the antilynching bills and other similiar racial issues that were debated in Congress. By 1944, organizations such as the Southern Conference for Human Welfare (SCHW)—organized in 1938 to promote underprivileged groups in the South—helped galvanize liberal, labor, and civil rights groups to support a federal anti-poll tax bill. At the Wilberforce convention, Virginia Durr, the White civil-rights activist who would play a significant role in the Montgomery bus boycott a little more than ten years later, pledged the support of other southern Whites in the struggle. Delta also went on record as supporting the FEPC—the primary government watchdog over discriminatory practices in industry, and an ally of Black women workers. Betwen July 1943 and December 1944, the complaints of Black women workers made up 25 percent of the total. Less predictable at the convention was the sorority's support, of the CIO's Political Action Committee, and the Negro Youth Congress, both of which were criticized by many for their leftist leanings. That the sorority's progressive political positions were gaining it a national reputation was evidenced by the more than three thousand who attended the convention's public meeting. Featured on the program was Dr. Charles H. Wesley, the eminent historian and then-president of Wilberforce.

At the convention Austin, who was ill and would not have another term as president, talked about both the status of the sisterhood and the direction that she thought the organization should take. She noted a "new sense of unity among Delta women," one that did not preclude "areas of conflict," but for a greater understanding of the "dangers of personal dominance, . . . and unfairness." Problems were remedied, she said, "without the sustained personal feud, jealous vindictiveness and malicious reprisal which have cost women so much efficiency and effectiveness." And sounding the new era of interracial cooperation, she affirmed that Delta "should be concerned with some prgram which will enlighten both white and Negro people. . . . Let us use our initiative, ability and good judgment to devise programs which go far beyond the old-time feeble interracial teas and discussions of differences." Austin—a member of the Baha'i faith, which gives emphasis to the oneness of God and the unity of mankind, and who would go on to a foreign service career with the U.S. Information Agency—concluded: "We must find new ways to bring people together in interested action for a bettered democracy and greater harmony."[16] Austin's statements not only reflected a large part of the national mood, but that of the Deltas as well. Two years earlier, for example, founder Bertha

Campbell was one of the primary forces behind organizing the Christian Friends for Racial Equality, a prominent interracial group in Seattle, Washington.

At the next national convention, set for Richmond, Virginia, December 27–30, 1945, the sorority—with the exception of Beatrice Penman who would be reelected treasurer—would have new national leadership. For the 1944–1945 period, Mae Downs, a former Baltimore chapter president, and national vice-president under Marsh and Austin, would be president. Downs was a Phi Beta Kappa graduate of Tufts University and received a master's degree from New York University. Dorothy Height, presently in Washington, was elected vice-president; Reber S. Cann of Cincinnati, a friend and mentor of the ailing Austin, secretary; Dorothy C. Lymas of Philadelphia, journalist; and Minerva Johnson of Nashville, historian. Of special note was the election of a student, Gloria Hewlett of Fisk, to the new position of undergraduate coordinator. The office had been created when undergraduates, demanding better representation in the policy-making body, petitioned the national office. The need to create a place for students dramatized the fact that those running the sorority command posts were no longer undergraduates or even younger graduate women. Delta was coming of age, in more ways than one. The coming years would find her playing a part in international affairs, expanding her programs, moving from a merely supportive role to becoming an intergral part of like-minded organizations, and increasing the breadth of her local chapter activities. And, as the newly elected president would note, these years would also mark the time when the image of sororities as "exclusive, black-ball based, social clubs, was in eclipse." More and more, Downs commented, they were being looked upon as an organization of women "with academic accreditation, social consciousness and sisterly devotion."[17]

THE PEACETIME EMERGENCY

In May of 1945, its war-machine routed, Germany surrendered unconditionally; three months later, the United States dropped the first atomic bombs on Japan, and by August 14, the Japanese also acquiesced. The Second World War was over, and so later that year was the life of Franklin D. Roosevelt. It soon became evident that just as the American involvement in World War II created new and sometimes unforeseen developments in the national body-politic, so would the exigencies of peace. The postwar years not only brought new political, social, and economic issues for Black Americans to the fore, they also brought about a new philosophy that guided their actions—all of which affected the sorority.

Among the most compelling issues for Black Americans was their economic status and future employment prospects. Black men and women who were able to take advantage of the wave of opportunity that swelled the manufacturing and government sectors experienced new levels of well-being. Bolstered particularly by the entrance of unprecedented numbers of Black women into the industrial and civil service labor force, there were, for the first time, enough Blacks earning sufficient income to make up a middle class. In the postwar period, the percentage of Black women working as domestics decreased, and those in the professions increased. By 1950 they comprised 58 percent of all Black professional workers. Beginning in 1940, more Black women received B.A. degrees than Black men, and by 1952–1953, the former were receiving 62.4 percent of all degrees from Black colleges.

But, of course, there was another side of the coin. The lesser skilled of the 800,000 Blacks who had migrated from the South to work in the defense plants found themselves at bay. The slower peacetime economy and the return of White soldiers resulted in their being downgraded, fired, or just left unemployed. About 20 percent of this category of workers were women. Studies found that the gains of Blacks had actually peaked between 1942 and 1945, and were now on a downward spiral. This was recognized by Delta's Job Opportunity Committee when it reported at the eighteenth national convention in Richmond: "If we ever wondered whether there was a need for this project, we can see the answer on the faces of those who stand in line at the United States Employment Service Offices seeking jobs. In most cities today a disproportionate number of Negroes stand in line with the jobless of other races. Already there is evidence that 'White Protestants Only' is creeping back into employment orders."[18]

Nevertheless, the jobs project would become weaker, not stronger. The "analysis" aspect of the program was problematic for many local chapters. Some were intimidated by the process, and southern chapters, especially, found it difficult to undertake the adversarial role that was often required—particularly when there was increased racial tension due to labor competition that was more imagined than real. There was also discomfort and tension around the direct involvement with unskilled workers. But the new philosophy of the period had an even more profound impact on the program. A more universal plea for equal rights replaced the more racially centered, strident tone of protest by the late forties. This was reflected in everything from literature—which abandoned the protest tradition—to political initiatives. The progress of a category of Blacks also put a new emphasis on individual behavior, rather than discrimination, as the major obstacle to upward mobility. Finally, there was a change in the attitudes toward the role of women in this era. They, for economic and social reasons, were urged to leave the labor force now that the war was over and return to more traditional roles. The pressure to return to traditional roles was also felt by Black women despite the fact that their income was desperately needed even by middle-class Black families. Though the less skilled lagged behind, Black women as a group were making tremendous progress. New positions, such as telephone operators, were available to them. And beginning in 1939 they would enjoy the highest percentage increase in median income of *any* group. Some found this an alarming development in terms of the Black family. Sociologists such as E. Franklin Frazier believed that Black men were becoming so dispirited by their relative lack of achievement that they were deserting their families.

All of these trends were reflected in the 1947 resolution, arising from the nineteenth national convention in San Antonio, that "the Sorority's national project be directed to a nation-wide effort to secure job opportunities for members of *minority groups,* and Negroes in particular" (emphasis mine). It made no mention of analysis, abandoned the focus on Black women, and even on Blacks, exclusively. Furthermore, the emphasis changed from directly challenging discrimination, to, as Helen Edmonds noted, "counseling and guidance" (i.e., personal development) as the "chief methods of proceeding."[19] As the historian further observed, by 1945 "Delta had redoubled its efforts toward job opportunities but had clearly laid down the premise that it was not enough to place continuing emphasis upon fair and just employment practices unless there was a corresponding degree of interest in better job-training on the part of Negroes."[20] And so although the sorority continued to advocate higher minimum wages, social security and full employment bills, a permanent FEPC, and the cutoff of federal aid to employers who practiced discrimination, there was equal if not greater emphasis on

"Hold Your Job" types of campaigns that stressed self-improvement through education and training.

In 1947, the sorority also turned its attention to college youth and vocational guidance, working closely with T. Arnold Hill, employment specialist of the National Urban League. The relationship evolved into joint projects of the two organizations, including an experimental program in Atlanta and Detroit that was to compare the vocational counseling needs of youth in a segregated and nonsegregated community; and the publication and dissemination of *Negro Heroes,* which contained biographies of outstanding Blacks, such as Jackie Robinson, in a comic-book format. The most dramatic successes of the new phase of the project, however, were the numerous vocational and guidance clinics held throughout the regions. In Maryland, for example, Job Opportunities regional chairperson Alma M. Harlee held a clinic that was attended by two hundred students from twenty-two schools who benefited from an array of consultants and specialists who also participated. In Roanoke, Virginia, regional chairperson Pauline Weeden conducted a career conference that drew nine hundred students from eight schools and two states, which won the praise of state education officials. And a Job Opportunities Conference in Kinston, North Carolina, which was attended by five hundred students, elicited an editorial from the local paper: "Such clinics should be encouraged," it said, "not only among Negro students, but white students as well. They give the young people an insight into problems and opportunities that will guide them in the choice of satisfactory vocations. . . . The sorority is to be congratulated on rendering a helpful service to the students and the State as a whole."[21]

There is no question that some important things were accomplished by the newly evolved Jobs Project, which continued into the 1960s. Although it ran more smoothly once it was better fitted to the proclivities of the membership—many of them in teaching and guidance fields—one wonders what would have happened if the sorority had not chosen the safer course and instead continued in the direction of its initial proposals.

Like other Black organizations of the period, Delta also turned its interest toward international affairs, which focused upon the establishment of the United Nations and its charter. Of immediate concern was the Dumbarton Oaks proposal that was to establish a framework for the UN Charter to be presented in 1945 at the San Francisco meeting, where representatives from forty-five nations were to discuss the charter's provisions. For many Blacks, the Dumbarton plan didn't go far enough to ensure the rights of minorities, either at home or abroad. The establishment of the United Nations, and the principles it would abide by, was seen by Blacks as a new opportunity to redress racism and discrimination—this time in the international arena. The conference was deemed all the more important because it took place soon after the death of Roosevelt, who had represented such hope to Blacks. There was the conviction, observed John Hope Franklin, that the international meeting could bring "world opinion to bear on their plight." There was also the rationale, which would later underlie the civil rights movement of the fifties and sixties, that racism at home was just as abhorrent as the usurpation of rights elsewhere—and should be viewed accordingly. "A national policy of the United States which permits disenfranchisement in the South," opined Charles Hamilton Houston, "is just as much an international issue as elections in Poland or the denial of rights in Franco's Spain."[22] Such deep feelings compelled President Mae Downs to authorize Bertrell (Collins) Wright—head of the newly formed Public Affairs Committee—to send a letter in the name of the sorority to each member of the United States delegation to the conference.

"The Dumbarton Oaks Proposals represent an excellent beginning," the letter said in part. "We feel, however, that the proposals do not go far enough to insure a lasting peace. Definite proposals should be made in regard to the minority groups and dependent nations of the world. They must be assured of the same rights and protections as other free people of the United Nations. The problems of these people cannot be continued to be overlooked, if justice is to be made the guiding objective of a peaceful world."

"Delta Sigma Theta, a National College Sorority," it continued, "is very hopeful that you are aware of the significance of the minority groups and dependent nations. We hope that you will see that adequate proposals for their protection will be made at the California gathering of nations."[23] The sorority received a response from each of the delegates, who expressed their assurances and became, perhaps, a little more sensitized to Afro-American concerns.

The foray into international affairs had an indelible impact on the sorority. Future conventions would use the theme of international human rights as their organizing principle, and pass numerous resolutions that spoke to the inextricable link between international and domestic quests for the "Four Freedoms." By the fifties, Delta's growing international consciousness would manifest itself in its programs and even in its reaching out to form chapters in other countries.

Of course, there was still much to do on the home front, and the sorority further consolidated its national initiatives by establishing a five-point program, authorized by the eighteenth national convention held December 27–30, 1945 in Richmond, Virginia. The five points—fostering education; employment; housing; race and intercultural relations—would be approached with vigor and the consensus of the largest convention in Delta's history. Under the theme "Design for Living in New Age," it was attended by four hundred sorors. The chapter roll of the sorority now numbered 144 and each was obligated, stressed President Downs, to promote one of the five points and report to the national office. Such accountability, a more defined approach to the national program, seemed to spur the chapters on as seen in their five-point-program reports.

Education, of course, was always a primary concern of the sorority, but it had a particular urgency in the mid-forties when the fight to realize the 1938 Supreme Court *Gaines* v. *Canada, Registrar of the University* decision, that states must provide equal facilities for its Black and White students—was in full throttle. Late in 1944, as the *Delta Bulletin* reported, a southern governors' conference that concluded that such provisions had become the White South's primary problem. "There must be a 'Victory for Negro Education,'" the bulletin continued, "because education is one of the chief instruments of racial understanding."[24] A related struggle was that of the equalization of Black teachers' salaries. By the forties there were increasing challenges to this inequity, including those of individual Deltas. Founder Jessie Dent successfully sued the Galveston Independent School District and won equal pay for Black teachers in that city. In writing of Delta's role in this issue, historian Rayford Logan no doubt had her in mind when he wrote in the *Pittsburgh Courier:* "Individual members of the [Delta] sorority dared to carry on the epoch-making fight of Southern teachers for equal salaries. In two of the most outstanding cases, Delta women were the plaintiffs. Another Delta woman lost her position in Virginia because of her dynamic efforts in behalf of equalization of salaries."[25]

The education effort also included the traditional granting of scholarship awards. For this purpose the $5,000 given by the national chapter for scholarships was supplemented by the $550 given by Ohio's Gamma Sigma Chapter and additional awards of between $100 and $500 given by numerous chapters. The two-decade-old Jabberwock program, used as a fund-raiser, was widely utilized as a means to secure scholarship funds. Another approach to aiding Black students was initiated by Beta Lambda Sigma Chapter of Okmulgee, Oklahoma, which helped lead a campaign to get a bond issue passed to build a new high school for Blacks. Yet another tack was taken by Charleston, South Carolina's, Beta Alpha Sigma Chapter when it—boldly for the time and place—endorsed a page in the local newspaper on the evils of the dual school system. As could be expected, fewer chapters centered on race and intercultural relations. However, Theta Sigma of Illinois cosponsored with other Greek-letter organizations an "Exhibit of Portraits of Americans of Negro Origin" put together by the Harmon Foundation. And the above-mentioned Gamma Sigma, perhaps inspired by a national convention address given by Eslanda Robeson, presented an original pageant to raise money for the Council on African Affairs. The council, chaired by Paul Robeson and based in New York, was the first predominantly Black organization that attempted to influence United States policy in Africa.

Under the employment category, one of the most interesting chapter activities not mentioned earlier in connection with the Jobs Project, was Beta Alpha Sigma's campaign aimed at the American Tobacco Company to end its discriminatory practices against its mostly Black and female work force. The tobacco industry had been the target of union organizers who led numerous strikes and walkouts since the thirties.

Most of the antidiscrimination in housing issues would be dealt with by the Vigilance Committee through supporting and keeping sorors informed on the battles being waged by the NAACP and others. There were also other aspects of this concern, namely supporting the NCNW's campaign (to the tune of $1,000) to maintain its national headquarters in Washington, D.C.; and the tremendous efforts of local chapters to purchase and maintain housing as childcare and youth facilities. By 1946, for example, Beta Beta Chapter in Texas had successfully raised over $7,000 for the purchase of a site and the partial furnishing of a child welfare center in Houston; and Beta Kappa of Virginia contributed $1,070 toward the building fund of a nursery school.

Two of the most outstanding projects were realized by chapters in Michigan and Gary, Indiana. Beta Nu Chapter in the latter city purchased a house at a cost of $13,500 for use by the sorority as well as community organizations, with further plans to establish a finishing school for young women. The most ambitious, and perhaps successful, purchase was the Delta Home for Girls in Detroit. Although the home would be open to girls of all races, Michigan's Alpha Pi Sigma and Tau chapters became interested in providing a boarding house for delinquent girls after the race riots of 1943, when a study of community needs revealed that there was "not one existing child welfare institution willing to accept a Negro girl." There were few boarding homes in Michigan for young Black women, and those who ran afoul of the law had no recourse save returning to an often unwholesome environment or being committed to the state's juvenile facility. It was the latter whom the chapters wanted to help. And, after much effort, they were able to purchase a twelve-room brick house with two adjoining lots, for recreational purposes, in 1946 for $18,000. By June 6, 1947, six young women, between the ages of fourteen and eighteen, left the Juvenile Detention Home to take up residence at the Delta Home for Girls supervised by a housemother and staff. And within a year, the number rose to ten, and included young women referred to the sorority by the Children's Aid Society and the Detroit Board of Education. Two of the young women were accepted in a local Catholic institution, and, as the article on the home noted, "agencies which previously closed their doors to those of color are now considering ways of extending their services to our group."[26]

Much had been accomplished under Mae Downs's administration, and there seemed to be a great deal of admiration for her quiet yet effective leadership. "So many of the sorors spoke of your efficiency, charm and the dignity with which you presided," wrote treasurer Beatrice Penman to Downs, a week after the close of the December 1947 convention.[27] After reading the final President's Report, Penman went on to say that "I can see now that because of your modesty others, in many instances, have received credit for what you have quietly planned, guided and executed. Your responsibility has been great and you have accepted it and quietly discharged your duties . . . Not only I, but many others, admire you for your loyalty and unselfishness." Nevertheless, Downs, who in subsequent years would be a specialist in instructional television (the only Black in that position in the state of Maryland), declined nomination for another term. Although her decision was met with disappointment—"they [the sorors] were reluctant to see you go," wrote Penman—there was some consolation in the fact that she would become the next president of the National Pan-Hellenic Council. Subsequently she would also serve as a vice-president of the American

Council on Human Rights, a soon-to-be-established coalition of Greek-letter organizations.

There was also understanding about Downs's reluctance to serve again ("I can't blame you," wrote Penman), because of the stress and strain and even financial obligations that accompanied the position. Penman, herself, had needed encouragement "in order to hold out even for seven months"—the length of time until the next convention, which was scheduled in August of 1948. Asking that a successor be sought soon, she wryly observed that "working in Delta too long will kill anybody, and I want to live a little longer." In fact, she was only "waiting to see how the presidency was going before I made any declarations as to my intentions." Penman was fully prepared, she said, to refuse the nomination if Dorothy Height, the vice-president and initiator of the Jobs Project, had not gotten the nod at the last convention. After "Dorothy got it," Penman said, "I couldn't let her down. . . . I'm glad that Dorothy succeeded you. She, too, is cultured, refined, well-poised, and a clear thinker. If she will work, as you have worked," Penman concluded, "Delta can still go forward."[28]

PART THREE

CHAPTER 10

THE MODERN SISTERHOOD

THE DOROTHY HEIGHT
ADMINISTRATION: 1947–1956

In a 1947 article in *The Delta*, Delta journalist Dorothy C. Lymas expressed her view about the status of national affairs and what the ideal soror should be doing about it. She wrote:

> *The national scene is pretty much as it's been since the end of the war—bogged down with the housing shortage, rising prices, labor problems, segregation, foreign chicanery and the whole gamut of peace busters that reflect us more like people of the past than of the present. . . . Liberties that rightfully belong*

to democracy are boldly reproved as un-American. . . .

The scarcity of living quarters that forces children and overworked parents to live in hovels is to her [the Delta soror] a needless infliction on human endurance, so she makes sure of the crusading efforts on the sabotaged Housing Bill, S. 866, which provides a program of housing for low and middle-income groups. Writing to her Congressman, her Senator, and to the President of the United States, she tells them how she feels about the matter. . . . Incidentally, she makes a notation of their responses, too, just for the record when election time rolls around. . . .

Seeing what can be accomplished . . . she joins the cooperative movement in her section of the city . . . Like all fair-minded citizens, she's been working on FEPC . . . to make it a permanent commission. She hasn't given up either because the opposition has borne down in a million ways.

In addition, she affiliates with interracial groups that are aiming . . . to bring harmony between races.

The foreign front she views with an open mind, and no foregone conclusions save the major premise that two ideologies seem constantly at variance. On one side is a so-called rule by the people, and on the other side is the rule by a central authority. But neither, she notes, is exactly what it is thought to be. . . .

She's alert to change, and willing to weigh its proposals. Most of all, she knows her civil rights and is unafraid to speak out in defense of them. . . .

Being aware that stagnation is the result of inactivity, she never stops studying, building, moving on toward new understanding."[1]

To many including Beatrice Penman, no one was better prepared to lead such women than Dorothy Height. By 1947, she had already had a successful career in a woman's organization, the YWCA. Height had been associated with the Y since her days in a teenage club under the leadership of Sorors Lulu Howell and Edna Kinchion. It was Kinchion, in fact, who influenced her to join the sorority. Height subsequently held positions as executive secretary of the Phillis Wheatley YWCA in Washington, D.C.; director of the Emma Ransom House, Harlem Branch, New York City; and director of the YWCA School for Professional Workers in Mount Carroll, Illinois. Height was remembered fondly by Pauli Murray, the late lawyer, writer, and Episcopal priest who became an honorary member of the sorority. While studying at Hunter College in the thirties, Murray stayed at the Harlem Y, and wrote in her autobiography that Height, among others, was one of her role models. Of the Y women she said, they "would not have called themselves feminists in the thirties, but they were strong, independent personalities who, because of their concerted efforts to rise above the limitations of race and sex and to help younger women do the same, shared a sisterhood that foreshadowed the revival of the feminist movement in the 1960s."[2] By 1937, Height was elected as a youth delegate to the World Conference of Christian Youth in Amsterdam, Holland, and in 1944 was a member of the Y's National Board. While on the governing body, she was a member of the leadership services staff and worked on the development of a training program for volunteers and staff of American YWCAs. Height was also interracial education secretary of the National Board staff. All of these experiences would be brought to bear on the sorority.

A straight-A student at Rankin High School in Rankin, Pennsylvania, near Pittsburgh, she won her first $1,000 scholarship from the Elks, a Black fraternal organization, by winning an oratory contest. Her academic training was in social work; she gained a master's in that field from New York University. From Height's election in 1947 to the end of her final term in 1956, the organization underwent significant, even fundamental, change. "The modern era of the sorority began with Dorothy Height," noted Jeanne L. Noble, who would become national president in 1963. "She brought us right up to what would be the most modern level of women's organizational development."[3] "It was Dorothy Height who got me interested in that field in the first place," Noble, who holds a Ph.D. in education, noted. It was a field that Height had learned well at the Y.

By 1947, the new president had already proven her "clear thinking" with the formulation of the Jobs Project. She had also shown some political acuity in keeping it alive as a national program. And although her initial concept may have been beyond the ability of the sorority as a group, the project nonetheless reached its highest potential under her administration. It was during those years that the highly publicized conferences took place in Roanoke, Virginia, and Kinston, North Carolina; and that *Negro Heroes* was published—an event covered throughout the Black press. Height had appointed employment specialist Es Cobedo Posey to head the project in 1948. Pauline Weeden, a guidance specialist, chaired many of the best-attended clinics. Height had a good eye for personnel.

The other national initiative, the National Library Project also reached its heights under her administration. What had at first seemed a wasted effort—Delta's tardy purchase of a bookmobile for North Carolina after the state voted to provide such a service—was turned into a coup when it was slated for Georgia. The launching ceremony for the vehicle was performed with great fanfare. NBC-TV featured the event on its program *Date in Manhattan,* on which the bookmobile made its "debut" at New York City's famous Tavern on the Green restaurant in Central Park.[4] There was a "Delta Promenade" at the Chatham Hotel, where an eleven-year-old actor who was currently appearing on Broadway's *Lost in the Stars* cut "the crimson and cream ribbons draped across the door of the bookmobile and intoned, 'God bless you and the children to whom you'll carry happiness.'" Perhaps they weren't among the young man's most compelling lines, but they were effective, nonetheless. Another festive occasion awaited the carrier's arrival in Georgia. It is such fanfare—in addition, of course, to the project's undeniable intrinsic worth—that gets the attention of award givers. The careful planning, securing the right support—which Height had already made sure of before her decision to send the vehicle there—and an understanding of public relations all came together in time for the American Library Association's prestigious award.

The late forties and fifties were a time of tremendous interest in international affairs, and here, too, Height took the Delta program to new levels. In fact, as Helen Edmonds observed, her administration "lifted Delta to the highest level of international thinking in its history."[5] The sorority had already had a good start in this direction, as the Vigilance and Public Affairs committees had raised the consciousness of the sorority by taking stands on such issues as the United States intervention in Haiti and the Dumbarton Oaks proposals, among others. As was true with other nationwide projects, neither the direction nor the substance of the initiatives changed under Height's leadership, but the breadth and interest in them did. One reason was her ability to organize a high-quality program; another was her use of wide-ranging contacts to bring before the group—and the public—some of the most prestigious personalities on the scene, Black or White, American or non-American. Of course, there had been highly touted programs before. Under the previous administration, the Deltas and Omegas cosponsored a forum in New York City's Town Hall entitled "To Secure These Rights"—a name adopted from the report of the Committee on Civil Rights created by President Harry S Truman in 1946. Participants in the forum included six members of that committee: Sadie T. M. Alexander, Morris Ernst, Franklin Roosevelt, Jr., Dorothy Tilley, Boris Shisken, and Channing H. Tobias. The moderator was Walter White. Nevertheless, Height's programs managed to include individuals whose agendas were not primarily those of domestic race relations.

In 1948, for example, under the theme "Human Rights—Our Challenge—Our Responsibility," a panel presented before the convention included not only such people as Sadie T. M. Alexander, Mary McLeod Bethune, and Urban League executive director Lester B. Granger, but also Homer P. Rainey, president of Stephens College in Columbia, Missouri, and Madam Rajan Nehru, wife of the first prime minister of India, who represented the East-West Association. The 1950 national convention that took place in Berkeley, California, also featured some new additions to the Delta roster of participants. Under the rubric "Human Rights—From Charter to Practice," a public forum included the World War II hero and UN public relations representative, Admiral Chester W. Nimitz, as well as Alexander, Dorothy Ferebee—a physician and member of AKA who had headed their Mississippi Health Project and was then president of the NCNW—and attorney Belfore Lawson, then president of Alpha Phi Alpha. It was also at that convention that a resolution was passed to admit any qualified woman to the sorority, regardless of race, creed, or nationality.

In August of 1951, Height took the Executive Board on a tour of the United Nations where they met members of the Department of Information and the Political and Economic Committee on the Rights of Women. By that year, the sorority would have a more direct concern with international affairs. In 1950, Height had gone to Port-au-Prince, Haiti, for the island's bicentennial exposition. After her return, arrangements were made to initiate the sorority's first international chapter: Delta Zeta Sigma, an alumnae chapter based in Haiti's capital, organized by Haitian sorors Jacqueline Coicou, an instructor in the teachers college in Port-au-Prince, and Marie Berger, a member of the UN's secretariat. In just four years, Delta, through the establishment of its Haitian Relief Fund, which was administered through the Caribbean chapter, would come to their much-needed aid in the wake of Hurricane Hazel—a particularly vicious storm that had brought death and complete destruction to many villages.

In 1952, Height accepted a teaching position in India, and again her travels would have a direct impact on the sorority. After spending four months as a visiting professor at the Delhi School of Social Work, she had arranged her schedule to return to the United States in time to preside over the convention that year in Cleveland. She gave an inspiring speech on how the Deltas could aid the newly independent nation; and in response, the Deltas, "moved by [Height's] description of the needs of Indian women, voted to establish a scholarship at the University of Delhi for two deserving Hindu women."[6]

Of course, there was also much activity on the domestic scene, and panels such as those featuring Senator Herbert Lehman of New York and other high officials and politicians of moment became common events at the conventions. In 1953, the year of Delta's fortieth anniversary, the sorority sponsored a "Town Meeting on the Air," with Stanley High, a senior editor of *Reader's Digest,* and Dr. Charles S. Johnson, the sociologist, founder of the National Urban League's *Opportunity* magazine, and president of Fisk University. Recently, the latter had been chosen as one of the ten American delegates to represent the United States at the first session of UNESCO (the United Nations Educational, Scientific, and Cultural Organization) in Paris. The topic of the town meeting was "Are We Losing Our Moral Courage?" with Johnson taking the affirmative and High supporting the negative side of the question. The town meeting, which took place in Washington, D.C., on May 12, to coincide with May Week, was attended by two thousand people and broadcast by ABC radio over 310 stations throughout the nation.

Another town meeting, this one taking place at the twenty-fourth national convention in 1956, showed that Delta was again on the cutting edge of political developments. Taking place in Detroit, its theme was "American Race Relations: International Implications," and in addition to featuring the president of the City College of New York, Buell Gallagher, it also had a panelist who had just emerged victorious in the boycott that launched the modern civil rights movement: Martin Luther King, Jr., president of the Montgomery Improvement Association.

As far as legislative issues such as the creation of a permanent FEPC, discrimination in housing, fair employment bills and federal aid to education, it was during Height's administration when a new initiative to pool the lobbying efforts of the Greek-letter groups was begun.

THE ACHR

Called the American Council on Human Rights (ACHR), it was an outgrowth of the National Non-Partisan Lobby, both of which were created by the Alpha Kappa Alpha sorority which in this period was far ahead of the other groups in this area. By 1948, there were eight national Black fraternal groups and all, with the exception of Omega Psi Phi, consented to become a part of the council.

The ACHR promised to be the most effective interfraternal effort since the 1920s, when the first attempts were made to coordinate the activities of the Greek-letter organizations. All of the groups were now more experienced in lobbying activities. Then, their memberships had grown considerably. In 1952, an ACHR meeting in Cleveland had an attendance of 3,000 delegates representing some 100,000 members of Greek-letter groups. Additionally, the "interracial" climate of the times virtually guaranteed that the positions of the council would be at least considered by the Truman and Eisenhower administrations, if not always acceded to. And finally, unlike the other efforts, the ACHR employed a staff to provide continuity of leadership and who were less vulnerable to internal politics.

The ACHR was fortunate to have as its first director Elmer Henderson, who had served as the director of the Committee on Fair Employment Practices that investigated violations of Franklin Roosevelt's 1941 executive order against employment discrimination. Henderson was not only the director of the committee; he had himself been a litigant in an important court case. When, in 1942, he was not allowed to eat with White passengers on a Southern Railway train whose regulations had been approved by the Interstate Commerce Commission, he promptly—and successfully—sued the federal government. Henderson's attorney was Belfore Lawson, president of Alpha Phi Alpha—and as this was one of the few major cases not handled by the NAACP, financial backing for the litigation was entirely provided by the fraternity.

Henderson's able assistant was a young woman by the name of Patricia (Roberts) Harris. Born in Mattoon, Illinois, Harris was a summa cum laude graduate of Howard University (where she pledged Delta under Jeanne Noble who was also a student there) and furthered her studies in political science and industrial relations at the University of Chicago. While in that city, she worked for the Human Relations Commission, the NAACP, and the YWCA where she first met Dorothy Height. Harris would be in charge of social action programs for the ACHR. In addition to Harris, other Deltas held responsible positions as officers in the council. As noted earlier, Mae Downs was its first vice-president. Height would be vice-president in 1952, and Delta representatives to the ACHR included Bertrell Wright—who was elected president for two terms in 1953 and 1954—and Charlotte R. Lewis.

The agenda of the ACHR included passage of the Fair Employment Act, desegregation of the armed forces, public transportation, and public accommodations in the nation's capital, the anti-poll tax and antilynching bills, federal aid to education with safeguards against discrimination, revision of the cloture rule that allowed filibusters in the Senate, federal appointments of Blacks, and abolition of racial discrimination in immigration and nationalization. Representatives of the new organization appeared before congressional committees, conducted research on legislative matters and the voting records of congressmen, lobbied individual representatives on Capitol Hill, and worked toward public support of their positions through the press.

The ACHR could count some successes by the fifties. Henderson, as the council director, was invited to tour Army, Navy, and Air Force installations to assess efforts toward desegregation. Using data he acquired firsthand, he and the ACHR played a significant part in defeating two amendments to the Selective Service Act—proposed by Senators Richard Russell of Georgia and Arthur Winstead of Mississippi—which would have slowed progress toward full integration of the armed services. It also helped defeat another amendment, introduced by Congressman John L. McMillan of South Carolina, which would have virtually endorsed a policy of segregation by the federal government in Washington, D.C.

The nation's capital, which had segregated public facilities and accommodations, was a target of civil rights groups in this period. The Coordinating Committee for the Enforcement of the District of Columbia's Anti-Discrimination Laws, for example, challenged the policy of restaurants and department-store lunch counters that refused to serve Blacks. The chair of the committee was none other than Mary Church Terrell, now nearly ninety, who led the group in sit-ins, distributed leaflets, spoke at public meetings, and picketed area stores urging a customer boycott. (As told by Dorothy Height, when a young woman who saw Mrs. Terrell offered to help her across the street, the irrepressible activist replied, "Oh, no, dear, I'm on my way to picket Thompson's Restaurant.") Thompson's Restaurant became the focus of a legal suit filed by the committee after it discovered that the city's segregation ordinances, though never actually rescinded, had not been on the "books" since the post-Reconstruction era. The ACHR had filed an amicus curiae brief in the case, which, in 1953, got a favorable ruling by the Supreme Court.

That the ACHR played an important part in the victories against discrimination in this period was acknowledged not only by other Blacks but by the Truman and Eisenhower administrations as well. On October 20, 1952, President Truman met with the council's board of directors in the White House. And it was before the same board that Secretary of the Interior Julius Krug chose to announce the new federal regulations against discrimination in Washington, D.C.'s parks, playgrounds, and swimming pools. In March of 1954, the ACHR received a message from President Dwight D. Eisenhower congratulating it on its "efforts to preserve and to strengthen our liberties," but, more important, to inform them that another of their objectives had been reached. "I know," continued the message, "you can also take pride in the service which your distinguished member, J. Ernest Wilkins has begun to perform in his new position as Assistant Secretary of Labor."[7]

The creation and the effectiveness of the ACHR had both a short- and long-range effect on Delta's internal organization. It allowed many of the activities usually relegated to the Public Affairs Committee now to be channeled through the interfraternal council, and in 1948, the Vigilance Committee was disbanded altogether. The relegating of the lobbying activities to the ACHR also had legal implications. Delta, as a tax-exempt organization, could not engage in what could be construed as partisan political activities. To Height's mind, the opportunity to streamline Delta's committee structure was a welcome one. She believed that the internal machinery had become unwieldy. Some of the committees had overlapping functions. Lines of authority and responsibility weren't always clear. Procedures changed with each new election of officers. There was a need for a complete revamping of the system, for a central office, for a staff person to handle the growing volumes of paperwork and other activities that had to be coordinated with some kind of continuity. Height's association with the efficient and hardworking Patricia Harris no doubt gave her an idea of who that staff person should be. But first things first. Delta needed to be reorganized after years of adding committees and boards in a patchwork kind of way. Now that the national projects were proceeding smoothly, and the legislative program was taken care of by the ACHR, it was a good time to focus on bringing the sorority to its next stage of development. "Dorothy Height always said that you cannot run an organization without a master plan," recalled Jeanne Noble.[8] The new president had one: First there was a need for internal reorganization; second, a national headquarters and the position of executive director had to be filled; and third, at some point Height would have to suspend the laws of the constitution that limited her to two terms in office. And, well versed on the methods of organization, she accomplished all three.

As early as 1948, the national president intoned the need for Delta to reevaluate itself. At that year's national convention in St. Louis, she observed that the sorority had to find ways "in which we can make Delta stand out from day to day; to take a look at ourselves, and see how we can have a stronger and better program; to see what we want to develop for Delta; and to work together, play together, yet find a kind of unity which can make the organization live."[9] The first step toward that realization was making the national office more efficient. In 1950, the Berkeley convention approved a recommendation for the reorganization of the Grand Chapter. And by August of 1951, arrangements were made for the Executive Board and appointed members of a reorganization committee to meet on the campus of Vassar College in Poughkeepsie, New York. Their task was to examine the constitution and the various boards and committees.

The result of what was called the "mending conference" was a streamlined sorority. For example, the Constitution Board was eliminated as a standing board; an appropriate committee would be appointed when a revision was necessary. The Judiciary and Standards boards, were both absorbed into the Executive Board. These moves alone eliminated much confusion, for in the past certain matters had had to be acted upon by all three boards before they were resolved. Not only was time lost, but one board often duplicated the functions of another, or had insufficient information to enable it to act effectively. The functions of the Standards Board that concerned academic criteria were absorbed by the Scholarship Committee—which, under the new plan, became the Scholarship and Standards Committee.

The historian's office was also done away with; the Public Affairs and Public Relations committees were combined into one Public Relations Board. And the functions of the grand journalist, the Pan-Hellenic representative, and the Jewelry Committee (responsible for the purchase and distribution of the official Delta pin) were all to be the responsibilities of a new staff officer: the executive director. The administration of the national projects was consolidated under a national projects committee (subsequently headed by Jeanne Noble) and there were small but important procedural changes in the collection of fees. Most important perhaps were the proposed changes in the composition of the Executive Board, which had become bloated with all of the past board and committee chairs. Now it would be made up solely of the president, first vice-president, second vice-president (who would be the undergraduate representative), secretary, treasurer, legal consultant, regional directors, and the heads of the Finance, Scholarship and Standards, Public Relations, and Personnel committees.[10] All in all, the number of Executive Board members was reduced from thirty to eighteen.

That the assembled committee could agree on such sweeping proposals—especially since it meant that a number of them would lose their own positions—was in itself an achievement. Dorothy Height had foreseen that particular problem and as early as 1950 spoke of the unique task of the Executive Board to "modify the basic framework of our Sorority so as to enhance the work of the organization, even though we know that such steps may mean that some of us may not be members of the Board at the end of this meeting."[11] It was the beginning of Height's own campaign to, as Jeanne Noble observed, "psychologize people to give up power."[12] But next, the reorganization would have to be voted upon by the 1952 national convention and this would hardly be a shoo-in. Not long after the reports were distributed, criticisms came pouring in. Many believed that the paring down of so many committees and boards diminished, in the words of Edmonds, "the general enthusiasm which diverse and widely separated official positions could engender."[13] There was also the fear that the reorganized national office gave the president too much power. Tensions ran high between those who opposed the new structure and those who saw the results of the "mending conference" as a tremendous boon to the organization: Administration would be much more efficient; the cutting down of the Executive Board would save a great deal of money in the form of expenses that could be put to better use for the national projects and the purchase of a national headquarters among other things. Height had eighteen months to make her case to the sorority before the next convention which would take place December 26-31, 1952, in Cleveland. As previously noted, she also knew that some of the time would be spent in India, where she was a visiting professor for four months. Nevertheless, by the time it was convened, and the vote on the reorganization plan taken, Height's objective was in hand. There was only one dissenting vote recorded!

The acceptance of the reorganization plan now opened the way for the employment of an executive director and the purchase of a national headquarters—which issues had been discussed by every convention since 1929. One of the obstacles concerning the former was the difficulty in defining the exact role of the director—since the duties of the grand secretary and other officers were so diffuse and had no clear lines of demarcation. By 1941, President Elsie Austin had authorized a committee to look into amending the constitution to provide for the position, then referred to as an executive secretary. Nevertheless, she had strong reservations about it. At the 1941 convention she stated: "I believe the appointment of such an office would be one of the most unfortunate steps we could take. I have studied and observed the function of this office in two national organizations. It has provoked nothing but the most antagonistic struggle for control of the organizations with the executive secretary on one side and the national officers on the other side. It has been a hotbed of feuds, friction and 'finagling.' An executive secretary is not the answer to Delta's administrative problems," Austin concluded.[14] Her words, it turned out, would be prophetic ones. Nevertheless, the reorganization hurdled the final obstacle: By February 1953, Patricia Harris would become Delta's first executive director.

Of course she needed someplace to work from. And the next stage of the master plan was well on its way. The purchase of a national headquarters had also been approved by previous conventions—and there was also consensus that it be located in Washington, D.C., because it was the hub of legislative activity. A frustrated Anna Julian, chair of the Vigilance Committee, had written then-President Vivian Marsh as early as 1937 that "we as an organization are extremely limited to take part in vital phases of our national life until we have a National Headquarters here in Washington. . . . Then, we shall have someone always at hand who can keep an eye on what's happening on Capitol Hill."[15] There was also the more basic problem of having files and other important documents in one place. Jeanne Noble recalled that the records of the secretary, Reber S. Cann, were in her garage in Cincinnati, and the money was in Oklahoma with Bea Penman.

Nevertheless, the war and the skyrocketing inflation of the postwar years—especially in a city like Washington—added to the delays in getting the headquarters. In the meantime, however, local chapters had shown that the deed could be done. There were Delta houses in Detroit and Gary, and in 1950, Alpha Nu Chapter in Illinois had purchased a sorority house at the University of Illinois. Former President Jeannette Jones, chair of the Chicago Delta Projects, had headed the campaign for the house; and Marguerite Alexander, then the only founder living in Chicago, was also a member of the housing group. The purchase of the house marked the first time that the sorority would assume complete responsibility for a campus residence, and both the Midwest Region—which raised more than $28,000—and the national office helped to finance it. And at the 1952 convention, the Deltas, now a member of the board of the NCNW, had come through for Mary McLeod Bethune when she pleaded for help to maintain that organization's national headquarters in Washington. She was in danger of having the mortgage foreclosed, she said, and in spontaneous response, the sorority pledged $3,000 to help her make the payments.

Obviously, Delta had the wherewithal and willingness to have its own headquarters. What was needed in the national organization was not only the desire to get a headquarters but fund-raising skills and the engendering of a sense of mission throughout the sorority. At least $50,000 was needed, the Executive Board which met in August of 1952 reasoned, to purchase and equip a building. To gather up such a sum required a well-thought-out, systematic campaign. It was decided to launch such a campaign forthwith—and to employ a seasoned specialist in such matters to lead it: Daisy Lampkin.

When she was called on to lead the campaign, Lampkin had already served as a field director for the NAACP for eleven years. In addition to organizing branches, she had also raised money for the association's legal work and for its various campaigns, such as the antilynching crusade of the thirties. Subsequently she was vice-president of the *Pittsburgh Courier,* a leading Black weekly. But the Delta "crusade" would be different from the others. For the first time she would try to raise a significant amount of funds wholly within one organization: an organization whose members, chapters, and regions had varying amounts of resources. Lampkin's "inside" help would be Gwendolyn Higginbotham, serving as liaison chairperson of the steering committee for the drive. Higginbotham, chair of the Finance Committee, and former National Budget Board chairperson, had also been the charter president of Epsilon Sigma Chapter of Bluefield, West Virginia, which was organized in 1936. Higginbotham's versatility extended to her being the director of the Delta choir at the 1952 convention.

The plan was to create categories of donations with specific sums and/or obligations attached to each one. "Pioneer Sponsors," for example, were expected to give $100 each, as was each individual chapter. Larger chapters with more resources were expected to give more. Each individual graduate soror was to give a minimum of $10, undergraduates, $5; and all contributions were to be written up on a "roll" of contributors and published in a permanent "Book of Honor." "Every Delta in the House of Delta," became the rallying cry, and Height provided an even more compelling rationale for contributions. "Once in a lifetime you have the opportunity to be an 'angel' for your Sorority," she wrote in *The Delta Newsletter.* "The time is *now*! Your gift goes beyond all requirements—it is a gift of love," she continued. "It expresses your desire to join your sorors to pioneer in Delta's greatest venture. It does what only love can do—it exemplifies the true spirit of the Delta woman."[16]

With Height running the headquarters campaign and the hiring of an executive director, it was difficult to conceive continuing without her at the helm. But she had already had two terms—the maximum according to the constitution. Nevertheless, on the third day of the 1952 Cleveland convention, the sorors heard the following from the Recommendations Committee: "In light of the importance of this transitional period, in implementing the Reorganization Plan, and establishing the National Headquarters, our Grand President, Dorothy I. Height, [is] requested and authorized to continue in office for an additional term of two years."[17] The recommendation of the committee, chaired by Frances Flippen, was adopted by the 760 delegates attending the convention that year.

For the next biennium, officers would include Reber Cann, former grand secretary, as first vice-president; second vice-president Ann Fisher, former president of Philadelphia's Gamma Chapter and a student at Temple University; secretary was Nancy Lee, a social worker who received her undergraduate and master's degrees from the University of Pittsburgh. To great approbation, Beatrice Penman was given the title grand treasurer emeritus. Though winning reelection, she had decided to step down—five years after writing Mae Downs about her intentions. At the end of the Treasurer's Report, which showed Delta's receipts to be almost $298,000 and a balance of just under $98,000, Penman wrote her farewell: "During the thirteen years and four months that I served you as your Grand Treasurer," she said, "I have made mistakes, but I have learned much; I have travelled to many places, and I have made many, many friends." She also left the sorors with the observation that Delta was "known throughout the country for the unusual service it renders. . . . Business people . . . are amazed that a group of college women have continued their interest in a sorority after leaving college, and have such a program as we have. Big things we have done," Penman concluded, "but we cannot rest on our reputation, we must continue to grow."[18] Taking her place was Dorothy P. Harrison, who was Penman's sister, and would succeed Dorothy Height as president. Harrison's undergraduate degree was earned at Ohio State, and her master's at Oklahoma A and M University. She was married to the president of Langston University, G. Lamar Harrison.

With Gwendolyn Higginbotham reelected to the Finance Committee chair, the campaign accelerated. In February, Patricia Harris officially became Delta's first executive director, and by March plans were made to purchase a house in northwest Washington at 1814 M Street. A Black architect and designer, David Byrd, a graduate of Hampton Institute, was employed to work on renovations and remodeling. Plans went ahead so rapidly because of the tremendous response, even outpouring, of Deltas to the fund-raising campaign. By October of 1953, treasurer Harrison reported 73 sponsors; 155 chapters and Pyramid clubs (initiation clubs) and 1,001 individual sorors had contributed. In less than a year, over $31,000 had been collected, with numerous pledges yet to be filled. By May of 1954, with some $37,000 raised, plans were made to burn the mortgage at the 1954 convention slated for New York City.

In the interim, Delta had much to celebrate by the year of its fortieth anniversary in 1953. And in May of that year, celebrate they did. Four days of activities were planned in Washington around May

Week. The aforementioned "Town Meeting" with Charles Johnson and Sidney High took place. There were addresses by Senator Herbert Lehman of New York, India Edwards of the Democratic National Committee, and Bertha Adkins of the Republican National Committee—whose assistant, Ruth (Mueller) Hill, was an active Delta. ACHR director Elmer Henderson was also on hand, and on May 9 a banquet, whose mistress of ceremonies was Eastern regional director Pauline Weeden, was held in honor of the founders who had come for a reunion. Ethel Black, Jimmy Middleton, Vashti Murphy, Eliza Shippen, Florence Toms, and Edith Young were all there. A recording of their reminiscences, "Delta in Retrospect," was arranged. The reunion was particularly significant because it was the beginning of a healing process between the founders and Delta's national officers. That there was a rift—reportedly due to the fact that the suggestions of the founders were largely ignored before the current administration—was indicated by Frederica Dodd in a letter to Myra Hemmings in 1950. Hemmings was writing to all of the founders to get their addresses so that they could keep in closer touch with each other and the sorority. Dodd suggested that Hemmings not write them on official stationery. "You know," Dodd wrote, "that some Founders resent too much Grand Officers' actions and although you are a Founder you are also a Grand Officer."[19]

On May 10, there was a formal dedication of the national headquarters attended by hundreds of people—non-Deltas and Deltas alike—the latter answering the call for a Delta "pilgrimage" to the nation's capital. For many, the highlight of the celebration was a reception at the White House as guests of Mamie Eisenhower, wife of the President, who was heard to say that the Delta women were among the prettiest she had received. Among the more than one hundred sorority members present for the reception was Mary Church Terrell, fresh from the victory of the "Thompson Restaurant case" that had desegregated Washington, D.C. Terrell took the occasion to recall coming to the White House with Frederick Douglass sixty years earlier to urge then-President Benjamin Harrison to speak out against lynching. Terrell and Douglass had asked for an appointment after the murder of one of Terrell's friends, Thomas Moss of Memphis, whose death was also the catalyst for the first antilynching campaign launched by Ida B. Wells.

The 1954 convention was scheduled for August in New York City's Roosevelt Hotel. To get such a large hotel for a group of Black women was a coup: It marked the first time that a Black group met in a downtown hotel in New York City, according to Dorothy

Height, who had gotten the personal okay from Conrad Hilton to book it. Up until the very end of the convention, the sorority would feel, rightly so, very good about its achievements and its future. Dorothy Height's presidential report, given before 1,030 Delta registrants, noted that $40,000 had been raised, for the Washington, D.C. headquarters, from 2,000 sorors in 194 chapters. "No organization of Negro women of our size can say that within so short a period, without appeal to the public, that it had raised [so much money] in a Headquarters campaign," Height intoned. "It shows we have strength, and what we can do if we must." Height, as she could do so well, also talked in spiritual tones about the Deltas' rising above the adversity they encountered. "We came to the Cleveland Convention with pictures of the one building we liked, but it was not long before we discovered that, through the reactions of people in the neighborhood, they did not want an organization of our kind there," she said. "So we had a staff with no place to go, no place to work . . . But for those who love Him, God moves in mysterious ways. There appeared a simple ad in the papers; Grand Officers went together to explore it formally. . . . We received the right to move ahead to a choice piece of property in the heart of downtown Washington, D.C. What a difference this made," she observed. "We not only had a good piece of property, but had a building with an income."[20]

During the convention, a 16mm film featuring the house at 1814 M Street was shown, highlighting its features and strategic location in the capital. The reality of a national headquarters "gave us a sense of really being a national organization," observed Anna Julian, "it provided the core from which we can reach out to all the chapters everywhere in the country."[21] That it was situated in Washington gave sorors like Julian an added attraction, for there the sorority "can feel the heartbeat of what was going on." There was something else, too. For Black women, the sense of well-being and accomplishment attached to finding a "home" had special meaning. It was the ultimate symbol of "belongingness" and communion, as well as the kind of material achievement denied to Blacks.

Another milestone had been reached with the hiring of the talented Patricia Harris as executive director for a not inconsiderable sum of $4,500 a year—with annual increments of $250. In addition, an administrative assistant, Letitia Johnson, a graduate of Bluefield State College, was also hired. The executive director reported on the mountains of work her office had accomplished since February 1, 1953, including planning the successful May Week celebration, representing the sorority at other conferences, receiving the dues of the

6,535 active Deltas (out of a total of about 11,000) and implementing the new procedures for handling the finances, and the circulation of more than forty thousand pieces of correspondence to the 231 chapters (124 graduate, 81 undergraduate, and 26 mixed) operating in thirty-eight states and the Republic of Haiti.

Other reports revealed that Delta had granted $33,000 in scholarships that year. The assets for the organization were $130,000. The Haitian Relief Fund had dispensed $1,000, and monies were still being funneled to the National Library and Jobs projects. The national reputation for Delta as a public service sorority was getting the attention of the major media such as *The Washington Post* and *The New York Times*. In addition, the sorority was continuing to draw influential persons and leaders to its forums, such as, for this convention, the well-known newswoman Pauline Frederick, and Robert C. Weaver, then an officer of the Whitney Foundation, and subsequently the first secretary of housing and urban development. Also on hand were Roy Wilkins, then the administrative secretary to the NAACP, and Kenneth B. Clark, the sociologist who had had such a pivotal role in the *Brown* v. *Board of Education* Supreme Court decision.

The invitation extended to Clark, then director of the Northside Community Center in New York City, may have been particularly significant to Height. As the president of an organization made up largely of educators, she was concerned, as others were, about the reaction of many Black teachers to the *Brown* decision. There was fear among many that integrated schools would mean the loss of jobs—a fear that did not prove groundless in the years to come. Nevertheless, such a preoccupation missed the larger issue and it was important that all of the ramifications be discussed. The question had been brought up at an Executive Board meeting in 1953, where ACHR director Elmer Henderson was in attendance. Dorothy Proctor, a member of the Personnel Committee, mentioned that some teachers felt "insecure" about attending protest meetings concerning segregated schools because it could jeopardize their jobs. Height observed that "even the best educated are not very well prepared" and asserted that "we as Negroes can not stop in our efforts to bring about equality even though we have to accept the possibility of some immediate risk."[22] Patricia Harris then asked Henderson if the ACHR could examine the impact of the decision "so that teachers will see that their jobs are not jeopardized," and Henderson responded favorably. And in the 1954 *Delta Journal* (now edited by Harris), an article entitled "Negro Teachers in 'Integrated' School

Systems" concluded that the number of Black teachers employed was growing in both segregated and nonsegregated (meaning, there were no statutory restrictions) schools, and that a favorable Court decision could in fact improve the numbers. And there was lots of room for that. Statistics showed that the Berkeley, California, public school system, for example, had only six Black teachers as of 1953; Lansing, Michigan, had four; and Elizabeth, New Jersey, had none.[23]

At the New York convention, Kenneth Clark also raised the issue, saying that a successful fight was a necessity. Although it should be taken for granted that "the educated individuals of any group are to provide the leadership," he was disturbed that "leadership has not come from the educated upperclass college-trained Negroes, but from the masses of the Negro people. The major opposition is from the educated," Clark asserted, "and must be brought clearly home to those of us who are seriously concerned."[24] After his talk, a discussion did ensue about the protection for teachers, especially in the South, and whether organizations such as the NAACP had worked out any FEPC kind of mechanism. Henderson, who was in attendance, replied that some teachers would probably lose out but more would be gained. The discussion ended when a soror expressed her opinion that "you don't get freedom cheap. If our whole concern is whether we are going to keep our jobs, then we don't want freedom."[25]

However, as was true with the Black student movement of the twenties, the criticism of Howard president Mordecai Johnson, even the decision to allow "B"-rated schools into the sorority, the school integration issue was yet another instance of the president of the sorority not taking a strong *public* stance on an educational issue. Of course working behind the scenes, as Height did, had its advantages. And the president was primarily a corporate leader, that is, one who reflects the constituency, which was divided on the matter. Not speaking out did prevent the Executive Board's becoming a flashpoint for division in an organization that was not created to become a political vanguard. Nevertheless, one must wonder at a lack of decisiveness on an issue that meant so much to the constituency.

But controversy would raise its head on another matter before the convention, whose theme was "Women in the Decade of Decision," ended. A controversy that would begin when Dorothy Height would seek yet another term as president. This time, though, her intentions were not known until the very last minute; farewell gifts of a travel purse and a leather-bound book with messages from sorors had even been presented. Up until the report of the Nominating Committee, everything seemed to be going smoothly. Nominated for president was Reber Cann, the present first vice-president who had served as secretary from 1944 to 1952. Active in the civic affairs of Cincinnati, she was a hard worker and popular among the sorors. And, she was loyal to Dorothy Height. The other nominee was Pauline Weeden, Eastern regional director, holding degrees from Howard and Columbia universities, and active in such organizations as the Y, the Virginia Teachers Association, and the NCNW. Others were put forth for the various offices, according to the standard procedure, but before the nominations could be closed, Height suddenly spoke up. Though the report had been made, she said, she realized that there had been a recommendation made by the Executive Board that should have been made before the report. It was then moved that the committee's report be tabled until the recommendation was heard. The recommendation, it turned out, was one that would upset the whole apple cart. It was that a chairman of the Nominating Committee be elected, as well as additional members, representing the various regions. So now there would be two votes cast by the delegates: one for a chairman, and another for members from each delegate's region. This dramatic change in procedure was moved and seconded so rapidly that it was difficult to believe it was wholly spontaneous. Then second vice-president, Ann Fisher, who had taken the chair during the discussion, nominated Dorothy Height for president. "We are at a crossroads," Fisher said, "we need something to steady us." Height then gave what can only be called a campaign speech. "I have served to the best of whatever ability I have," she said, and then talked about the accusations that she was trying to "impose" the idea that "one Dorothy Height thought that she is indispensable to Delta," that she had pressured the Nominating Committee. "I have no intention, no desire, no will . . . to bring anything of shame or disunity to Delta," Height intoned.[26]

Following her speech, there were praises for Height and motions to suspend the bylaws. This was countered by others who challenged the legality of such actions. At one point even Patricia Harris tendered her resignation, citing the terrible things being said about Height. And in the midst of the heated debate, Osceola Adams observed, "I am able to read between the lines, to know that something ugly is at work with Delta Sigma Theta."[27] Finally, when Height was nominated once again, Reber Cann said that "I would not think for one minute of allowing my name to remain as a candidate if my beloved Dorothy Height would just consent to be president." Helen

Edmonds then spoke up to ask Weeden if she would continue as a nominee for grand president "in order to show that democracy is still at work." Weeden did keep her name in nomination, and was promptly charged by some with disloyalty to the organization. "I have been a Delta for over twenty-five years," she riposted at one point. "Why is my loyalty being questioned? I am and always have been a true Delta."[28] Nevertheless, the sorority would suspend the bylaws and vote Dorothy Height in once again.

There was considerable fallout from this precedent which created the most serious division that the sorority had faced in its history. There was a great deal of bitter feeling and serious questions were raised. Catherine Middleton, for example, a physician and one of the daughters of founder Jimmie Middleton, wrote the Executive Board about her "grave concern" as to how the constitution and bylaws could be suspended "to suit the purpose of the moment, then picked up again." She went on to say, "It is my opinion that our Grand President now holds office illegally . . . it will always be, in my mind and in the minds of others, suspect, because of the casual rearrangement of the constitution which allowed her nomination."[29] Middleton wrote another letter to Dorothy Height. She had come to the convention, Middleton wrote, "with the feeling that Delta had benefitted from your administration, as from previous administrations, and that you as retiring Grand President, had a long, honorable and challenging record to leave to a new president.

"I left New York," Middleton continued, "a disillusioned and disgusted person. . . . Your apparent inability to control at least the constitutional abuses from the chair seem to me to have soiled a brilliant record unnecessarily and beyond repair. This exhibition seems to me to have hurt Delta, not irreparably, but certainly deeply. . . . Unlike some of the other sorors," she concluded, "I intend to remain active and to do what we must all work for now—work for the healing of ugly wounds and for the assurance that this will not happen again."[30] And, in fact, Middleton would be a member of the next Board of Elections, representing the Eastern Region, at the following convention, slated for 1956.

It is a reflection of the strength of the organization—and the sisterhood—as well as Height's administrative abilities, that the sorority didn't bog down for the next two years. The Executive Board, though divided about their loyalties to Height, nevertheless maintained a constructive working relationship with her. At the 1956 convention, held in Detroit, the president counseled: "You know, first hand, what it means to be part of a chapter in which the officers are unable to work together, what a difference it makes when each sees herself as part of the team . . . willing to see the job that has to be done and to put the accomplishment of the task beyond her own personal interest. . . . Such has been the experience of our Board," she asserted. "It doesn't mean that we all see eye to eye on every point, but it does mean, that somehow together, women whom you have chosen to be of service to the Sorority, have found the way to work together."[31] Height helped the situation by head-on confronting the criticisms. At a 1955 Executive Board meeting, she herself brought up the Middleton letter as well as one written by Jean Murrell Capers, a councilwoman in Cleveland, which expressed similar concerns. "In the kind of organization that we are," Height explained, "if we hurt any part of us, we hurt the whole."[32] The president then instructed the secretary elected at the last convention, Nellie G. Rouhlac of Memphis, to acknowledge the letters.

The biennium, 1954 through 1956, was not a particularly active one however. On the national level, much energy was directed toward fine-tuning the relationships between the executive director (Harris withdrew her resignation) and the grand officers. In 1954, the "blackball" was abolished: Now an initiate was accepted with two thirds of the vote by chapter members. New awards were established in the name of Juliette Derricotte, a national student secretary for the YWCA and dean of women at Fisk University, who died when a southern White hospital wouldn't accept her after a car accident; and Julia Bumry Jones, one of the early women columnists for the *Pittsburgh Courier*. The awards of $500 each were given to a soror who achieved in the fields of social work and journalism, respectively. Citizenship seminars, at which chapter members met with elected and appointed government officials, were instituted.

The most innovative project was that of establishing "leadership institutes," where sorors spent an entire day considering the components of leadership in the sorority. In 1955, twenty-seven institutes in as many cities were conducted with almost one thousand participants. As Jeanne Noble noted earlier, the focus on organizational development and skills—including even the breaking up of conventions into small groups—was a tremendous boon to the functioning of the sorority. Association with Black and civil rights organizations continued, and at the 1956 convention, a meaningful workshop was conducted featuring the dean of women of several colleges who explored the topic: "Membership in Delta—Its Meaning and Effectiveness and Motivating the Undergraduate Potential."

Such a discussion had come at a crucial time, as the pros and cons of Greek-letter organizations were once again being discussed by college administrators and others. Morgan State College in Baltimore had even gone so far as to suspend all groups because it was said that they had a negative effect on scholastic achievement. Through the urging of Height and officers in other fraternities and sororities, Morgan did reinstitute the societies, but it was important to deal with the matter head-on. Such questions and issues as the college attitude toward the sorority, whether sorority members promoted the growth of student governments, the need to reevaluate chapter programs, the role of faculty advisors, resolving the conflict between loyalty to the institution and loyalty to the sorority, and the fine line between selectivity and snobbery were discussed. Among the panel members, representing both predominantly White and Black schools, was Sadie M. Yancey, dean of women at Howard University. In the near future she would head an important evaluation program that analyzed the status of the undergraduate sorors on campuses.

It was evident that Height understood not only the dynamics of running an organization, but the needs of the sisterhood as well. Once she noted that "twenty-two young women [the founders] gave us something more than an organization; they planned it to be a sisterhood. . . . We could not be here today if they had not faced the issues of their time as they came." Sisterhood, Height observed, had a special dynamic all its own. "Friends love us at all times," she said, "sisters are made for adversity."[33] In 1956, she admonished that "it is so much easier to pick apart, than to put together, and that a sisterhood like ours, has to find its way and its place in a divided world."[34] And, in 1956, she observed, "I think that because we love Delta, we love each other so much that together we can say that we may not have all the answers but we certainly try to get to the real question and not baffle each other, but rather to help each other deal with our questions that is [sic] worthy of us."[35]

Nevertheless, however justifiable the ends—Height did, as Noble observed, give the sorority the machinery to deliver its own broad objectives—the means for sustaining power threw the organization into chaos. The 1956 convention, which from the beginning was riddled with controversy because Delta had chosen the Sheraton-Cadillac Hotel instead of a Black-owned facility, also ended on a controversial note. There was the perception by many that Height, despite her denials, would attempt to run yet again. The suspicion mounted when a recommendation from the floor sought to provide an alternative to the strict two-term limitation for grand officers. The recommendation was that "a term of office for Grand Chapter officers shall be for the biennium except for those Grand Officers whose terms of office are otherwise specified."[36] Needless to say, the recommendation didn't go unchallenged, and it was voted down. But another proposed amendment would ensure Height's continued influence and leadership in the organization. It was that the Executive Board now include the immediate past president among its members. Efforts by some to limit the years that a past president should so serve was defeated.

Height would not only serve on the Executive Board, but her closest allies would be grand officers: Dorothy Penman Harrison, from 1956 to 1958 and Jeanne Noble, 1958 to 1963. There is no question that Height, as a result of her organizational skills, had a more discernible impact on the sorority than any other president. Her quest to remain in office was certainly nothing new in the history of Black women's organizations. Two of the most important leaders, who in fact had passed away in the mid-fifties, Mary Church Terrell and Mary McLeod Bethune, were also loath to give up power—much to the benefit, many felt, of their respective organizations. Nevertheless, there is always a down side to the assertion for power. The activist/journalist Ida B. Wells, who once fought Terrell's seeking of a third term in the NACW despite a two-term restriction, wrote that Terrell, though successful, had lost influence and respect among many of her colleagues. The perception that power is concentrated in too few hands also invites apathy and negatively affects the infusion of "new blood" into the leadership of a social-movement organization—a danger that the Delta membership evidently understood regardless of their admiration for Dorothy Height's accomplishments. In any case, by 1957, Height would go on to become the fourth president of the National Council of Negro Women—a position she has held for thirty years.

CHAPTER 11

DELTA IN THE MOVEMENT YEARS

Prior to Dorothy Height's presidency, Delta "was a fine, scholarly organization of highly moral, respectable women who had some philanthropic ideas, but not the structure to deliver these things," observed Jeanne Noble.[1] Now the structure was indeed there, even if it still needed some fine-tuning. Subsequent Executive Board meetings continued to devote a great deal of time and discussion to clarify the responsibilities of both elected officers and staff. Height's administration also furthered the concept that Delta, as she would often say, was not "a federation of chapters" but a national organization whose chapters worked in the interest of the whole. The further development of the Five-Point Program, designating specific areas of concern—job opportunities for youth, mental health, community service, international goodwill, and library service—would go a long way toward realizing that idea. The five-point strategy, in fact, had been painstakingly designed by Height and the National Projects Committee—headed by Jeanne Noble—by consulting experts in each of those fields, and polling the views of chapters about their own needs and those of the communities that they served. Also there was an ongoing analysis of the effectiveness of the sorority's programs. This systematic approach, offered by Height at a 1957 Executive Board meeting, had resulted

in, she said, the "strongest clarification of what we have been trying to do as a national body." And the convention program, which
included prominent deans of women at various colleges, mental
health experts such as the famed Allison Davis, and Martin Luther
King, Jr.—still flushed with the Supreme Court victory that desegregated Montgomery's buses only six days before—all attested to
that fact.

At the same time, that the convention's attendance was only a
little more than half of the one before revealed the need to resusci-
tate the enthusiasm and sense of sisterhood in order to effectively
exploit what Height had put in place. And those elements would be
needed for the sorority to navigate the next two tumultuous decades—for the civil rights movement, spurred by the success of the
Montgomery bus boycott, was ready to explode. School desegregation, followed soon by civil disobedience, and the cry of "Black
Power" would force the sorority to question the very core of its
values and purpose. During the administrations of the next four
presidents, the questions concerning how to respond to these
changes would take the organization through some of its most critical
years.

Dorothy P. Harrison would head the so-
rority between 1956 and 1958, and provide the needed transition
that both calmed the waters and continued the progress of the
sorority. Although Harrison was grand treasurer between 1952
and 1956, she was seen more as an "inheritor" of the office
(she succeeded her sister, Beatrice Penman) than an ambitious
contender for a leadership position. "I had no idea of becoming
president of the sorority," Harrison said,[2] and she was hesitant to
accept the entreaties from the nominating committee to run. Her
husband urged her to do it, however, and encouraged the committee
to keep asking until she agreed. Her reluctance and perhaps her final
acceptance was due, at least in part, to her attempting to recover
from the death of two sons in recent years. Her decision to return to
graduate school and deeply involve herself in Delta activities provided the "much needed therapy," that helped her through this
period.[3]

As president, Harrison was a quiet-spoken woman whose interests were more in line with "administration and detail than con-
ceptualizing new programmatic initiatives," she observed. Also
important at this stage of the organization's development was Har-

rison's belief in delegating authority to her officers and the "equal partnership of staff and volunteer workers."[4] Under her administration, the sorority would inaugurate *The Delta Newsletter* in an effort to improve communications. Her willingness to marshal Delta's resources to the Little Rock crisis would also set a pattern of the organization's involvement in the movement.

Harrison was followed by Jeanne Noble, who presided over the sorority between 1958 and 1963, was an assistant dean of students at City College in New York and only thirty-two years old when she was elected to office. She was first vice-president under Harrison, a protégée of Dorothy Height's and proudly admits to being one of those who helped "mastermind," as she put it, Height's continuance as president. Noble, from Albany, Georgia, began her teaching career at Albany State College—later to become a pivotal college in the movement—and was a former dean of woman at Langston University in Oklahoma. She earned her B.A. degree from Howard, and a master's and Ph.D. from Columbia University. Noble's doctoral dissertation, "The Negro Woman's College Education," was a ground-breaking work and full of progressive notions about the role of women in the society. Her youth and advocacy of the student movement was an important element in Delta's participation during these crucial years.

Under Noble's administration greater ties with Africa and African women were established, which resulted in the sorority's support of a maternity wing in a rural Kenyan hospital, and a chapter established in Liberia. Her administration would also create the "Teen Lift," a mentoring project. Passionate, articulate, and, like Height, undistracted by marriage, Noble would expend much of her professional and personal energies in Delta, and subsequently in other Black women's organizations.

It would fall to her successor, Geraldine (Pittman) Woods, (1963 to 1967) to fill the vacuum left by the dismantling of the ACHR in 1963. In the early sixties it had instituted a Student Emergency Fund, whereby its more than one thousand chapters across the country

---

*Other officers at the period included: grand secretaries: Nellie G. Roulac (1956–1958), Ann L. Campbell (1958–1963), Marie Fonsworth (1963–1967), Lennie M. Tolliver (1967–1971), Gloria R. Scott (1971–1975); grand treasurers: M. Lucia James (1956–1958), Vivian E. Washington (1958–1963); Thelma Daley (1963–1967), Phoebe LeSesne (1967–1971), Betty Williams (1971–1975); grand second vice-presidents: Mary Rucker (1956–1958), Gloria Scott (1958–1960), Miriam Stamps (1960–1963), Claudette Franklin (1963–1965), Constance Rolison (1965–1967), Jacquelene Sharp (1967–1969), Jayne Ware (1969–1971), Patricia Ann Milligan (1971–1973), Matta JoAnn Lewter (1973–1975).

raised money to pay fines and bonds of those arrested during sit-ins and other demonstrations. It also paid tuitions for students, including the young North Carolna A & T students who staged the first student sit-in of the era and the first women who sought to integrate the University of Georgia—one of whom, Charlayne (Hunter) Gault, was a Delta. The ACHR's last presentations were scheduled, ironically, on the evening of November 22, 1963, the day President John F. Kennedy was assassinated. That evening $1,000 was given to the Prince Edward County Free School Association of Virginia, which was fighting recalcitrant school segregationists; an equal amount was accepted by Stokely Carmichael on behalf of the Student Nonviolent Coordinating Committee (SNCC); and a third presentation was made to the Reverend Walter E. Fauntroy for the Leadership Conference on Civil Rights. The ACHR leadership had agreed to disband the organization amidst some interfraternal conflict; the reluctance of the fraternities to give it adequate financial support; and pressure from the NAACP, which saw it as responsible for a "brain drain" of leadership and energy from its own organization. Additionally, by the sixties, the Delta leadership believed that its resources could be better used to support organizations such as the National Council of Negro Women, now headed by Dorothy Height, which had a more broadly based membership.

Under Woods's administration, a Social Action Commission would be established to act much as the Vigilance Committee had before it. It would be especially important in lobbying for landmark legislation, including the Civil Rights and Voting Rights acts, which were passed largely as a result of the pressure from Black groups. Geraldine Woods, who had been first vice-president under Noble, was a member of Phi Beta Kappa and had been educated at Howard, Radcliffe, and Harvard, with a concentration in neuroembryology.

While serving as first vice-president in Woods's administration, Frankie M. Freeman became the only Black and the only woman appointed by President Lyndon B. Johnson to serve on the six-member U.S. Civil Rights Commission. She had become well known as the attorney who brought and won the case that desegregated public housing in St. Louis in 1952. She also had served as assistant attorney general in Missouri and associate general counsel of the St. Louis Housing and Land Clearance Authority. Before becoming president from 1967 to 1971, she had also served as chair of the nominating committee and of the housing and property committee. While national president, Freeman had to provide a steady course through the period when nonviolent tactics were challenged and the Delta constituency was more politically polarized. But she would be well served by a straightforward, take-care-of-business attitude that was displayed when she was denied service at an airport coffee shop in Louisville, Kentucky. The year was 1954, and Freeman was changing planes there on the way to her mother's funeral. When told she wouldn't be served, she challenged the waitress to arrest her, because she wasn't moving. "I'm a lawyer," she said, "and I know that this is illegal." And, she had thought to herself, "my mother wouldn't want me to get up."[5] She called a Black lawyer she knew in town who filed a complaint against the host chain restaurant. After the funeral, Freeman learned that the coffee shop had become desegregated.

Lillian P. Benbow, who presided over the organization from 1971 to 1975, would have the most controversial and innovative administration since that of Dorothy Height. She created the National Commission on Arts and Letters whose primary project was the sponsoring of a full-length feature film with political import. During her administration she had to contend with excesses in hazing, resistance to her political perspective, and conflict over several aspects of the Arts Commission itself. Benbow, a graduate of LeMoyne-Owen College in Memphis, who also studied at the University of Michigan and the Detroit College of Law, had been first vice-president under Freeman and was an assistant director of housing programs for the Michigan Civil Rights Commission. Tall, charismatic, and forceful, Benbow's leadership left an indelible impression on many of those who knew her.

The next phase of the sorority could be said to have begun in August of 1957, when a rock was hurled through the window of the home of Daisy Bates, president of the Little Rock, Arkansas, chapter of the NAACP. Tied to the rock was a note, which would later prove to be prophetic: "Stone this time, dynamite next." The warning had come as a result of the efforts, led by Bates, to integrate that city's Central High School with nine Black students. Before that was to happen however, Bates's home would be bombed; the *State Press,* a newspaper that she and her husband published, was shut down; women and reporters would be viciously beaten; the schoolchildren, themselves, threatened and attacked; and the National Guard would be brought in. Finally, President Dwight D. Eisenhower, no sympathizer of integration, would be forced to enlist paratroops from the 101st Airborne Division to quell the violence and uphold the Supreme Court's *Brown* decision passed three years before.

Little Rock and the first stages of the school integration battle was fought in the arena where so many Blacks pinned their hopes for the future: the right to education. Delta's leadership knew that they had to respond—despite the fears, despite the fact that it would mean stepping onto a political battlefield and using weapons that the organization had never before attempted to arm itself with. But it would be moved along both by the forces of history, as Noble observed, and a growing consensus of its members—particularly the younger members—toward more direct involvement on the part of the sorority. Little Rock, observed Jeanne Noble, was the turning point for that involvement.

As first vice-president during the crisis, Noble called President Dorothy Harrison. "I want to go down there," she said. "Yes," Harrison concurred, "go there, call me back, and then let's see what we can do." Noble found the young Deltas there were, typically, "pillars of polite society," as she called them.[6] They were concerned but cautious. Most were studying to be teachers, the occupation of some 90 percent of the membership, and one particularly vulnerable to recrimination by state authorities. And before the sixties, overt confrontation was not sanctioned by large numbers of Blacks nor was it clear if inciting such racial passions would, in the end, be productive. Already, a number of chapters were "banned" by southern state authorities along with other Black organizations such as the NAACP, keeping legal advisor Sadie T. M. Alexander busy communicating with chapters, and easing anxieties. It was agreed that the first actions of the sorority couldn't be overly zealous—but that they should be meaningful.

A good place to start, it was believed, would be to turn the traditional Christmas parties given by the sorority into a fund- and consciousness-raiser for the Little Rock students and Daisy Bates. In addition to providing some one hundred gifts and $300 for the nine young children, the sorority gave direct aid to Bates herself. Advertisers who kept the *State Press* afloat now refused to continue running ads, so the sorority responded with eighty-three chapters buying advertising space in the paper, thus extending its life as a vital organ of information.

More important was the fact that the sorority had given public moral support during the crisis. In the fifties, before the sit-ins, before the national press gave sanction to defying state authorities, before going to jail or losing one's job became a badge of honor, before, even, the NAACP had become entirely "comfortable" with Bates's methods of direct challenge, Delta had supported Bates when few others did. "Even today, every time that I see Ernest Green," noted Noble, referring to one of the "Little Rock Nine" who subsequently became an assistant secretary of labor in the Jimmy Carter administration, "he tells me that 'I will never forget that the Deltas were there.'"7 At the 1958 convention, Daisy Bates herself would make a surprise appearance to thank the sorority for their help. She would subsequently become an honorary member, but the greatest appreciation was expressed by several of the young women who had helped lead that struggle as high school students there. They became Deltas.

Still, it would be some time before the organization saw itself as a potential agent of change. Its primary role was to prepare its members for the inevitability of integration, even within their own organization. In 1954, West Virginia State had asked the sorority to certify that they did not discriminate in terms of the criteria for membership. The organization's perspective was evident in the theme of its twenty-fifth national convention (1958): "The Challenge of Changing Patterns of Living." Of course, Delta activities were always directed toward self-development both for sorors themselves and those whom they served. But the Supreme Court decision of 1954 added another dimension. Though much of the country's focus was on how the decision would impact on Whites and their social institutions, there was an issue of even greater import. How would it affect Blacks, who had so long been pressed beneath the heels of segregation, exclusion, and racism—especially in the South? Tremendous social adjustments would be needed, and it was important that there be some knowledgeable guiding force in the communities to design appropriate programs. The sorority, which had a constituency of professionals, which was well established in communities throughout the country, and which was in a better position than ever before to deliver those programs, was a good candidate for the job.

By the time of the twenty-fifth convention, much had already been done in this area in the form of projects and activities that fell under one or another of the categories of the Five-Point Program. The concept of the National Library Project, for example, was expanded to include the Southern Regional Hearing Project, which had been developed in 1957 by the Atlanta Alumnae Chapter.

Under the guidance of the regional director, Thelma Cobb, it focused on improved services for children with impaired hearing and reached some 200 children throughout the Southern Region. In addition to the traditional aspects of service, there was also the more subtle motive of helping such children, many of them emotionally disturbed because of their handicap, adjust to the demands of a society in the midst of change. The same was true for the highly touted "Ride the Winged Horse," (named after Pegasus), developed in the same year by the Tuskegee Alumnae Chapter in Alabama. Like the hearing project, the concept was a familiar one: a cultural enrichment program, involving parents, teachers, and other professionals, to motivate elementary and junior high students to improve reading skills. But it was also seen, in this stressful time, as a way to help provide the children "with a means for maintaining emotional stability in a troubled adult world."[8]

Other aspects of the Five-Point Program reflected a similar perspective, and effectively melded tradition with a post-1954 reality. "The Delta Volunteers for Community Service," for example, not only affirmed the sorority's cooperation with both Black and White service organizations such as the YWCA, the American Red Cross, and the National Urban League, but put new emphasis on the emotional implications of volunteerism. As Mary Elizabeth Vroman observed, being a volunteer was "an expression of self-respect," and declared to others one's "potential value to society." Volunteering, especially for predominantly White organizations, meant, in many instances, successfully overcoming fears of rejection. That those fears were often justified wasn't the point. More important, as the thinking of the time went, they could cripple one's self-development. So, in addition to the services the sorority could deliver with its twenty thousand members by the mid-fifties, volunteerism was also seen as a means of enhancing individual potential. Therefore, in March of 1956, when several agencies that were part of the New York-based Social Welfare Assembly were targeted for a pilot project in the Eastern Region—whose director was Jennie (Douglass) Taylor—there were also provisions made for leadership training. These "selected Delta women all were qualified and successful workers in various fields of social work," observed Vroman, "and their background of understanding helped them to groom themselves further for more effective leadership in the conferences."[9]

The most widely touted aspect of the Five-Point Program was the Jobs Project which, by the mid-fifties, focused on youth through Parents' Clinics; Ninth-Grade Clinics; Search for Future Scientists, which attempted to target students with potential in that field; and

Conferences of Counselors. The latter, particularly, reflected the idea of establishing interracial contact and information to counselors who in turn had an impact on race relations among youths. A number of conferences were held in cities across the country, involving not only the Deltas but other experts in the field. One held in Indianapolis, for example, caught the particular attention of Allison Davis, then professor of education and a member of the Committee on Human Development at the University of Chicago. The success of the conference moved him to write executive director Patricia Harris that "I feel that Delta has struck 'pay-dirt' in the field of educational counseling in Negro-White relations. No other organization, I believe, is directing its efforts to this specific need, although the Anti-Defamation League is working on integration as a whole. Counseling and clarification of the psychological factors involved in integration are at the very center of the whole process, it now seems clear," Davis continued. "Delta had great insight deciding to concentrate on this pivotal area. You have the most effective and enlightened organization I know—bar none" was his glowing conclusion.[10] The letter was proudly read by Harris before the sorors who had come to Washington, for the 1958 convention, held August 17–23. But the events in Little Rock the year before, growing evidence that direct action was the most effective response to intransigence of the South, and the speakers invited to the convention itself all presaged a change in focus.

A panel discussion on the theme of "Womanpower," for example, not only focused on the status of women and the psychological and social implications of the desegregation era, but concluded that "goals cannot be reached by social service alone. They will require social action."[11] One of the panelists for the discussion was Kate Mueller, a professor at the School of Education at Indiana University. She was the same Kate Mueller, in fact, who had given the Deltas such a difficult time in the late thirties when they attempted to establish a chapter there, and who had "wiped her hands on her dress" after shaking hands with several of the young ladies' parents. As late as the forties when there was still the unsullied hope that integration would proceed smoothly, there was the tendency to give those who had "sinned" in the past the benefit of the doubt, to let bygones be bygones. Then Mueller's presence might not have stirred so deep an emotion. But by 1958, when it became clear that most of the battle—and racial hatred—lay ahead, some were not so sanguine about it. That attitude prompted a letter to President Harrison from Mary Johnson Yancey, who had been on the campus while Mueller was dean of women there. "To those of us who were present . . . this news [of her appearance at the convention] is disheartening and to those of us who braved the storm and became Deltas in spite of her prejudiced attitude it is heartbreaking," Yancey wrote. "I have lost sleep over it . . . I had many contacts with Dean Mueller . . . I was a member of the YWCA Council and an AWS counselor. Upon being urged by the president of AWS to ask some Negroes to attend our opening dance, which we did and were received, Dean Mueller sent for me a few days thereafter and threatened my expulsion if it happened again . . . and if her attitude toward Negroes has changed it has taken all of seventeen years! . . .

"I don't want to upset the program," continued Yancey,[11] but . . . [Governor of Arkansas] Faubus may have been a better speaker for our convention. . . ."[12]

Another indication of changing attitudes was the words of E. Franklin Frazier, the sociologist who had recently published the landmark *Black Bourgeoisie* and who spoke at the August 22 luncheon. Frazier emphasized that the role of the educated, intellectual class of Blacks should not so much be integrating into society and its institutions as they now stood, but changing the status quo. In the "present world crisis when there is so much talk about preserving a world that is falling apart," the sociologist said, "the Negro intellectual should see that he has no stake in a world that rested upon colonialism and exploitation and prejudice. He should use his intellectual energies in formulating ideas about a new world which is coming into existence rather than repeating meaningless platitudes," he concluded.[13]

That platitudes were a luxury Black organizations could ill afford was reflected in the resolutions passed at the convention. In the past, many of those resolutions did not go very far beyond commendations and words of support for the activities of organizations such as the NAACP, the National Urban League, the Association for the Study of Negro Life and History, and others. In 1958, however, they resonated with the urgency of the times—so much so that legal adviser Sadie T. M. Alexander cautioned that some of the more controversial subjects might be toned down in view of the organization's tax-exempt status. The Resolutions Committee Report included, for example, a recommendation that a telegram be sent to President Eisenhower urging that "he be more forceful concerning the attempts of circumvention of the laws pertaining to civil rights." Also, they would ask the President to "urge the Supreme Court to meet in immediate session to overrule the appeals court stay [that immediately affected Little Rock and schools in Arlington and Norfolk, Virginia] and make integration the law of the land."[14] Such strong sentiments would push Delta also to confront Frazier's more substantitive mandates concerning the role of educated Blacks. With her youth and iconoclastic tendencies, Jeanne Noble was suited to lead the sorority in new directions.

1958–1963

"I wasn't supposed to be up there, you know," said Noble, thinking about her age and experience when she was elected at the twenty-fifth national convention as the twelfth national president of the sorority. It was Dorothy Height who set her on that road, she says. "I was this poor, no-money Black student at Columbia on my way to not identifying with anything much," Noble said. "Dorothy's way of getting me involved was, 'Could you do this little thing?' or 'Could you come up to my office?' Before I knew it, I had embarked on this scholarly study of the bookmobile in Georgia; I became fascinated with that and some parts of the Jobs Program."[15] By the forty-fifth year of Delta's existence she would preside over nearly seven thousand active members (about a fourth of the total membership) and 247 chapters in thirty-eight states and Haiti; and assets in excess of $166,000. But recent events had raised new questions, as Harrison noted in her final presidential address. "What is demanded of us, if we are to move ahead?" she asked. "How shall we face the future? What are the major challenges which confront us as a national organization of college women?"[16]

Before one could look too far ahead, there were several pressing concerns. Immediately following the convention, an Executive Board meeting was held with the new officers, including Geraldine (Pittman) Woods, who succeeded Noble as first vice-president; Gloria (Randall) Scott, who would inherit the second vice-president (student representative) spot from Mary Rucker; Anne L. Campbell taking the place of Nellie G. Rouhlac as secretary; and Vivian Washington replacing M. Lucia James as treasurer, as well as the regional directors and the committee chairs—twenty-two in all. One of the first orders of business was to start internal planning for 1963—the year of the fiftieth anniversary. Dorothy Height proposed the idea of a Golden Anniversary Committee, which she would cochair with Gwendolyn Higginbotham. The purpose of the committee was three-fold: to find ways to come to a deeper understanding of the women in Delta; to realize their mission as a public service sorority in "these changing times"; and to strengthen the financial foundation.

The latter would be in the form of a continuing fund-raising program to establish an endowment to raise $250,000 by 1963. Understanding the changing constituency and mission was initiated by gathering statistical data and surveying attitudes about the Delta program. The results of a questionnaire read at the 1958 convention revealed that the majority of graduates held the active membership was between the ages of twenty-one and thirty, which told them that their programs had to appeal to this group. Over half of the more than four thousand sampled were either teachers or students. And the majority of graduates held masters' degrees—not an insignificant finding for a Black women's group in 1958.

The high degree of education brought into sharp relief an issue that the sorority would face again and again: its scholastic standards. What raised it this time was not the prospect of students from state land-grant colleges, but the increase of Black students on interracial campuses where, with few exceptions, White Greek-letter groups had lower standards. In her president's address, Harrison had broached the issue by asking whether "we should become merely another social sorority or struggle to retain our uniqueness among Greek-letter societies on interracial campuses as a social service group with an emphasis on scholarship?"[17] As president, Noble would have to answer the question in short shrift. In October of 1958, she received a letter from the assistant dean of women at the University of Pittsburgh, who was also the advisor to the Pan-Hellenic Council there. She pleaded that Noble allow three pledgees to become initiated into Delta despite the fact that their averages weren't up to the sorority criteria, since they met those of the university. If they were not allowed into the campus chapter, whose numbers were already small, there was a possibility that Delta could no longer be active on the campus, the dean said. "If your sorority is to continue to have an active chapter on this campus," she concluded, "I feel sure that a change will have to be made in the policy of the national sorority regarding grade requirements."[18]

But Delta, as yet, was not prepared to so easily give up the solid ground that had served so long as its foundation. In her presidential speeches, Noble continued to talk about maintaining its scholarly standards, not only for their own sake but because of the role she believed Blacks and Black women were to play in the coming years. "We must identify ourselves with scholarship as an academic concern," she wrote in *The Delta*. "We as Deltas owe an allegiance to the world of ideas. We must be more related to the ivory tower . . . we need to align ourselves with the intellectual concerns of our times."[19] But it would be increasingly difficult to stave off the forces that attempted to push Delta in the direction of lowering its standards. In addition to the pressure from interracial colleges, there was an increasing overall challenge to the "ivory tower" standards that had unfairly excluded Blacks for so long. More serious were the pressures coming from the inside—from the growing numbers of students in interracial colleges upon whom continued growth largely depended. At Pittsburgh, it was the campus chapter itself that had brought the issue to the assistant dean. (This was an ironic twist, of course; in the past it had been those very students who were in the forefront of demanding that the standards be maintained.) And finally, there were organizational pressures. The sorority's membership was losing ground. It just wasn't keeping pace with the growing numbers of Black students attending college. As Mary Elizabeth Vroman noted in her book *Shaped to Its Purpose,* published in 1965, "Ten years earlier, the enrollment in a particular college was 2,000 and the probation line 20; why in 1960 was the probation line still 20, when the college enrollment had risen to 6,000?"[20] Was one of the reasons too high an academic standard? Should the sorority maintain it at the expense of a rapidly growing membership, which in turn provided its budget that enabled the organization to carry on the services that were also an essential aspect of its sense of identity and mission?

Even though the sorority was trying to hold the line on standards, it was, ironically, also suffering from an image problem that was keeping more serious-minded students away. Despite the national office's painstaking efforts to implement meaningful programs, many of which were successful, the primary image of the sorority came from the activities of local chapters. And too many of them still engaged in traditional social activities rather than the more substantive projects that required more resources and administrative skills. A "chapter audit" initiated in 1958 and designed to find out how effectively chapters were implementing the national program confirmed this. Over half of the chapters, for example, had no projects committee to implement the Five-Point-Programs. Only 1 percent had initiatives in all the program areas; about a third had them in one or two of them. Their budgets were still largely spent on traditional social affairs and programs like the Jabberwock, which, though used for scholarship fund-raising, were still not substantive in content. And few chapters had publicity committees that touted the more meaningful projects that were undertaken. As a result, as Noble observed, "far too many highly intelligent girls refuse membership because they think a sorority is 'child's play.' Too many Delta daughters now at Radcliffe, Mt. Holyoke, and other silk stocking colleges say, 'the sorority serves no purpose.'"[21]

All of this prompted the need for further study to understand and resolve these problems. The Yancey Commission on Undergraduate Development was established in 1958 to have a deeper look at Delta's primary constituency: its students. The commission, named after the woman who proposed it—Sadie M. Yancey, longtime dean of women at Howard University and chair of the sorority's Scholarship and Standards Committee—was to also look at how the Delta program impacted on its young members. The commission itself was headed by Sara-Alyce Wright, staff member of the Leadership Services Unit of the National Board of the YWCA. It prepared an extensive questionnaire, which more than 66 percent of the undergraduates filled out. The responses answered some of the immediate questions that had been asked about the decreasing membership. The standards did not seem so bothersome. The overwhelming majority had B averages, though less than 9 percent had A averages. There was overall satisfaction with the sorority's regulations, including, one assumed, the grade point averages. Restrictive personal budgets didn't seem to be a factor. About half said that they had sufficient money for expenses and emergencies; however, 40 percent had a job to defray expenses and 52 percent received scholarship aid. More than half also depended on parents for both initiation and dues payments.[22] The responses to the questionnaire also revealed a great deal of personal satisfaction derived from sorority life. More than a third said it provided "security, friendship, sisterhood and status." About a third said that they gained "inspiration toward academic, social and spiritual achievement," though only 5 percent said that they gained intellectual benefits primarily. And nearly one fourth of them selected the Delta national president as a "prominent role model"—a higher figure than the 20 percent who cited their own mothers, and nearly twice as many as those who selected such prominent women as Mary McLeod Bethune and Eleanor Roosevelt!

Where the problems seemed mainly to lie were in the sorority's chapter activities. Over 90 percent said that their chapters needed help in implementing the national projects. Taking into consideration the findings of the chapter audit, including the complaints about the chapter's inefficiency, lack of organization, and uninteresting agendas, one could see what had to be worked on the most.

Picking up on a concept introduced by Height, Noble instituted a series of Officers Roundtables, comprised of local chapter officers, undergraduate advisors, and local Golden Anniversary committees, as well as national officers and staff in key sites around the country to aid in the implementation and administration of projects and programs. The Roundtables were intensive leadership development workshops. Other efforts to increase membership included systematic "reclamation" efforts, which were already finding success under the supervision of Geraldine Woods, first vice-president and chair of the Scholarship and Standards Committee. Under her direction nine hundred Deltas were "reclaimed" by local chapters and brought back into the financial fold. Noble also pushed the concept of a membership-at-large category similar to that of the past, which would include Deltas who did not belong to a specific chapter. But there was resistance to this idea due to the fear that "floating" Deltas would not participate in chapter activities whereby the bonds of sisterhood were strengthened. Yet it would certainly be a means to increase the rolls dramatically. The push and pull over this issue, which would last for decades, was another instance of the needs of the "sisterhood" clashing with those of the "organization."

But the most important findings of the Yancey Commission indicated the need for a subtle but fundamental change in the sorority's mission: to see itself as a public service organization. Although the sorority always saw service as a central theme of its activities, it still defined itself as an exclusive organization whose purpose was to foment bonds among women of similar experience and achievement. Becoming an organization with public service as its *raison d'être* was something else again. It carried implications about its membership, about the thrust of its activities, about its social status in traditional terms. "I used to tease the Deltas," said Noble. "I'd say, 'all you-all are annoyed with these little babies because they can't pour tea with their gloves on' which at Howard University, you know, we had to learn. We needed to take them and teach them what they needed to know," she continued, "you take the raw talent and mould it."[23] Lynnette Taylor, who in 1967, would become Delta's executive director, also reflected the new thinking. "It was easier for those who grew up in middle-class families and always saw themselves becoming doctors and lawyers and so on to talk only to each other," she said. "But the migration of Blacks from the South to the Midwest and Southwest and elsewhere during the thirties to the fifties imposed a new obligation," she opined. "I lived in Detroit and saw people coming there who could barely write, and then see their children in two years time go to college. And I welcome the fact that the sorority was drawing such students. I feel the organization owed it to the Black people of this country to pass on whatever mores were 'acceptable' to 'society.'"[24]

For many, however, though empathetic to that struggle, there was fear that the presence of the "new" middle class, as well as these new organizational goals threatened the very foundation of the sisterhood which had been heretofore based on social bonds among those with similar social backgrounds. This would explain why, Height, as she recalled, was criticized for such programs as the Jobs Project on the basis that it diminished the "sisterhood" dimension of the organization. Her response was that sisterhood did not have to be sacrificed in the name of public service. Nevertheless, it did mean that the basis of that sisterhood would have to be changed.

Noble continued this new direction. "Dorothy [Height] had laid the groundwork," she said, "the next big move was to be able to say that 'We are a public service organization. We are a sorority in that we are a sisterhood bonded to certain values, but public service was the mission.' There was resistance," Noble continued, "there were those who said that if I'd wanted to do all of this, I'd just have worked with the NAACP. And there were those who dropped out, preferring to be with more status conscious and social oriented organizations. But we were able to reach the point where we could articulate that we were a public service organization, that yes, it was important to bond together and develop good human relations skills and be caring about each other, but that we are first sisters *doing* public service."[25]

If Deltas were lost during this transition period, many more would be gained. Now the organization attracted such women as Lynnette Taylor, executive director from 1967 to 1980, who as a young assistant principal became interested in the organization because of its substantive goals. "I liked the fact that the Detroit chapter had a policy that there wouldn't be any dances for two years," she said. "Instead they had decided to concentrate their activities around the Detroit Home for Girls."[26] Future national president Frankie Freeman, involved with civil rights cases in St. Louis, also joined the alumnae in that city, and later national committees, on the condition, she said, that their activities would be meaningful. She had little time for social affairs.

The change in direction also corresponded with the changing constituency, and probably assured the continued viability of the organization. For as the Yancey findings showed, the undergraduates and increasing numbers of alumnae were composed more and more of what E. Franklin Frazier had defined as the *new* middle class—which had emerged after World War II—rather than the old bourgeoisie that had had several generations of college-educated members. By the sixties 43 percent of the undergraduates' parents had less than a high school education; 30 percent were high school graduates and only 14 percent had a bachelor's degree or higher. This, in turn, had deep implications about the collective attitude of the membership. As the scholarship on the new middle class was saying, it showed less reverence for "achievement for achievement's sake" or for social status in the traditional meaning of the term. The older bourgeoisie put more credence in such things because, at least in large measure, they were the primary weapons against notions of Black inferiority and inability to "fit" into American society. But by the late fifties and sixties, the achievements of the bourgeoisie made the need to establish such proof less compelling. In addition, as Frazier and subsequent writers such as James Baldwin postulated, it was unhealthy to try to "fit" into a society still warped by racism. It was more important to try to change it.

Organizationally, the first efforts in this direction combined traditional programs with those elements of change. This was initiated with the Christmas parties that supported Daisy Bates in Little Rock. In 1959, material and moral support was given to the "lost class of Prince Edward County High School" in Petersburg, Virginia: Fifty-seven seniors who would not graduate on time because county officials closed the schools rather than obey a Supreme Court order to desegregate. In conjunction with the National Council of Negro Women and local groups, Deltas raised scholarship money for the students to attend schools elsewhere. In 1960, the Christmas party supported the four six-year-old girls who were the first to desegregate the elementary schools in New Orleans.

But by 1961 and 1962, the support for students in McComb, Mississippi, and Albany, Georgia, signified a new development—and a less conventional posture of the sorority. The latter was evident when Delta supported students in both places who were not only trying to implement the new law of the land but confronted authorities with direct-action campaigns that landed them in jail. The new development was a student movement that added fuel to the smoldering embers of change.

Just two months before the Yancey Commission questionnaire was distributed to the membership in April of 1960, four North Carolina A and T students quietly sat in at a Woolworth lunch counter in Greensboro, North Carolina. Within a week, student sit-ins spread to fifteen southern cities in five states. In less than two years, some seventy thousand young people had participated in the movement. Among them were a significant number of Deltas. Responses to the questionnaire found that a full 35 percent of the undergraduates had taken part in the sit-ins. Furthermore, many of the remainder said that they might still participate in them. Only 2 percent were unsympathetic to the sit-ins. And that times were changing, for all generations, was evidenced by the fact that only 2 percent said that their parents objected to this new wave that was engulfing the country.

By April of 1960, when the Student Nonviolent Coordinating Committee (SNCC) was born, yet a new phase of the movement would be inaugurated: direct nonviolent confrontation with local authorities accompanied by a "jail-no-bail" strategy. Additionally much of the activity would take place outside of the more cosmopolitan areas where the NAACP held sway, or in the larger southern cities that were the bailiwick of the Southern Christian Leadership Conference (SCLC), headed by Martin Luther King, Jr. SNCC activities penetrated the rural reaches of the South, focusing attention on places little known to any except those who lived there—attention that brought the rest of the movement with them. In McComb, Mississippi, for example, a fifteen-year-old by the name of Brenda Travis was arrested when she sat in at a Whites-only area of a Greyhound bus terminal as a participant in the Freedom Rides, begun in 1961 to challenge the segregation of interstate travel facilities. Seventy high-school students who protested in support of the jailed Travis were expelled from the McComb public schools. In response the Deltas raised over $3,600 to aid the teenager and enable the students to attend private schools in Jackson.

Albany, Georgia, the birthplace of Jeanne Noble and Osceola Adams, was the scene of one of the most important demonstrations in this period. Again, they were precipitated by attempts to integrate interstate facilities. This time it would be initiated by the youth chapter of the NAACP there. SNCC joined them and so did SCLC. Before it was over, more than a thousand had been arrested. Of particular interest to the Deltas was the participation of a soror,

Marion King, who, though visibly pregnant, was knocked to the ground by police when she attempted to bring food to some of the teenagers who had been arrested. Mrs. King lost the child. Not only physical but economic reprisals were heavy in Albany. Many were fired because of their participation or suspended from Albany State College. Deltas provided money for those who had lost their jobs, and also aided voter registration efforts.

These activities were combined with more traditional ones in these years. The Delta "Teen Lift" was inaugurated where groups of southern young people with few resources were taken to cities such as St. Louis, Los Angeles, and Detroit to become exposed to new experiences and sorors who served as mentors. The program was derived from the minority youth counseling projects and fully developed during Geraldine Woods's administration. The compelling testimony of one of the twenty-nine members of the Teen Lift at the 1965 convention attested to the importance of maintaining constructive traditional roles as well as exploring new ones. "We have gained something that we believe is valuable to us now and will be valuable throughout our lives," said Teen Lift participant Criseta Seals. "We have found ourselves, we know who we are." Saying that the experience with the project erased their feelings of inferiority, Seals added that they now had "the faith and self-confidence needed to meet their responsibilities. Our minds have been opened. When we return to our communities, we are going to be more determined to claim our rights."[27]

Combining the new and traditional in its national programming was also evident in its international initiatives which attempted to aid the struggle for independence among African nations. In 1957, Ghana was the first to declare its self-rule and with that declaration came a concentrated focus on strengthening ties between Africans and Afro-Americans. This was true of Delta as well, which in 1960 established an alumnae chapter in Liberia during the inaugural ceremonies of Liberian president William V. S. Tubman. Soon following were Delta-sponsored African tours, and meetings with the likes of Ghanaian president Kwame Nkrumah, and the Kenyan leader Tom Mboya. His wife, Pam Mboya, would become a member of the sorority as did Mrs. George Padmore, wife of the well-known Pan-Africanist. In 1959, Delta sponsored a twenty-seven-year-old political leader of the Tanganyika African National Union, Lucy Lameck, to observe women's organizations with the view of helping those in her nation toward social and economic development. Delta also provided institutional aid as part of its Five-Point Program. When the plight of Kenyan women who received little pre- or postnatal care came to their attention, it was decided to raise $5,000 to equip a maternity wing in that country's Njorge Mungai Hospital. At the 1958 convention, Dr. Mungai, its director, appeared to accept the gift at a ceremony where the sorority's newest honorary member— the singer and actress Lena Horne—cut the ribbon around a replica of the maternity wing, which was named after the sorority.

Subsequently, Deltas took on the responsibility for the building of the wing itself and in 1961, Jeanne Noble was invited to Kenya to witness the ground-breaking along with other sorors. "Each of us was first anointed with an African name," the president recalled. "And after the naming the Kenyan women would dance a few steps in our honor. Then they formed a trail which stretched as long as the eye could see, and they passed the bricks, one by one, and laid the foundation before our very eyes. Can you believe it? I can remember standing on that sandy hill, just standing there while they built the foundation brick by brick with singing, with dancing, with happiness."[28]

By 1963, the year of its fiftieth birthday, the organization would be challenged once again to reassess its role in the movement.

CHAPTER 12

CHALLENGE AND
CHANGE

The twenty-seventh national convention marked Delta's fiftieth anniversary and it was a triumph. The 1963 Golden Anniversary Jubilee had actually begun in January, the month of the original founding, with the founders, now in their seventies, being honored on the twelfth and thirteenth. Osceola Adams, then a director of the Putnam County (summer repertory) Theater in New York, and who had directed a dramatic presentation at the last convention, came to Washington for the occasion.

Ethel Black was also there. She had retired from the New York City school system, and ten years before had assisted in the chartering of the Queens Alumnae Chapter (which, in her later years, provided for her care in a nursing home). Naturally, the irrepressible Bertha Campbell wouldn't have missed the event for anything in the world. She was no doubt pleased to see the "blustery" Myra Hemmings, Alpha Chapter's first president, still showing her leadership: She was the cochair for the Golden Anniversary celebration. Hemmings had also helped to charter the San Antonio Alumnae Chapter, served on the National Judiciary Board, and was a former grand vice-president and director of the Southwestern Region. The "inspiration" for the whole Delta movement, Madree White, was also in attendance. To no one's surprise, White had continued her journalistic career as the publisher of a small newspaper in St. Louis, and had also been an associate editor of the Omaha *Monitor* in Nebraska for twenty-five years. Since 1955, White had lived in Cleveland. Among her Delta activities was the chartering of Lambda Sigma Chapter in 1926.

Campbell's old roommate, Winona Alexander, who had had an outstanding career as one of the earliest Black social workers to work in public welfare agencies in New York and Florida, also came. Alexander had also been active with the YWCA, and was a past president of the United Presbyterian Women's Organization. She then lived in Jackson, Florida, where she had returned after the death of her husband in 1943.

Eliza Shippen, who received her Ph.D. from the University of Pennsylvania, retired as professor of English and chair of that department from Miner Teachers College in 1954. She remained active with the D.C. Alumnae Chapter and various professional organizations. Her Washington "cohort" Florence Toms, former assistant principal of Garnet-Patterson Junior High School, was also there. The still-feisty Jimmie Middleton, who had conquered arthritis and the problems of sending herself and her daughters through graduate school after separating from her husband, came for the celebration. In 1936, after a long struggle, she received her master's degree at the same Howard graduation ceremony at which her daughter Amanda received her B.A. Wertie Weaver also was there. She had not been active with the sorority since 1923 when she moved to Los Angeles. But for this celebration, Geraldine Woods, then first vice-president, brought Weaver with her to Washington.

All were sorry to hear, however, about the death of Pauline Minor, only days after the January meeting. Like Olive Jones, Minor had lost touch with the sorority. After teaching in Alabama, South Carolina, and Pennsylvania, Minor wrote and published hymns and became a missionary in the Apostolic Church of Philadelphia. She seems also to have experienced tragedy in her life. A letter written to Myra Hemmings, probably in the fifties, mentioned the illness of her husband; and it was soon after that when she lost contact. Though she died on January 23, 1963, it was not known to the sorority until sometime afterward—when mail was returned to the national office, marked "Deceased." There seemed to be no immediate family: A death certificate revealed that a friend, Emma C. Thompson, notified the coroner's office. The certificate showed her marital status as divorced, and especially disconcerting was the fact that under the space provided for "Usual Occupation," Minor—who had graduated first in her class—was listed as a "domestic." By 1963, of the original band of twenty-two, Jessie Dent, Marguerite Alexander, Edna Coleman, Olive Jones, Vashti Murphy, Mamie Rose, and Ethel Watson had also passed away. The losses made those in attendance reflective of the past; but at the same time the celebration underscored the brightness of Delta's future. Those who attended were exhilarated to see the evidence of the organization's growth not only in numbers but in importance as well. The luncheon speaker on January 12 was President John F. Kennedy, who praised the sorority's achievements. Others included Vice-President Lyndon Johnson, Associate Justice William O. Douglas, and Congresswoman Edith Green (a honorary Delta) from Oregon. Also in attendance were many distinguished guests from government and the diplomatic corps.

The national convention, taking place the following August in New York City, also drew a panoply of those who represented the organization's past and future. Present were six former national presidents and two additional founders—the latter including Frederica Dodd and Zephyr Carter. Carter still showed much of the good-humored nature she had had as an undergraduate student fifty years before. Dodd, who was a prominent figure in Dallas, must have been filled with thoughts about Jessie Dent, with whom she had formed a lasting friendship that endured throughout their lives. Since neither had heirs, in their latter years each made out a "survivor's will," which stipulated that whoever survived the other would receive her estate. Dodd would outlive Dent by twenty-four years.

A sense of urgency accompanied the deliberations, which were held practically on the eve of the historic march on Washington. "The Past Is Prologue," the theme of the convention, was more than appropriate. Noble had described Delta as an "adolescent" at the previous convention—a "searching and sifting stage prior to adulthood." That rite of passage would begin in 1963. By then civil rights leader Medgar Evers had been murdered in front of his home in Jackson, Mississippi, with "a shot fired into a leader's heart heard around the world," as Noble said in her presidential address. "We may have come to greet each other, to transact Delta business," the president continued, "but lest we forget the subordinate goals of our existence as an organization, we do well to remember that the single most pressing issue of 1963, as it was in 1913 and 100 years ago is the need to expand the drive for *freedom!*"[1] So, just as Delta had attained the largest total assets in its history ($225,000); had the kind of attraction that would make one of its honorary members, the musical prodigy Phillipa Duke Schuyler fly in from Rome for the convention; attained the kind of influence that made U.S. Attorney General Robert Kennedy, though not formally invited, "drop by" the convention to talk about civil rights; just as convention registration was up again—to 1,322; and just as it celebrated women such as the lawyer Constance (Baker) Motley, who received the Mary Church Terrell Award for her role in the *Brown* court case, and Daisy Bates as an honorary member—Delta would have to turn on its heels once again.

The convention's "Youth in Action" luncheon helped them do it. Four college students, two of them Black—including the future sociologist Joyce Ladner—and two of them White, including Joyce Barrett, a Delta, movingly told the assembly about their experiences in the Deep South: the beatings, the torture, the jailings, the fears that had to be constantly conquered. They also talked about what the sorority could do: provide tuitions for expelled students, or simply provide food and shelter for the SNCC workers who had very little money to work with. Most important, several of them stressed, was for Deltas not to resist the forces of history, as they had heard chapter complaints about sorors who spent "too much time bringing the movement into the chapter." And there was criticism about the standing ovation given to Robert Kennedy, whose Justice Department was criticized by SNCC. "Why did you applaud?" one of the White panelists challenged. "He talked about the drop-out rate. What has the federal government done about the kids who are forced to drop out in Prince Edward County? You could have stood in silence, or you could have applauded without standing."[2]

"The young people were constantly challenging," Noble recalled. "And without them, I don't think that we would have been as involved in civil rights as we were. They told us not to give these symbolic messages to people. They asked me why I would let Robert Kennedy come in the first place. And they made us think in a different way." Two years later, at the 1965 convention in Los Angeles, held in the wake of the Watts riots, the lesson had been learned. "When [Los Angeles] Mayor Sam Yorty came to speak at the Convention, Gerri [Woods, the succeeding national president] found herself in the same position," continued Noble. The mayor "got up and said, 'Well, I know you people don't approve of what is going on in Watts.' And he finished the speech and *silence* covered the whole place. Not a hand was lifted. And afterward, several people said, 'You know, I thought over what that kid had said at the last convention.'"[3]

By 1963, Delta also mandated a Social Action Commission "to

provide information and direction to the membership on current civil rights issues." By the end of the convention, said Noble, "when Gerri Woods became president, we didn't miss a beat. I mean, the gavel struck, the convention was over, and when she opened it up, we were marching."[4]

LEGISLATION AND
CONFRONTATION, 1967–1971

Delta joined the hundreds of thousands who participated in the historic March on Washington, held in August of 1963, which was designed to apply pressure for the passage of civil rights bills. Lobbying had been a tradition of the sisterhood and during these years it was refined into an art. Of immediate concern was the 1964 Civil Rights Act, with its Title VII provision that also prohibited sex discrimination and became the legal foundation for the women's movement. And in 1965 there was the all-important Voting Rights Act. "We worked very hard with Clarence Mitchell, then chief lobbyist for the NAACP," said Geraldine Woods. Mitchell's influence concerning civil rights legislation in that period was so powerful that he became known to his colleagues and congressmen as "the 101st senator." As Woods, who resided in Los Angeles, remembered: "Many a night I would fly to Washington and go to the Capitol, and Clarence Mitchell would be the only person sitting in the gallery, looking down at the Senators. He would be pointing out to whom we should write. When the gallery was full, you were supposed to move out every twenty minutes or so. But Clarence would say, 'Let her stay,' so they would let me stay."[5] The mid-sixties were the years of the "march on the mailbox" where the sorority's regional conferences would hear a speaker such as Daisy Bates, Mitchell, or Wiley Branton—then a special assistant in the Justice Department—after which stationery and stamps would be handed out. "We would advise the sorors on the form the letter should take and then wait until they wrote and addressed it," recalled Woods. "Then we'd physically get up and march to the mailbox."[6] Respect for the organization would grow in these years because of its ability to mobilize opinion so quickly and have it heard at a time when the government was particularly sensitive to lobbying power.

"We became very effective monitors for legislation," said Lynnette Taylor, executive director who succeeded Patricia Harris, Marie Barksdale, and Allene Tooks in that position. At a 1964 board meeting the decision was made to individually visit key congressmen on the Hill. "I remembered on one occasion going to the Hill with Barbara Jordan," who was a member of the Houston chapter and once chair of the National Finance Committee, said Woods. "And she said to me, 'You know, Gerri, one day I'm not only going to be visiting Congresspersons, I'm going to be one myself.' And I said, Barbara, knowing you, I bet you are."[7]

The highlights of these efforts came in 1964, when the Civil Rights Bill was pending. "We got a room in the capital," said Taylor, "about fifteen members of the Board were there and each called on their Senator or Representative and made arrangements for them to come and talk to us. The Senators came in, and they were scared, too," Taylor remembered with a smile. "After a while others started coming in to see us on their own." Clarence Mitchell told the Deltas that they were the only Black group actually operating on the scene. "We were so effective," observed Taylor, "that Senator Bill Hart later told us that he thought our presence was the decisive reason why it passed."[8]

Nevertheless, the leadership would have to go even further if they were to rise to the occasion of the deepening crisis, which would soon take another turn. It was a turn that especially affected Delta's primary constituency and traditional focus of concern: the students of the nation. For 1964 was also the year that SNCC launched its Freedom Summer in Mississippi, where Black and White students, mainly from the North, would come to that state to help with voter registration and the "freedom schools," where civil rights workers engaged the local population in political awareness as well as standard courses of study. The Freedom Summer was also calculated to focus nationwide attention on the movement in one of the nation's most intransigent states. The strategy included Black and interracial organizations coming to Mississippi to bear witness to the injustice and brutality and the nonviolent efforts to redress both. President Woods was among those who represented the Deltas on one of those trips to the state when tension was particularly high. Three civil rights workers, James Chaney, Michael Schwerner, and Andrew Goodman, had been arrested, released, and were now missing in Philadelphia, Mississippi, the scene of a recent freedom school bombing. "We weren't even to tell our families the names of those in Mississippi who we were staying with, in fear that it would put them in jeopardy," Woods recalled. "The Blacks and Whites whom I traveled with were separated and we were to pretend that we didn't even know each other for the same reasons.

"We visited several freedom schools in the area," she continued. "But our main assignment was to meet with a group of Blacks and Whites at a church in Meridian; to hear about the situation first-hand so we could get a better idea of what we could do. The Whites didn't show, they were too frightened of the retaliation." At a subsequent mass meeting where Martin Luther King, Jr., was booed when he came to address Blacks there, Woods and her compatriots also decided to exercise the better part of valor, and left the site. "The young woman I was staying with said she would drive me home," Woods recalled. "Well, I looked up and I saw a police car behind us, and I said, 'Oh, good, the FBI is watching us.' (I was more naïve in those days.) "The young woman said, 'Uh-huh, just shut the door.' And she put her foot on the gas and we got home and we flew into the house."[9] But it was obvious that they were still not completely out of danger. The car stayed outside of the house for several hours. Woods would learn several years later that she along with many others had the honor of having an FBI file in her name.

The college campuses were also feeling the heat. Delta's Christmas parties became directed more toward raising money for bail bonds for students such as those at South Carolina State. Other kinds of legal, financial, and moral support were given to those involved in the confrontations at Jackson State, where students were killed, as well as at other schools. In 1965, after the violent retributions of the Selma to Montgomery march, Alabama State, Lynnette Taylor's alma mater, was poised to erupt. "The state police were bullying students who wanted to go into town to demonstrate," she recalled. "I was already on the plane by the time that word had come that I shouldn't go down there. When I arrived, I was met at the airport by the police who escorted me to Montgomery." Taylor arrived on the campus and talked to students about the civil rights movement, about the role students were playing, about how people were thinking in different parts of the country. When the confrontation between the state police and the students ensued, "I ended up having to stay in the president's house for three days."[10]

The sorority was also prepared to engage on another front. In 1964, Frankie Freeman, then first vice-president, was nominated to the six-member U.S. Commission on Civil Rights by President Lyndon Johnson. The commission was charged to investigate complaints, gather information, and appraise federal laws and policies as they affected equal rights protection. The group conducted hearings all over the country, and members of the sorority took an active part in them. "Everywhere Frankie Freeman appeared, she involved the Delta leadership in the local community to either appear or give testimony," observed Lynnette Taylor. "So we were very much a part of the activities of the Commission, in the school desegregation cases, the busing cases, the causes for women's rights. Freeman gave us an organizational role in this vital movement which was really the conscience of the country."[11] In the mid-sixties, not all "consciences" were equally moved by the hearings. Those who testified were often threatened with the loss of their jobs and other forms of retribution. It could have been worse for those holding the hearings. At a commission meeting in Jackson, Mississippi, in 1965, Freeman was understandably shaken when a bullet was fired into the hotel room where she was staying, shattering a mirror. It was an incident that she is reluctant to talk about, even today.

At the August 1965 Los Angeles convention, the organization itself would come face to face with the rawer aspects of racial confrontation. Still flushed by its lobbying successes, the sorority was nonetheless made to realize that this was no time to rest on its laurels. From the windows of the elegant Ambassador Hotel in that city, the registrants were literally able to see the smoke from the insurrections that had begun in Watts and spilled over into Los Angeles proper. "They said Watts was burning," recalled Woods, "but much more was burning at that time in Los Angeles than Watts. It was a tragic situation, but in a way, I think, it showed a lot of sorors what we were facing. And so though it was unnerving, it also inspired us to get things done."[12] Things would be "done" in a very emotional environment. There was the sad news that two founders, Jimmie Middleton and Madree White had passed away. Even more shocking was the news that the relatively young Mary Elizabeth Vroman, an honorary Delta who had written *Shaped to Its Purpose,* a Delta history published in 1963, had died. So, too, did Phillipa Schuyler who had met an untimely death in a helicopter accident.

Immediate events were no less compelling. At the luncheon, money was raised, spontaneously, to provide relief for local Black families in need. Then there were threats of being held hostage by the Black Panthers, a radical California-based group. Mayor Yorty was greeted by silence after his insensitive speech. Young SNCC panelists challenged that the cost of the luncheon could have paid the salaries of several civil rights workers to teach in the freedom schools. Martin Luther King, along with lieutenants Andrew Young, Bayard Rustin, and others, made a surprise appearance. So, too, came Patricia Harris, who had just been named the first Black woman ambassador, and assigned to Luxembourg.

The former executive director of Delta gave an impassioned speech: about the obligations of the Black middle class; about the self-confidence gained as a result of her relationship with the sorority; about pressing the case of discrimination and racism. She was also critical. Too many chapters were conducting "business as usual," Harris noted. And, she warned, "we must avoid any shame about Negroes, who do not meet middle-class standards of morality and middle-class standards of behavior."[13] Although some members of the middle class, such as herself, were no longer affected by the cruder forms of discrimination, it was important to remember the past, she intoned. Just six years before, Harris recalled, she had been turned out of a Whites-only apartment building. It was important to retain this memory of racism, to articulate it to others, to understand the sense of identity with all Blacks through the common experience of discrimination, she said. That is why she did not tire of being touted as the first *Black* woman to be appointed to the ambassadorial ranks—a Black woman who despite her credentials had also felt the sting of racism. "I want everybody in the world to say over and over again, 'Pat Harris is a Negro; Pat Harris is a Negro; Pat Harris is a Negro. . . .' "The remembering that I want to urge upon all of us who have been able to take advantage of the opportunities which, in most instances, we carved out with our fingernails and with our teeth and with our grit and with our work, is the hurt of being black, she concluded."[14]

By the sixties, there was the realization that piecemeal donations to the disadvantaged wasn't enough to heal the hurt. As Charlotte Lewis, cochair of the Social Action Commission, noted in her presentation at the 1965 convention, it was also important to use the "power leverage" of the organization to make more substantitive contributions.[15]

With the implementation of the War on Poverty during the Lyndon Johnson administration, Delta would have the opportunity to use that leverage. Its lobbying activities, its increasing service orientation and sensitivity to the needs of poorer Blacks, and its ability to reach into the communities of the country made it a prime candidate to administer many of the initiatives of the Office of Economic Opportunity (OEO). "I was contacted by Mrs. [Lady Bird] Johnson," remembered Geraldine Woods, "and she said that she had a new program. She invited me to a White House meeting in February of 1965 with a number of other heads of organizations. The program she wanted to talk about was Project Headstart. I immediately sent our chapters across the country the information about it and asked that they send proposals."[16] By August, eight alumnae chapters had initiated the program, which focused on underprivileged pre-schoolers (and among the most successful of all the antipoverty projects) in Akron, Ardmore (in Oklahoma), Grambling, Houston, Jacksonville, Los Angeles, San Antonio, and Chicago. Los Angeles, the home of Woods, had sixteen Headstart sites.

Project Headstart was the beginning of a close association with the Johnson administration, an association that had been presaged by the appearance of John F. Kennedy at the 1963 convention, and a subsequent invitation for the Delta Executive Board to meet with him for a briefing. In August of 1966, the board was invited to the White House for a briefing about the Demonstration Cities Bill that was subsequently passed by the Congress. The Delta board met with the President in the Cabinet room for nearly two hours and on the same day, they were also received by then–Vice-President Humphrey. It was not the last such meeting. Deltas were called in once more by the President, and there was also an additional meeting with Humphrey. During the first term of Freeman's administration, "Vice-President Humphrey asked six of us to come to his office," recalled Taylor. "And he talked for two hours, about what it was he wanted to do and how he had run across our members as he had moved around the country. He just wanted us to know where he was going, what he was doing, what kinds of things he expected—which was quite something: that we had developed this kind of rela-tionship." Also on other occasions representatives met with the Civil Rights Division and other agencies to discuss judicial appointments, or to develop bills, particularly those involved with education. "We were always being brought in on the planning stage of legislation," said Taylor.[17]

All of this activity brought on the need for the Social Action Commission, "to bring into sharper focus our diffuse activities and our concepts of Delta's 'place' in the civil rights movement."[18] To do that, there was also the need to bring into "sharper focus" the very premises of the organization, whose "principal purposes and aims" were, as stated in its constitution, still exclusively cultural, moral, and educational. However, by the 1965 convention an amendment was proposed by Constitutional and Bylaw Committee members

Charlotte Lewis, Hilda Davis, Marie Fonsworth, Helen Richards, Dorothy Height (who received the Mary Church Terrell Award in 1965, and now counted among the major organizational civil rights leaders), and Dorothy Harrison to broaden that concept. "The principal purposes and aims of this *public service* organization shall be cultural and educational; to establish, maintain and encourage high cultural, intellectual and moral standards among its members; to engage in *public service programs,* and to promote and encourage achievement in education"[19] (emphasis added). The amendment was officially approved at the following convention in 1967. And it could be said that the sorority not only was looking at its role differently, but was beginning to see itself differently as well.

C H A P T E R   13

TOWARD A NEW
IDENTITY

. . . We have looked good . . . We have used good English, we have talked about Delta women in the first person, and at times we talked about poverty in the third person. We have analyzed, theorized and we have seconded the motions . . . We have not condoned lawlessness and violence here, but we have not dared to unequivocally abhor and condemn it as a methodology for progress and achievement. . . . We have glibly discussed the communications gap between the black man and the ruling power structures, but somehow we have not come to grips with the gap between the black middle class and the black underclass. . . . Will you return to your hometowns and take up business as usual? . . . Change is the word that must precede all meaningful dialogue, and I ask you to make that work a part of what you take from this place.

—Texas state senator Barbara Jordan, speaking before the national convention, Cincinnati, Ohio

Frankie Freeman's precipitous rise to the presidency in 1967 indicated the sorority's desire for the change that Barbara Jordan spoke about. Unlike the presidents before her, she was a relative newcomer to the sorority. Freeman had been inducted in the St. Louis Alumnae Chapter in 1950, and had not previously held elective national office. Her leading role as a civil rights activist, and her appointment to the U.S. Civil Rights Commission, undoubtedly hastened her rise to the top. In fact, she became the first and only national president whose nomination came from the floor rather than from the official slate of the Nominating Committee. And she won by a 3–1 margin. Such unconventional tactics, it seemed, were needed in the first year of the organizations becoming a public-service sorority and with the necessity of having to respond to the concept of "Black Power" and further urban upheavals.

During Freeman's presidency, from 1967 to 1971, there was a growing restlessness among the membership despite the glowing progress reports heard at the conventions and regional conferences. In these years, those attending the meetings heard, for example, that the Social Action Committee had held twenty-four leadership seminars in eighteen states during 1966. Delta was doing its service: the Wewoka Alumnae Chapter in Oklahoma had been instrumental in providing a day care center for mothers there. In Baltimore, there was a major program, directed by treasurer Vivian Washington, of counseling unwed mothers—some time before the issue had captured the nation's attention. As individuals, Delta students were still leaders on their campuses. A foundation study of student leaders on fifteen Black campuses found that 85 percent of them belonged to Delta. And in the report of Claudette Franklin, second vice-president, she noted that Deltas made up the majority of Greek-letter students in the *Who's Who in American Universities* for 1965–1966.

In addition to their own scholarship programs and the continuing Teen Lifts, which forty-one chapters sponsored by 1968, the sorority received funding from both private and government sources for additional projects. For example, OEO gave the St. Louis chapter money for the College Test and Application Fee Program for low-income students, which helped those who could not afford the testing fees. Subsequently, the sorority would be on line for grants totaling several hundred thousand dollars, much of which came from the Federal Office of Education, for such programs as "Discover Scholastic Talent"—designed to recruit school dropouts. Again the Baltimore chapter, a model for such programs dating back to the Jobs Project's earliest days, executed it most successfully. In one year, 2,251 students received motivation and counseling; and nearly $90,000 was given in financial aid. Sorors heard comments from recipients that underscored the project's importance. "I think my walking over to your table on college night was the best thing that ever happened to me," a young high-schooler testified before the sorority. "If it were not for your encouraging me to come to the office, I never would have made it into college."[1]

By the seventies the sorority had established a reputation that superseded its known Democratic party loyalties. The Richard Nixon Justice Department, for example, created a $500,000 program to be administered by the Deltas; the United Church of Christ and the federal government in a joint effort were to provide rehabilitation for female law offenders. The pilot program included five months of intensive guidance and vocational training for women, who, unlike men, had fewer available work-release programs and halfway houses. Deputy Attorney General Richard Kleindienst had come to the 1971 convention to announce the program. When at the same convention, a former prisoner talked about the needs of the women, she was received with a standing ovation and a spontaneous singing of "If I Had a Hammer."

The organization also continued to respond to the era's unfolding events. "When they started the Poor People's Campaign we were in Atlanta at a regional conference," remembered Lynnette Taylor. "By the time the mule team had gotten to Georgia from Mississippi, it had bogged down because there wasn't enough money. They couldn't buy the food for the animals," she continued. "It was just about to deteriorate, and at that point the southern regional conference took up about four or five thousand dollars and gave it to [SCLC's] Hosea Williams and Andrew Young. And that was the money that got them to Washington."[2] The Campaign was originally to be led by Martin Luther King, Jr., before his assassination in April of 1968. Its purpose was to demonstrate to the nation the plight of its poor and it was important that the plans for Resurrection City, as the encampment in the nation's capital was called, be carried out despite—and because of—his murderous death. "The Deltas also made up much of the volunteer force of Resurrection City,"

Taylor recalled. "Those who were employed in the Social Services in D.C., helped to get food and clothing."[3]

Still, Delta as an organization wasn't wholly comfortable with itself or its image. Of the latter, Geraldine Woods observed that even in the late sixties the image of individuals was good, but that of the chapters—many of which were still conducting business as usual—was still lacking. More disturbing were the growing signs of tension concerning color within the sorority itself. The situation was deemed serious enough for Jeanne Noble to conduct sensitivity sessions, beginning with the Executive Board in 1968, which stressed "the need for debrainwashing in relation to our concept of 'Black' and the meaning of fair skin."[4] There had even been some mumbling heard about the appearance of Frankie Freeman, who was darker than most of the presidents before her and showed little desire to be a fashion plate. And there was still some resistance, Freeman recalled, to being "brought in to the civil rights movement" and the "resentment of the word 'Black.'"[5]

On the other end of the spectrum, there was increasing pressure to be more in keeping with the Black Power movement. Two letters written to Freeman by Patricia Rice Press, then associate executive director of the sorority, in March of 1968, illuminated this development. "Alumnae chapters as well as undergraduate chapters are asking, 'How involved can we (Delta chapters) become with civil rights in our communities?' . . . The Black Power advocates have been left out there by themselves for too long. The Black Movement needs women and also needs an organization like ours," she wrote. "As you [Freeman] told the audience at the Baltimore Founders Day Program, 'I've read about your Delta programs—they're good programs, but are they enough?' I ask a similar question: Is it enough to wrap bandages, to March to the Mailbox, to tutor children, to entertain foreign visitors, to conduct Negro Heritage Seminars, to visit the sick, even to vote? . . . Can we afford not to support certain activities?" Press continued. "Must we as a public service organization straddle the fence and always take the safe, tried, and conservative stand 'after the fact?'"[6]

The questions were all the more urgent because of the increasing criticism of the Black middle class, which had lagged behind or resisted the Black Power initiatives. "Middle-class Negroes," said Press, "continue to be indicted, continue to be accused of being asleep. . . . We are the group who intellectualize, who verbalize, but do nothing." Citing the progressive positions of past presidents on racial issues, and the political motives of the founders, Press recommended that Delta take a stand on Black Power and Black unity, that they comment on the President's Commission on Civil Disorder, and that they push themselves and other Greek-letter organizations to make more meaningful contributions to the current struggle.[7] In just a few short years, integration, as conceived in the fifties and even early sixties, had become an anachronism.

As the letters indicated, Blacks were of several minds, and so were the Deltas. There were the integrationists who believed the Black Power notion dangerous and counterproductive. Black Power advocates themselves differed over the degree of separatism the term implied. There were also divergent views over whether more emphasis should be placed on poverty issues, or of developing the leadership potential of the middle class. Class and color were intertwined into much of the thinking, often subconsciously. For the Deltas, these divisions affected the meaning of public service, of membership requirements, of the direction that the organization should be taking. That the sorority was composed of women of different generations as well as of other diverse experiences made the issues all the more difficult to resolve.

At least there was a broad consensus, articulated by Frankie Freeman in her "Call to Convention" statement, that "The real issue is not whether change will occur, for it will. . . .The question for us sorors, as we convene, is will we be caught up in change or will we be creative and responsive to the needs of our people, our community, and participate in bringing about change?"[8] Nevertheless, there were different views about which direction that "responsiveness" should take. The thirtieth national convention, held in Baltimore, in August of 1969, became the crucible where all of these impassioned ideas would play themselves out.

Its theme, "One Nation or Two? . . . One Nation!" with a subtheme of "Rage and Racism," reflected two streams of thought that contested for dominance. The first reflected Freeman's own public position in a supplementary statement to the February 1967 report of the U.S. Commission on Civil Rights. In the statement, she had written that "we are now on a collision course which may produce within our borders two alienated and unequal nations confronting each other across a widening gulf." A year later her conclusion was incorporated into the report of the National Advisory Commission on Civil Disorders, which warned that "Our nation is moving toward two societies—one Black, one White—separate and unequal."[9]

The idea of continuing to strive toward one nation was expressed by founder Osceola Adams, then seventy-nine years old and still elegant in dress and manner. She gave an eloquent speech criticizing those who would abandon the drive toward integration. "Voluntary segregation is an open invitation to compulsory segregation," she said in her firm voice to applause from the assembly. "It can well be the first fatal step down to a South Africa brand of apartheid." She went on to say that "the proposition of separatism is negative and defeatist. By implication, it is an admission of inferiority. . . . I am beginning to feel like a mad Cassandra," she continued, "but I feel so strongly that if we lose this struggle to preserve the concept of 'One Nation' everything we have ever worked for will be destroyed—the hopes, the dreams, the labor of our Frederick Douglasses, our Sojourner Truths, our Mary Church Terrells, our Mary McLeod Bethunes, will amount to nothing and all of Delta's splendid public service will be destroyed. We are now beginning to emerge from compulsory segregation. . . . We still have a long way to go," she concluded, "but we are on our way. Let us not turn back now,"[10] she said to a standing ovation.

In keeping with this idea, Frankie Freeman then spoke of the need to reverse the "trend of racial, class, student and administration polarization" and called for a reassessment of the Five-Point Program. She announced that, "after six years of a successful teen-lift, our 1969 teen-lift would be expanded to include Black and White, affluent and poor, because racial and social class isolation will be eliminated only to the extent that each person works affirmatively and aggressively to include all races."[11] The concept was already realized in the membership of the sorority, which included several Whites, most notably the outspoken SNCC worker Joyce Barrett. There were also White honorary members such as Congresswoman Edith Green, and Esther Peterson, assistant secretary of labor in the Kennedy administration. In 1969, LaDonna Harris, of Native American descent and wife of Senator Fred Harris of Oklahoma, was also inducted.

Other mainstream perspectives which spoke of faith in the political system, and the role of the middle class to articulate to White America "that this land belongs to Black people too . . . that we are going to be free in Marks, Mississippi, in Harlem, in Watts . . . all over this land,"[12] was movingly expounded by guest speaker Vernon Jordan, then assistant to the executive director of the Southern Regional Council—and known to the Deltas during his former NAACP days as the man who escorted soror Charlayne Gault through the screaming mobs at the University of Georgia. And pride of heritage was spoken about by Dorothy Height who recalled Mary McLeod Bethune's deep conviction of the physical and spiritual beauty of Black people long before the sixties; as well as by Alex Haley's impassioned quest for his African ancestors, which years later would be written about in *Roots*.

The giving of the Mary Church Terrell Award to the indomitable Fannie Lou Hamer, the Mississippi sharecropper who helped found the Mississippi Freedom Democratic party was testament that she had become the symbol of racial justice in the mid-sixties. She spoke with pathos, humor, and wisdom, the likes of which has rarely been recorded in the annals of speechmaking. Reflecting the commitment to poor Blacks, the Baltimore Alumnae Chapter gave a grant as well as recognition to a local group called the Rescuers of Poverty that aided Baltimore's indigent, especially welfare, mothers. The convention program was a brilliant one, and had sanctioned more racial perspectives, perhaps, than any before it.

At the same time, the more radical questions concerning Black Power, and the charges of elitism and political uselessness leveled at the Black middle class were not directly broached by any of the speakers. And as the Patricia Press letters showed, they were the most bothersome issues of the moment. The latter issue was brought up only once, indirectly, over a debate on whether Delta, which was an affiliate of the National Council of Negro Women, should have each individual become a dues-paying member as well. When there was resistance, Jeanne Noble fired back, "We can do better in NCNW because the black community doesn't trust us, because they feel as if we are alienated from them; and we will never have a Fannie Lou Hamer in Delta Sigma Theta. The National Council as Dorothy [Height, the president] was talking about, is broadly based."[13] Of course, as someone brought out, Hamer could be an honorary member—which she in fact soon became—but the point was made. The thorny question of the Black Power mandates was, typically, brought up by students. At a sensitivity session conducted by Noble, students voiced their concerns about the need for Delta to be "more forcefully involved in social action . . . and that chapters affiliate with such organizations as the Black Student Union and the Black Panthers." At an undergraduate luncheon, where three students talked about their role in the college community, the most assertive of them, Jayne Ware, confronted the class separation issue. "Have we disassociated ourselves from the Black community?" she asked.

"Do you place your academic and social status so high that you forget the original environment from which you came? Sorors, what have you done or what do you do to bring about Black awareness not only in the community but within yourself and your sisters?"[14] The three participants were all candidates for the second vice-president spot, reserved for student representatives—and Ms. Ware won. These most emotionally wrenching of issues would also be addressed, more indirectly, in the delegates' deliberations concerning the bylaws and resolutions of the convention.

Though not mentioned specifically, the elitism charge was undoubtedly in the minds of those who favored "tampering" with one of the sacred cows of the historic sorority movement: its academic requirements. Proposed before the assembly was that a student with "good academic standing from the appropriate university or college official" be eligible for membership. In the past, of course, it was required that that student have an 80-percent or B grade point average. The rationale for the change was that the diverse grading systems made it necessary to be more flexible.[15] The meaning of the change, of course, went far deeper. Many who advocated it were well aware that numerous colleges, especially interracial ones, had lower standards of eligibility for membership in Greek-letter organizations than the Deltas. It was inevitable that the grade point average of the organization would drop. So, the proposed change reflected the fact that the organization's public service responsibilities now eclipsed its scholarship mandate, not only in the programs of the sorority itself, but in its very membership. Some would interpret this as a willingness to lower its standards in the face of outside pressures, plain and simple. Jeanne Noble, for example, talked about "those of us who teach on interracial campuses . . . in the heat of the battle trying to take [more] of a total look" at prospective members. And there was the suspicion that Delta was giving in to its needs to increase the membership. This brought the charge from a delegate: "I do feel from the general tone of the discussions that . . . you are considering increasing the numbers as the most important change and by increasing numbers, this will bring more money into the national body."[16] Another believed that "good standing" did not adequately safeguard the possibility of members being poor students who might be forced to drop out of school. This, in turn, would not augur well for a college-based organization.

But most agreed with the change. Many believed that the tradition of scholarship would not be affected by it. A delegate from the University of Houston, for example, cited that although the requirements on her campus were as low as 2.0 out of 4.0, Delta attracted the good students, who had the highest collective average of both the Black and White Greek-letter groups. Most seemed to agree with the perspective of the delegate who said: "I would like to point out that we are a public service organization, not a scholarship organization, per se. Sometimes students are so busy passing exams, that they cannot get out into the community."[17] Character and service were in these years deemed more important than the GPA. The amendment passed with the required two-thirds majority.

Similarly, the criteria for the acceptance of alumnae members, who formerly had to have "distinguished [themselves] in a particular field and in the life of the community," now only had to have "rendered service in a particular field and in the life of the community." The rationale for the change was that it would be more in "line with the community service requirement of the sorority."[18] The amendment was also adopted with the two-thirds majority.

The hottest debate was reserved for discussions of proposed resolutions. There were the usual ones: commitment to an effective welfare program, escalation of the withdrawal of troops from Vietnam, support of Black mayors and other elected officials, encouraging women to run for office, support of a national observance for Martin Luther King, Jr.'s, birthday, the extension of the Voting Rights Act. Under the chair of the well-known judge, Juanita Kidd Stout, the Resolutions Committee, however, did not "escape" with the usual commendations. An undergraduate who said that this was her first convention relayed her opinion that "it had been a waste of time and money." A "group of Black women," she said, should take "a more active and direct position in the Black community—not urging, not sending letters and telegrams of recognition for Black people who had gotten out of the struggle."[19]

One resolution, however, went beyond such parameters and as a result became the center of debate. It "deplored the advocation of separatism" and resolved the sorority "to strengthen American democracy by implementation of executive, judicial, and legislative actions which unite all people into one nation—indivisible."[20] It reflected, after all, the theme of the convention. Although there were those who agreed with the principle of that theme—"I think that separatism would defeat all that was done in the name of Civil Rights which included integration," as one delegate said—more had problems with it. "On a university campus," observed Jeanne Noble, "this [resolution] means a put-down of the Black movement . . . [a criticism] of a Black student organization that asks for a separate place to hold their meetings. . . . I think it will look very conservative to those who read that we came in and passed the same kind of resolutions. . . . It's not that I'm against integration," she continued. "We have a problem because of the [implied] self-hatred of doing things alone."[21] To applause, Noble suggested that the resolution be reworded or rejected. After unsuccessful attempts to come to consensus about its rewording, it was withdrawn.

Despite the disappointment of the young delegate about the convention of 1969, it was a demonstration of why the organization was able to maintain its viability in a period when others were not as successful. It consciously confronted these issues and encouraged young people to take them to the cutting edge when others, especially the major civil rights organizations, were suppressing them. At the same time, though its final corporate pronouncements may have frustrated many as not going far enough, neither did they alienate any significant part of the constituency. And in fact, Delta had come a very long way in meeting the needs of its changing constituency in changing times. Consequently, between 1961 and 1971, the number of active members rose from 8,317 to 18,226 and its chapters increased from 269 to 408. Although the active or financial membership was still only about a third of its 60,000 total members, it was a larger percentage than in the past. That most of Delta's growth took place in the mid to late sixties, when the organization was most active in the civil rights movement, was also significant. Finally, though the convention debates may not have resulted in the resolution of the particular issue, they often planted the seed for developing, through its programs, a new phase in the thinking of its membership. This was evidenced in the reactions to the Treasurer's Report. Like the resolutions, the report was usually accepted without much discussion. But in 1969, Jeanne Noble, reflecting the concerns of many of the delegates, questioned the organization's investment in U.S. Savings Bonds, which it had done virtually throughout its history. The traditional way of handling the money, she said, raised questions "about our concern for Black capitalism and investments in the areas that would in some way be helpful in terms of . . . the Black community."[22] It was a question, replied treasurer Phoebe LeSesne, that the Executive Board and the Finance Committee were looking into.

In fact, by the seventies, economic development became a key concern of the sorority. Not only was it touted by Blacks who were becoming more aware of their purchasing power, but, for the Nixon administration's own reasons, it was also encouraged in legislation that was conceived to further "Black capitalism." For the Deltas, it also accommodated all of the various perspectives of the Black movement in this period. Whatever one's views about separatism, integration, Black Power, or the role of the Black middle class, all agreed with the need for Black economic development. Its emergence as a Delta concern was seen in an annual report of the sorority's chapter activities. Although chapters still responded to issues like school desegregation, unemployment, and the need for library services, the 1970s stressed economic development—as well as issues like the increasing drug problem and the strengthening of the Black family. Fifty-six percent of the almost four hundred chapters had a program that reflected the economic concern, according to the survey conducted by Thelma Daley, then chair of the National Projects Committee. It would be taken to new levels by Frankie Freeman's successor, Lillian Benbow.

THE LILLIAN BENBOW
ADMINISTRATION, 1971–1975

Like Frankie Freeman, Lillian Benbow did not come up through the usual ranks before becoming the fifteenth national president of Delta. The usual route consisted of being president of a local chapter; followed by a position on the National Executive Board; a regional directorship, and/or the chair of a national committee; and finally an elected national office which led to the national presidency. In her first Executive Board meeting, Benbow thanked the board members for their patience. She had been nominated from the floor for first vice-president at the 1967 convention in Cincinnati, and in that position, served on the board for the first time. The only previous national experience she had was serving on the National Projects Committee.

Unlike Freeman, however, Benbow did not have national visibility either. At the time of her election she was assistant director of the housing program for the Michigan State Civil Rights Commission. A native of Vicksburg, Mississippi, and a graduate of Le-Moyne-Owen College in Tennessee, Benbow was a former president of the Detroit Alumnae Chapter, and chaired the board of directors for the Delta Home for Girls. She was also a member of the YWCA board. What had catapulted her to the Delta presidency was a charismatic personality and an ability to inspire the constituency, a growing number of whom were challenging traditional ways of thinking and middle-class mores. Though Lillian Benbow was conventional in many ways, she also personified the new generation. She had a close-cropped hairstyle (which would become a full-fledged "Afro"), and a warm exuberance that filled a room. The Deltas loved it. "I remember teasing Lillian," said Noble, "saying, God, with such adulation, what do you plan to do with it? You know, when God gives you this, you have to take it to another level. You just don't say, 'Oh, how nice it is to have all these people desperately in love with me.' You've got to move on it."[23] And Lillian Benbow would, in a number of ways.

"Before I knew her very well, while she was first vice-president, I once mentioned to her that I liked her hair, that I would love it if I could wear one [an Afro]," Noble, who has straight hair, recalled. "Well, I appreciate the fact that you mentioned that," Benbow said. When urged to have a full one, however, Benbow wondered whether it might keep her from getting nominated for president. "I think you should go for it," the past president said, "because the reaction will either let you know if you would want to be president of an organization that can't accept it, or it will push you that much further ahead." Typical of her personality, Benbow chose to go ahead despite the fact that it would create controversy. "A chapter *actually* wrote Lillian to ask her when she spoke before them *not* to wear an Afro," recalled Noble.[24] But she not only refused to desist, but would go so far as to publicly criticize columnist Carl Rowan, who wrote an article that implied that Afros atop many heads substituted for brainpower beneath them. Benbow challenged that the pride an Afro symbolized didn't diminish "brainpower" but probably increased it. She also challenged the underlying notion of the article: that the natural hairstyle invited even more oppression and alienation from the mainstream. After all the years of conforming to White standards, she concluded, it was obvious that straightened hair did not ameliorate the condition of Black people. If it did, "our generation of pressed and processed hair-wearers would have made this a time when . . . our progeny would not be judged by the kink or straightness of their hair."[25]

She was also the first president to publicly raise the issue of sexism among Black men. "Black sisters are quietly discussing this situation," she wrote in *The Delta* in 1974, "but it is now time to say to our Black brothers openly that we will not take any more kindly to a *third* oppressor than we do to the original two. . . . Many sisters are also expressing concern about the insensitivity of some of the Black politicians who having gained national and local offices are demonstrating an unwavering devotion to the sexist patterns established by their white predecessors: ignoring the female voter who was instrumental in putting him in."[26]

Echoing past criticisms made by Delta presidents, Benbow reemphasized more strongly than any president before, the wastefulness of a sacred fraternal activity: "the dance." She called for a moratorium on them, and for the eight Black fraternities and sororities with their three thousand chapters, and approximately 500,000 professionals, to channel those costs—which she estimated to be $1.5 million a year, not including the cost of the gowns, tuxedoes, and accessories—into more substantive programs.

And, it fell on her administration to have to take a more critical view of the White House in a time when Delta was, as noted earlier, utilizing government and private grants at unprecedented levels. But it was also a time when the less empathetic Richard Nixon administration was in full gear and turning back past civil rights initiatives. At the convention of 1971, the year she was elected, she lambasted Nixon for his stand against busing to achieve integration. "President Nixon is now standing in the doorway of every school in the nation," she was quoted as saying in the *Houston Post*. The Nixon administration's position, she opined, "is coercive and punitive. . . . We strongly protest and condemn [it]."[27] Though in the past, federal administrations had been criticized in resolutions; and presidents were urged to realize the promises of equality, Benbow's direct criticisms in the press marked a new departure. And it led the way for other members of the sorority to take on the administration while wearing their Delta "hats." The newspaper also quoted state senator Barbara Jordan's speech at the convention, which attacked the governmental surveillance of private individuals. Jordan, who was the convention coordinator, would become a U.S. congresswoman the following year, and in that capacity play a similar role to Mary

McLeod Bethune and others before her in apprising the sorority of behind-the-scenes political events.

In terms of the social needs of the organization, Benbow's interpretation of the meaning—and obligations—of the sisterhood also filled a need. The swirling events of the sixties called for the focus of attention to be on the organization dimension of the sorority. Its "sisterhood" aspect, the emotional glue that held it together spiritually, had been relatively neglected. Benbow's passionate persona, her reiteration again and again of the love of the sisterhood, filled this void. In her first speech after being elected at the 1971 national convention in Houston, she told the delegates who had welcomed the election results with a standing ovation: "Let there be no walls around us, my sisters. . . . Teach our eyes to see each other as we are, for in each other we see ourselves. When I look at you, I see myself. If my eyes are unable to see you as my sister, it is because my own vision is blurred. . . . I am my sister's keeper and my sister is mine. The keeping, my sorors, is not only to know the physical comfort, the verbal expressions of fellowship, it is the keeping somewhere in the quiet recesses of the mind, those silent, unexpressed and unexposed feelings known only to the heart."[28]

For Benbow, this idea went beyond that of serving those less fortunate in the spirit of noblesse oblige, but was in the spirit of one-to-one identification. For example, the prisoner rehabilitation program should be seen in the light of mobilizing "our criminal justice and personal security concerns, as if we ourselves were locked inside a huge stockade, prison or jail . . . that we speak with the same indignant concern against the brutal injustices that are visited on our brothers and sisters . . . as if we were they, because my sisters, we are they."[29] It was a question of feeling a deeper responsibility, she intoned often during her administration. "How many letters have come . . . objecting to the personal conduct of sorors—or persons considered for membership—but the letter does not come that says, 'I saw a hungry child this morning and I counselled my chapter to feed him, but because it was not in the budget we couldn't respond and I charge my chapter with immoral conduct. . . . My chapter rejected the opportunity to present to the community library a collection of works by Black historians and I charge it with cultural negligence.'"[30]

"One of the things that she worked on was a sense of reaffirmation and internal development," commented Lynnette Taylor, whose thirteen years as executive director included the Benbow administration. "She came in at the end of the civil rights movement and at a time when many needed direction."[31] There was also a more painful phenomenon that emerged in this period when much of the movement was in disarray and racial passions turned inward. Hazing had taken an ugly turn. In a few instances, pledgees had felt violated enough to sue the organization.

Of course hazing had always been a part of the initiation period—of all Greek-letter organizations—but may have a particular meaning and character among Blacks. For example, there is special emphasis on the line of initiates acting in unison, whether through the dance steps that they perform, dressing alike, or even walking across campus in a kind of lockstep. As in many such organizations where group action must supercede individual ones, many of the pledging activities were of conscious design. The stripping away of individuality is achieved through activities that are designed to "humble" a pledgee (some would, accurately, characterize it as humiliation). A "one for all, and all for one" mentality is further developed through the knowledge that if one pledgee does something "wrong" the whole "line" is punished; if one is unable to perform a certain task, someone on the line will have to perform it twice. Hazing activities also force creative responses to "impossible" demands from a "big sister." The idea is to learn how to satisfy the "request"—not literally, but through some other means. For example, if told to jump out of a window, an initiate might either find a ground-floor window or hastily draw a sketch of one, then "jump" through it. Also inculcated is the unconditional respect for those who are already in the sisterhood. All of these things—the need for unity, for taking responsibility for another's actions, for understanding that one's own actions will affect the entire group—have a particular resonance in terms of the Black experience. Though physical abuses such as paddling were not unknown, they were prohibited; most often—for the women at least—such threats were psychological in nature. But there were excesses, and they were seen in a harsher light by the sixties, when there were growing questions about the nature of the pledging period.

There was, after all, an inherent contradiction between the more humiliating aspects of initiation and the values and demands of the civil rights movement—and of Delta itself. "Are we young women who invite other young women with creative and intellectual abilities to join our ranks so that we can subjugate them to all manner of indignities and inconsiderations," asked a writer in *The Delta*. "Do we exist on the premise [of] . . . having the unique ability of trans-posing months of subservience into immediate sisterliness and service with one ceremony?"[32] The concern led to much formalized discus-sion between Delta leaders and the membership, and eventually a new "intake" or initiation process designed by Jeanne Noble. Never-theless, in the early seventies, complaints of abuse were more nu-merous. Whether this reflected greater sensitivity to them; the increasing refusal of pledgees to quietly withstand abusive behavior; or was a reflection of the anxieties, frustrations, and bitterness of Blacks in the wake of a movement that had been fragmented by assassinations and had turned in on itself, is not known. But their implications in terms of the "sisterhood" was too much for Lillian Benbow to bear.

One particular incident was particularly troubling, and at a 1973 board meeting, Benbow was visibly distressed by the activities of a chapter whose "zeal" had resulted in an injury to a pledgee. "We're talking about what has happened to a young woman seeking sis-terhood, wanting to be a sister . . . a college woman, seeking to be a part of her peers," said Benbow. "It should never have been. . . . I have begun to feel that maybe we can never purge ourselves. . . . Our soul has been invaded with it," she continued. "She trusted us . . . and the responsibility lies with us. . . . We are a sisterhood. We believe in sisterhood. We prohibit any acts of brutality. . . . We have our constitution, we have our ritual which speaks about compassion, courtesy, temperance, you know. We have to recognize the old ways, the old harassment, brutality, we cannot carry along. Some beautiful traditions we had will always be with us. The brutality and harass-ment we will throw that off. We can't afford it. We cannot carry it. We cannot bear it. [Applause] We cannot bear it, my sorors. We just cannot bear it."[33]

Immediately, she proposed new bylaws that suspended and/or levied heavy fines on *each* member of an errant chapter. (By 1979, thirty-eight chapters would be disciplined, and four suspended.) The severity of the punishment, the debates over what constituted "ha-rassment," and the interpretation of the power of the president and national chapter to deal with the infractions became the object of some controversy. The debate was not so much about pledging as it was about maintaining tradition at a time when so many traditions were under siege. But Lillian Benbow was determined to move for-ward. Her reaction to the controversy was typical of others to come and was reflected in the phrase, "Breaking New Ground," the theme of the 1973 national convention held in Atlanta. "We dared to risk the 'turning off' of some young sisters and the 'tuning out' of some older ones by espousing a hard line on illegal intake activities," she said before the assembly. "And we moved to the place of NEW GROUND."[34]

But in that year, another part of the new ground's landscape had come into view. At the convention, a resolution was passed for the sorority to become involved with the "development of telecommunication technology among Blacks." It was a timely idea. Delta could envision the effective use of that technology to improve communication and dissemination of information throughout its hundreds of chapters. "The 32nd Convention will be a skills-building, consciousness-raising event," announced Lillian Benbow in the 1973 preconvention issue of *The Delta*. "Technical specialists will discuss and demonstrate such world breakthroughs as direct satellite educational instructions systems, informational systems for the retrieval and dissemination of educational data . . . and telephonic and microwave communications—even a presentation on earth stations!"[35]

With both human and economic resources, it would not take Delta long to become programmatically engaged in this new frontier of activity—or for its membership to come up with a rush of new ideas on how to use it. On Delta's roster, and involved with the workshops in telecommunications at the convention were Ruth Bates Harris, an administrator of NASA; Gloria Anderson, appointed to the Corporation for Public Broadcasting; Grace L. Hewell, who was involved in the telecommunications field as a program officer in the Department of Health, Education and Welfare (HEW); and Phoebe LeSesne of the IBM Systems Research Institute. Significantly, many of the activities of the Social Action Commission, cochaired by Hortense G. Canady, a future national president, and Doris Haley, were also devoted to this area. The commission put into immediate operation, for example, a Delta Resource Bank, which computerized and identified the skills and educational background of the membership, to be used for the planning of programs or as a kind of instant resume to be used for referrals. There was also interest in chapters' using telecommunications technology for information on all aspects of social issues. The first experiment of the kind was the distribution of a taped panel discussion on feminism entitled, "Who Is My Sister."

Once introduced into the program of the sorority, the telecommunications concept would gather a quick momentum and billow in other areas. The resolution had also included the use of telecommunications to combat racism and sexism. "As instruments of positive change in the conditions of Black people we must insure that *human* and *social imperatives* are programmed into the operations of these future world technologies," the president wrote.[36] The transmission of the Black image, which was still largely negative despite recent gains, could tie technology and social action together, Benbow knew. So DST Telecommunications, a nonprofit corporation was established, and its first project would be the production of a full-length feature film. It was an intriguing idea. The early seventies were a time when the growing consumer power of Blacks was having an impact on the marketing of music, books, song, and film. Black artists, particularly women, who had emerged in the sixties, were becoming national figures and, in many ways, the cutting edge of Black thought and aspirations. Anticipating the presence of several of them at the Atlanta convention, such as the poet Nikki Giovanni, and actress/writer Ruby Dee, Benbow had written in *The Delta* that the confab would reflect these times: "a time of poets, of singers, of dreamers, of futurists, of idealists." Out of the mix came the idea of how to incorporate these initiatives within the organizational structure of the sorority.

"When we initiated Nikki Giovanni and Ruby Dee in Atlanta," recalled Jeanne Noble, "they spoke, and I mean, they turned the place out. It made me think about the great interest that we've traditionally had in the arts. And thinking about the artists who were members and honorary members, I wrote a memo to Lillian that we had a natural goldmine."[37] The gold mine turned out to be the Commission on Arts and Letters, officially born on September 24, 1973. Its purpose was to act as an advocate for arts that projected the Black experience. Its objectives also included the inclusion of Black women on cultural boards and entities, and support for artists. In addition to its very serious purposes, it was also one of the more "glamorous" commissions that the sorority had ever created. Cochairs were Leontyne Price, and Lena Horne. Noble was its chair. Other Deltas on the thirty-one-member commission included founder Osceola Adams, Giovanni and Dee, Roberta Flack, Novella Nelson, Charlayne Gault, journalist Ethel Payne, archivists Jean (Blackwell) Hutson and Dorothy Porter, as well as others who were editors, television producers, musicians, members of arts councils and foundations, communication specialists, and advertising account executives. There were gala receptions, and in its first year there were successful events such as the book party held at several regional conferences, featuring Nikki Giovanni and Margaret Walker whose "conversation" book, *Poetic Equations* had been published by the newly established Howard University Press. In addition, a record, entitled "Roses and Revolutions" was produced that featured readings and poetry by well-known actors, and Delta artists. The commission, it as soon realized, would also be a resource for the planned film.

During the period, the only acknowledgment in the film industry of the Black consumer market was the production of what became known as Blaxploitation films: movies that featured Black principals who were hustlers, pimps, or violent-prone detectives. The women in these films were either prostitutes or Amazonlike "warriors." Why not produce a film that would depict the positive values of the Black experience and history; and at the same time expose the "system" that was designed to denigrate it? Such a film would not only advance Black cultural aspirations in general, and invest Delta and, by extension, all Greek-letter organizations with a positive image, but it also would represent the highest form of the sorority's thrust toward Black economic development and telecommunications. On the surface at least, the sorority seemed to have all the resources necessary. In addition to those who had experience in films and media, there was certainly the capability to raise a substantial amount of funds from its hundreds of chapters and some sixty thousand members. The organization had additional financial leverage: Its assets were now more than a half-million dollars. Scripts were submitted and the Commission on Arts and Letters selected one that reflected important political issues. Called *Countdown at Kusini,* its plot revolved around the attempt to assassinate the leader of an African revolutionary movement, who is struggling against colonialism and multinational corporations. An Afro-American musician, who becomes politicized by the events unfolding around him in Africa, also becomes involved with the revolutionary's efforts. The script attracted well-known actors and actresses, who enthusiastically accepted the roles. The musician would be Al Freeman, Jr.; Ruby Dee would be the principal and politically aware female character, and her husband, Ossie Davis, not only would star, but would direct and write the screenplay. The film would be shot on location in Nigeria and, taken with the idea, Columbia Pictures agreed to distribute the film.

"You've turned on the imagination of a film company which, by the way, only *seems* to deal with the imaginary but whose hard experience is rooted in the bedrock rules and regulations of business reality," a letter to Lillian Benbow from David Begelman, president of Columbia Pictures read.[38]

Now the project would have to be "sold" to the membership. It would not necessarily be an easy task. There was a great deal of money involved, there was risk, and this kind of project was untried and very different from the traditional ones that the organization had implemented before. There was also some resentment about the Arts and Letters Commission in general. To many, their beloved Lillian seemed to be so caught up in the film that she was neglecting other Delta business. There was tremendous attention, both within the sorority and in the press, focused on the "stars"—many of whom had not been active in the sorority, and had certainly not participated in any of the nuts and bolts work that kept it going. And here they were, being flown in from all over the country, being catered to, getting their pictures in the newspapers and on television. Nevertheless, Benbow's leadership style and charisma was difficult to resist—and so was the excitement of the press when it got hold of the story. Benbow "stumped" the country like a candidate. Often people like Lena Horne would accompany her for fund-raising events for the film. And always, always, there was the infectious enthusiasm and sense of challenge that she was so capable of expressing. "My sisters," began her editorial in *The Delta* in 1975, "there can be no Delta woman who does not see that 'Countdown to Kusini' is more than another movie; it is a new *feeling*—a new *lift of the head*—yes, *the planting of a new flag on a new summit* for Black people." She *could* create a vision. "We shall have great moments with its World Premiere: the name of Delta Sigma Theta looming big in the credits." But the greatest moment, she intoned, was when "that collective voice of the sisterhood said, 'Yes, Delta women *must* dare to venture! Must dare to break new ground!'"[39]

Though, there may have been some hyperbole in the cheerleading, Lillian Benbow believed deeply in the meaning of Delta's support for the film. "Delta's move to the competitive enterprise of image-building through "'Countdown to Kusini,'" she soberly wrote, "was again using the gift of possibility—the possibility to transform rather than merely to conform."[40]

The press knew a story when it saw one. As early as 1973, *The New York Times* carried an article about the Arts and Letters Commission, and when the plans for the film had been formulated, *The Washington Post* announced: "The country's largest Black woman's service organization . . . has entered the expanding Black filmmaking field."[41] In the *Post* as well as other papers throughout the country, much was made about the fact that most of the projected budget of $800,000 would come from the chapters and individual investors of the sorority; that other investors, including George Johnson, the Black millionaire cosmetics king would also be involved; that the film would be written, produced, and directed by Blacks. Benbow and others were quoted concerning their efforts to change the negative Black image, "to alter past injustices"—especially those regarding Black women. Perhaps the one most thrilled about it all was Osceola Adams, who, upon receiving an award from Detroit mayor Coleman Young at a Delta-sponsored event, spoke about the prospective film and then told the audience, "Now I know why I'm still living." These were heady times in the history of the sorority. And the membership responded, financially and personally. The actors, directors, distributors, and investors were in place; production began.

Although the film was the dominant event of Benbow's second administration, from 1973 to 1975, it wasn't the only one. Delta business carried on with its plans to march for the ERA; articulate and develop programs concerning health and jobs; discuss and explain to the membership the implications of Nixon's resignation in 1974; take a position for freedom of choice concerning abortion; and maintain its strong stand against harassment of pledgees. A new national headquarters was purchased; and aid to Black colleges was instituted. Delta gave $10,000 to Tougaloo College in Mississippi for its Civil Rights Library.

There were also additional indications that the sorority was redefining its image. "Sorority" was dropped from official usage—heretofore the organization would be known as Delta Sigma Theta, Inc. The change had legal significance related to its nonprofit corporate status, but also, as Benbow noted, it was another move away from the "social image" that the word "sorority" implied. This was not accepted without some discomfort by the membership. It symbolized another large psychological step away from tradition. Though Lillian Benbow was not confronted directly, the issue was raised from the convention floor with questions such as why she so frequently used "sister"—a term associated with cultural nationalist types—instead of the more traditional "soror." It was only a question of semantics, Benbow impatiently answered, but combined with

the huge step the sorority was taking with the film; the new styles of
dress and the increasing numbers of Afros seen at the conclaves; the
increasing presence of iconoclastic writers and artists; the nontradi-
tional living styles being touted; the changes in many of the women's
own lives into new occupations and the demands for more feminist
ways of thinking; and the redefining of the pledge process—things
were happening very quickly and the pace was out of the control of
the membership. And it wasn't in the mood for another dramatic
break from tradition. Nevertheless, Benbow tried to introduce one.

Because of production delays, the film was not due to premiere
until the spring of 1976 and because she was limited to two terms in
office, it would not be released while Benbow was president. That
prospect might not have been so critical to her if everything had been
running smoothly. But things weren't. The film was running into
trouble. There were cost overruns. It was encountering logistical
problems in Nigeria. One of the actors who was first cast for the film,
Al Freeman, Jr., dropped out, and was replaced by Greg Morris.
The distributor had replaced its "turned-on imagination" with "bedrock business reality." The board of DST Telecommunications, none
of whom had had any hard experience with the business of filmmaking (in fact no one in the sorority did) began to balk. After all, they,
were faced with the very real prospect of all kinds of indemnity. And
hundreds of thousands of dollars of the sorority's money was on the
line.

At an Executive Board meeting in 1974, Benbow proposed that
the sorority's national convention scheduled for 1975 in Seattle—
which would mark the end of her administration—be postponed for
a year. Although she cited as the main reasons the terrible recession
that was taking hold in the country, the fact that Seattle was not
easily accessible, and the need to prepare for Bicentennial celebra-
tions scheduled for 1976, many suspected that her real motive was to
remain in office an additional year to see the film and the new corporation through. At first the committee appointed to investigate the
possibility of postponing the convention suggested that it go on as
scheduled. Conventions were planned and looked forward to long
before they actually happened, they said. Hotels in Seattle had already been booked, and cancellation would be disastrous for the image of the sorority, not to mention the money that would be lost.
And though unspoken, there were, undoubtedly, still memories of
the divisions created when Dorothy Height maneuvered to stay in
office beyond the two terms, with much the same rationale. Like

Height, Benbow was a very forceful president: Through a long, tedious, and emotional executive session, she convinced the committee to recommend that the next convention be postponed. But unlike Height, Lillian Benbow did not have the organizational skills—and at this point, perhaps, the patience—to pull it off. The membership had to vote on the proposed postponement, and they voted it down. "She didn't follow up on it," recalled Jeanne Noble, "while those who wanted the convention were proselytizing for it. Lillian was kind of ethereal about things like that."[42] But her real miscalculation was, perhaps, failng to understand that Delta had undergone fundamental change and painstaking efforts had to be made to help the membership understand or feel an integral part of that change. Though Lillian Benbow's popularity remained intact, there were mounting suspicions that she was becoming dictatorial and egomaniacal. What did appear to be true was that she began to take criticisms so personally that she lost sight of the organizational dynamics that had created them.

Then came the previews of the movie. The reviews were disastrous. Headlines such as "KUSINI": INEPT, SHODDY and A LIMP TALE OF AFRICAN UNREST were common. They talked about the film's bad technical quality, the wooden acting, the poor script and direction. The most sympathetic review was perhaps from *The Washington Post,* which said it wasn't a "bad film. While its intentions were good, its results are primarily boring and pointless." And although the numerous chapters who held premieres did not lose money, many of the personal investors, of course, did.

In retrospect, the view of Lynnette Taylor seems to be the predominant one. "The problem was that we were all novices. We didn't have the margin of funds needed when problems arose. We really didn't understand distribution. Those involved had to learn about technical aspects of filming. But there are lots of films that aren't successful, and I think that it should be accepted as a historical fact that we made the effort. We were the only group that I know of who attempted to deal with a film that talked about issues such as the effect of multinational corporations and cartels in Africa. It was a courageous thing to do."[43]

The problems with the film did not diminish the popularity of Lillian Benbow, as evidenced by the unprecedented outpouring of affection at the end of her last term. The parting words of the editor of *The Delta Newsletter,* Norlishia Jackson, represented the feelings of many. She wanted to thank her "idol," she wrote, "who among many things helped me see and therefore interpret, the significant and exciting force Delta has the capacity and responsibility to be."[44]

CHAPTER 14

DELTA SIGMA THETA, INC.:
THE CONTEMPORARY
YEARS

In the seventies, Delta Sigma Theta marshaled its formidable resources to meet the new challenge of social concerns through the instruments of a technological age. It had dared to venture and though the venture itself fell short, Deltas in sixteen cities continued to premiere the film. In most instances it became a successful fund-raiser. St. Louis, for example, raised $10,000. The Arts and Letters Commission may not have turned out the way Lillian Benbow had envisioned it, but through her urging, it remained intact and its various activities diffused through its chapters.

The commission's evolution was emblematic of how the organization not only managed to survive crises, but continued to thrive.*

*Presidents: Thelma T. Daley (1975–1979), Mona H. Bailey (1979–1983), Hortense G. Canaday (1983–1988); first vice-presidents: Mona H. Bailey (1975–1979), Hortense G. Canady (1979–1983), Yvonne Kennedy (1983–1988); second vice-presidents: Michelle McRae McNeill (1975–1977), Elsie Cook (1977–1979), Barbara Bagneris (1979–1981), Linda C. Redd (1981–1983), Octavia Matthews (1983–1985), Karla Bailey (1985–1988); secretaries: Ruth Taylor (1975–1979), Shirle M. Childs (1979–1983), Nancy Randolph (1983–1988); treasurers: Inez Kaiser (1975–1979), Lorine S. Samuels (1979–1983), Dolores Sennette (1983–1988).

The ultimate success of Delta has been its ability to maintain tradition and continuity, while meeting the changing needs of the times and the membership. There were periods dictating that attention be focused on the quickened pace of societal change. This was true in the Depression years, and in the sixties. In other eras, the internal organization took priority. That was true of the fifties, late seventies, and most of the eighties. Always, however, there has had to be an alert balancing act between the two which ultimately resulted in expansion of program and membership. And indeed, between 1977 and 1981, the number of chapters grew from 584 to 685; by 1983 there were 712, and at last count, in 1985, there are 730 chapters, including 350 undergraduate and 380 alumnae chapters.

The key to that growth has been the sorority's uncanny ability to sense its own exigencies in each period. Certainly, Thelma Daley, whose administration lasted from 1975 to 1979, had the experience to understand those needs. She had served as Delta's treasurer, first vice-president, and chair of the National Projects Committee. "I went through twenty years of serving on the Board . . . practically *all* my life, do you realize that?" she asked as if she had just realized it herself. In the mid-seventies, there had been a brief decline in membership. Like the administration of Dorothy Height, Benbow's innovative leadership had also produced division, alienation, and the sense that power was too concentrated in the presidency. In the mid-seventies, after the experience with the Arts and Letters Commission there was a need, Daley believed, to "design programs so that people of the grassroots level can play a major role and feel a part of it. . . . I felt it was important to cement the organization. Mine was a kind of bridging period to build up the base, to bring back the membership, bring back the projects."[1] Especially during her first administration, she would bring the organization back to basics: refocus on the tradition and continuity of the sorority; create programs that all could comfortably take part in; and reestablish the administrative boundaries of the powers of the president and the Executive Board, which had become blurred under the previous administration.

Though her theme for the 1977 convention was "An Agenda for Change," it was an agenda that reaffirmed many of the organization's traditional values. There was, for example, renewed focus on the past national presidents and the founders—three of whom, Osceola Adams, Winona Alexander, and Bertha Campbell, spoke. There were tributes to Zephyr Carter, who had died the year before. The more than four thousand sorors who attended the convention in Denver that year witnessed a rededication ceremony emphasizing sisterhood, the meaning of the Delta ritual, the time-honored concerns for public service and social justice. During her administration a twelve-and-a-half-foot steel sculpture called "Fortitude" was commissioned to symbolize the "strength, courage, hope and wisdom" of the twenty-two founders. "Heritage reclaimed is invigorating," Daley noted in her report at the 1977 convention. "We look to the past for a renewal of our faith, for renewal of the bond that binds and for strengthening of a heritage that took us on to forceful movement."[2]

Daley's orientation toward building upon tradition was also evident in the innovation of Life Development Centers. Conceived by the National Projects and Social Action committees, chaired by Dorothy Stanley and Constance Clayton, respectively, the idea was to transform sorority houses into community centers that would become the focus of Delta's public service programs in the area. So in places such as Durham, North Carolina, and Houston, Texas, sites of the first model LDCs, the sorority house now became a center, making it more accessible to the community, and the focal point of services such as the Teen Lifts, library services, and the other projects.

Most symbolic of the return to tradition was the reestablishment of tighter academic criteria. At the 1977 convention grade point averages of 2.5 out of 4.0 or 1.5 out of 3.0 were once more required. GPAs had dropped significantly in the previous years. In fact, Daley's administration pushed education in general to the forefront. She, herself, was an educator in Baltimore and directed the Career Education Program for that city's school system. She also served as president of the American Personnel and Guidance Association until 1976. And, as the Delta president during the years when Black education was entering a new phase in many areas, Daley was able to utilize her professional background as well as her long Delta experience to bring new initiatives into the Delta program—and enhance traditional ones.

The years of Thelma Daley's administration came in the wake of a virtual explosion in the growth of the Black college population. Between 1967 and 1975, she informed the membership, it had increased from 370,000 to 948,000.[3] And as in the past, when there were such dramatic increases, there was also a backlash—though less overt than in eras like the twenties. "In an era when education is so very important," she wrote in The Delta Newsletter, "the future of our undergraduates is of paramount concern. Tuition is up; financial aid is down. Word has come that the ranks of Blacks are gradually dwindling on white campuses and many Blacks are being discouraged from applying to professional schools. There seems to be an increasing pattern of racism," she concluded.[4] She further talked about the importance of the case of Allan Bakke against the Regents of the University of California, which challenged affirmative action and had great implications on "the whole question of educational access." At the same time, historically Black educational institutions were also suffering from financial problems and lower levels of financial aid. Daley developed a two-pronged attack on the problems.

Assets of the sorority, which were in excess of a million dollars between 1975 and 1979 (representing an increase of about 95 percent), allowed greater financial aid to students. In those same years about $73,000 was given to undergraduates, exclusive of contributions to the United Negro College Fund and other similar programs. In addition to grants to seven Black colleges, Daley created the Distinguished Professor Endowed Chair, which provided funds to Black institutions to employ professors whom they could not otherwise not afford. The first recipient was Tuskegee Institute in Alabama, followed by Benedict College in Columbia, South Carolina. By 1979, the trust fund for the chair, provided by national and local chapter investment, totaled $202,734.[5]

In addition to the heightened educational concerns during the years of Thelma Daley's administration, the election of President Jimmy Carter in 1976 brought new intensity to Black political aspirations. Though Delta had remained an active political "player" throughout—as evidenced by the president's participation with other leaders in a meeting held by Secretary of State Henry Kissinger concerning South Africa—the election of Carter promised even greater involvement for the sorority, about 90 percent of whom were Democrats. At the end of her administration, firmer ties were being made with the Congressional Black Caucus and the major voting registration campaigns, such as Operation Big Vote, that were being implemented in the period. Daley's successor, Mona Bailey, who was elected at the 1979 convention in New Orleans, would further carry that political impetus, as well as other initiatives, during her administration from 1979 to 1983.

In 1981, in fact, Walter Fauntroy, a veteran civil rights activist and then chair of the Congressional Black Caucus, said at Delta's convention in Washington, D.C., that "there is no national organization in this country today that is better organized and worked more effectively on the national political scene . . . and on questions of serious concern to the nation, than Delta Sigma

Theta."[6] It was such a reputation that drew many major political leaders to a historic panel discussion at its 1983 convention in Detroit. The issue on everyone's mind was the candidacy of Jesse Jackson, a former Martin Luther King, Jr., lieutenant and director of the Chicago-based Operation Push. It was the main topic discussed by an unprecedented coming together of major Black officials on one stage: Mayors Andrew Young of Atlanta—on whose behalf the Deltas had sent three thousand letters of protest when his resignation from the United Nations was announced—Coleman Young of Detroit; Harold Washington of Chicago; Johnny Ford of Tuskegee, Alabama; and Richard Hatcher of Gary, Indiana. Journalist Ethel Payne served as moderator, and one of the commentators was Chuck Stone of the *Philadelphia Daily News*. The mayors also addressed the convention, as did Congresswoman Shirley Chisholm, Walter Mondale, and Jesse Jackson. Other political issues were broached when Randall Robinson, head of TransAfrica, the lobbying organization, talked about the exigencies of support for legislation that would benefit African and Third World countries. And panels on Black education, closer cooperation among Black women here and in the Third World, among other panels, were emblematic of the overarching theme of Mona Bailey's administration: self-determination and the best means to achieve it.

Of course self-determination was not a new concern in the history of Afro-Americans, but it had a new resonance in an era of access that now was concurrent with the Reagan administration's philosophy of decreasing federal aid. Harsh lessons of the *Kusini* film, the realization that access into the system did not readily affect the negative impact of institutions on Blacks—a fact brought home by Ronald Reagan's election in 1980—and the reluctance to break away from dependence on others made it evident that new skills, knowledge, and even ways of thinking were needed. Instead of the litany of complaint about Reaganomics—which Mona Bailey noted was well known—she emphasized another theme. "I must confess that I find it ironic," she said before the almost seven thousand in attendance at the 1981 convention, "that some of President Reagan's loudest critics retain their positions of leadership because their organizations are almost totally subsidized by federal funds. That is not self-determination, that is community supplication," she concluded.[7] Bailey urged that energy shouldn't be spent only in opposing the administration, but in developing one's own initiatives toward independence. Instead, for example, of fighting the diminution of federal support for projects—including the sorority's own—one should look toward supporting entities such as the Black United Fund and Black banks.

Bailey also articulated a greater emphasis on the distinct role of Black women. "Only when Black women become full partners will Black communities realize the grandeur of dignity that has always been ours to command," she opined.[8] The concept, of course, was reflective of Black women activists of the late nineteenth century who emerged during another period when progress, political conservatism, and the rise of racism were intertwined. And as in the past when Black women activists came together to form, in 1896, the National Association of Colored Women, the Deltas called a "Black Women's Summit" in Washington, D.C. Held in January of 1981, the summit was the idea of the Social Action Commission, which recommended to the Executive Board the need to bring together representatives from various groups throughout the country to focus on Black women's concerns. They were concerns in keeping with the theme of the biennium: "Delta Impacts on the 1980s: Black Youth and Women." What needed to be confronted was the fact that poverty was becoming more and more associated with Black women, especially single mothers and their children. The cochairs were Gloria Scott, who was past second vice-president and secretary of Delta; and subsequently the first Black president of the Girl Scouts U.S.A. and president of Bennett College in Durham, North Carolina—and Social Action chair Constance Clayton, presently the superintendent of schools in Philadelphia. Over seven hundred attended to hear issues discussed by community leaders; politicians; heads of fraternal groups; education administrators; and representatives of civil rights, labor and advocacy groups that included the full range of social, political, and economic concerns.

What also became apparent to Mona Bailey, who is assistant superintendent of schools in Seattle, was that a similar broad coalition of those working in the field of education should come together to try to impact on the system as it affected Black youth. The result was a two-day conference entitled "Educating Black Youth for Survival and Advancement in the 1980s" held in Detroit, April 24–26, involving participants from twenty-six different cities—just four months after the Black Women's Summit. It was an ambitious undertaking, but Mona Bailey was well versed in running conferences. In fact it was her successful coordination of the contested 1975 national conference in Seattle that was largely responsible for her being nominated from the floor for the first vice-presidency in 1975. Tall, articulate, and forceful, and a former Far West regional director, she was highly visible in that successful convention, allowing another against-the-odds victory over the candidate nominated on the slate that year.

Like a national convention, the educational conference had several purposes. "I wanted to make the conference a demonstration project on the national level," observed Bailey. "And the idea of this educational conference was not to invite individuals, but teams, from each of those twenty-six communities. For example, a team might include the superintendent, the chair of the school board; we asked for parents to be on the team; we asked that one or two students be on the team." Another group included major institutions that set policy that impacted on Black youth: Colleges were represented, for example, the federal Department of Education, and those who headed compensatory or other programs where the majority of those affected were Black. "It was a time, you remember, when people like Marian Wright Edelman [founder of the Children's Defense Fund and a Delta] were saying that 'Our children are falling through the cracks.' She was one of our keynote speakers," Bailey continued. "Part of the conference was informational, for all the participants. But then we also broke off into groups. We would get the superintendents into a room together and talk about the need that they take on leadership, that they must create positive programs for youth. . . . And we asked students about their needs, about what they weren't getting from the system."9

The information was immediately processed, noted Bailey, so each team could discuss how the situation in Miami, for example, related to that in St. Louis or Detroit. Finally, there was the follow-up by Delta chapters in the twenty-six cities, as monitors, and many of the young people who participated also spoke at the convention in August of that year. Though it is difficult to quantify the impact of the two conferences, they both showed Delta's stature and its ability to bring together professionals to focus attention on issues of dire concern. They were also experimental in that the decision to have them came out of Bailey's tact of asking the Executive Board and committee chairs their priorities within the Five-Point Program and concentrating on them. The approach was a recognition that, as Patricia Harris, who at the time of the 1981 convention was secretary of HEW and came to receive the Mary Church Terrell Award that year, observed that "diffusion of concern and activity is a luxury that Black people can no longer afford."10 Of course the sorority continued many of its other programs, some of which, like the Search for Talent, expanded to new levels. In 1979, it was superseded by the

Maryland Educational Opportunity Center, funded by HEW, to encourage low-income persons and minorities to pursue postsecondary education. But the leadership saw new value in, and the need to concentrate its resources on, educational and social needs—particularly those that affected Black women.

That beat would be continued under Hortense G. Canady who was elected Delta's eighteenth national president in 1983 at the thirty-seventh national convention in Detroit. The summit idea, for example, was continued as "Summit II: A Call to Action in Support of Black Single Mothers," announced in January of 1984. As Hortense Canady noted, it represented a follow-up to many of the recommendations from the previous meeting. Summit II was a response to the rise in the number of Black families headed by single women, from 21 percent in 1960 to 47 percent by 1982. And as the Delta president understood, the poverty of women was testimony that the War on Poverty, though ameliorating the plight of male-headed families, had not reached Black women.

But the philosophy behind the program went beyond that of the poverty and welfare issues associated with the statistics (less than half were dependent on welfare), and to the prejudices and perils Black women had to face. Many were heard to talk about sexual harassment from landlords, for example, when it was already difficult to find decent housing. And there was the fact that they and their children were stigmatized because there was no father in the home—regardless of the circumstances that had caused the situation. "That was something I hadn't really thought about before the summit," said Canady, "it was one of the most devastating pieces of information that came to my attention. Again and again we heard that not only the women, but the children were treated differently, in the schools and elsewhere. And the children were very aware of that fact. The victims very often were being blamed for their predicament," Canady continued, "and it is often made to appear as if our morals were less and our standards were less, when the truth may be the very opposite. We are less inclined to have abortions, for example, because we value that life." Where things may go awry is when the value of having a child becomes the only one in the lives of women who have little else to look forward to or contribute. In that situation, Canady says, a baby becomes "probably the single, best thing, that's ever going to happen in their lives."[11]

Canady's programmatic emphasis came from both a political and a personal concern. There was a need to look at the plight of Black single mothers from our own perspective because of the way they were often inaccurately and negatively portrayed. As she observed in a *U.S.A. Today* interview conducted by Barbara Reynolds (who was also an editor for *The Delta*), the stigma had a purpose. "If you want to discredit a whole family or a whole people, discredit the mother," Canady said.[12] There was also a personal identification. As she recalled, "I grew up in a single-headed household, where my mother was a widow and moved back with her parents . . . because there was no support system in place for help with care of her children. There are many dimensions to the issue."[13]

Those dimensions became so readily apparent because of the way the summit was designed by Canady and the three committees responsible for its implementation: Projects, Program Planning and Development, chaired by Lynnette Taylor; the Social Action Commission, chaired by Bernadine Denning; and Publications, Public Relations/Communications, chaired by Grace Hewell. Pilot projects were first conceived to be instituted in two cities from each of the seven regions.

However, interest in the project was so great that 128 chapters would take part. The idea was for the Delta chapters to host summits, which included the mothers themselves talking about their particular needs. The objective wasn't just informational, but success would be measured by linking the single mothers to appropriate agencies and services. The structure of the summits reflected the recognition, as Canady would observe, that "there is an abundance of empirical and hard data defining the programs of single motherhood, but a dearth of support systems designed to ameliorate the problems."[14]

This was evident at the summit in Auburn-Opelika, Alabama, for example, held at Auburn University, where participants included chapter members of the Auburn Alumnae and Kappa Upsilon undergraduates, single mothers and fathers, and the workshop leaders. The agencies represented included Auburn Headstart, the Alabama State Office of Pensions and Securities, Alpha Kappa Alpha sorority, and the National Organization for Women (NOW) who heard, among others, the testimony of a twenty-six-year-old single mother of three children who reported frequent anxiety attacks. After the birth of her last child four years before, the young mother developed a heart-valve condition, stomach difficulties, and migraine headaches. She was also under financial stress because of the lack of support from the father of her first two children. Though she had gone to the courts, the judge had ordered the father to pay just twenty-five dollars a week, and the mother rarely got that, she testified. "I have a lot of anger inside," the young woman confided to the group. In fact, her physician recommended that she get counseling to relieve her stress. She did attend one session that was helpful, but the forty-dollar-an-hour cost of the sessions were prohibitive.

The young woman's testimony brought out a number of issues. The coordinator of the conference, Bernice Rutledge, commented that the state's public assistance office "almost discourages fathers" from supporting their children. "The state takes the father's support check and gives the mother $124 monthly, no matter how much the father has paid," she observed. And it was revealed that if a woman works more than ten hours a week, she becomes ineligible for rent subsidies and very likely Medicaid and Medicare benefits. The participants in the conference concluded that efforts had to be made to reform the welfare system by forming a coalition for that purpose. Just as importantly, the young woman was exposed to people and resources that became available to her as a result of the meeting.

A different kind of testimony was heard at the Kansas City, Missouri, summit, coordinated by Inez Kaiser and Renee Kerr of that city's Alumnae Chapter. The program included remarks from Myrlie Evers, widow of the slain NAACP leader, Medgar Evers. She commented that the issues of single motherhood, long hidden because of the stigma attached to it by such studies as the 1965 Moynihan report, was now "out of the closet." Her theme was the commonality of experience among single mothers, no matter their station in life or the circumstances that created their situation. What drove them all was doing what they had, and were able to do, to provide for the children. In her case, she left her home in Jackson, Mississippi, found a job as a vice-president of an advertising agency and subsequently moved to California where she earned a bachelor's degree from Pomona College. "I really had no interest in living after Medgar was killed," she said, recalling how she and the children watched in horror as his stricken body lay across the doorway of their home. "He was my life. But I had these three children depending on me so I had to make it for *them*."[15]

Summit II follow-ups were also instituted, and the organization has created a network of about one hundred lawyers who are focusing on the issues of the summit. In the short term, a pamphlet called "Know Your Rights" will be distributed for use by single mothers. In addition to believing that the project had a discernible impact on the problem, Canady, a former first vice-president, cochair of the Social Action Commission, and Midwest regional director, saw the summit as meeting the organization's internal needs—something recent presidents were particularly aware of in this period. "We are such a diverse group," she noted, "as both individuals and in terms of the levels of chapters. This was the kind of project, she said, "where everyone could see something in it that they could address, regardless of their level of expertise or sophistication."[16]

There is also the need, as Canady knows, for independent scholarship and research on these issues and others if they are going to ultimately have a major impact on public policy. For these reasons, the president resuscitated an earlier project idea that never reached fruition. It was the Delta Education and Research Foundation, first conceived in 1967 under the administration of Geraldine Woods—who acts as president of the foundation. The idea behind it is to provide a means for research and education projects for Black women scholars. The goal set by Canady is to endow the foundation with $5 million primarily raised through chapters. "We often neglect the ideas of one administration, even good ones like the foundation," said the president, who has made a point of appointing past presidents to administer the Delta projects—such as Woods (a Mary Church Terrell Award recipient in 1979) for the foundation and Thelma Daley to the Distinguished Professor Endowed Chair committee.

An initiative that also is related to the advancement of scholarship on several levels, proposed in 1985, is the four-year international program, the Black Diaspora, which focuses on study, international travel, and awareness—highlighting the "debt owed to African culture," Canady said. The design of the Black Diaspora program is typical of her multidisciplinary and multitiered approach, in which all levels of the membership can find an interest and relate to. Thus far the program has included a lecture series by recognized scholars, in which a number of universities and community colleges have participated; programs providing awareness of legislative and foreign policy issues related to Africa, the Caribbean, and South America; and air and land tours scheduled throughout the diaspora, which will be accompanied by historians and scholars.

In fact, the late seventies and eighties is a period in Delta's history that can be characterized by a great deal of internal reflection and search through the past—both externally and internally. Especially in the eighties, that reflection has been made all the more poignant by the illness and passing of many of the sorority's standard-bearers. The first national president, Sadie T. M.

Alexander, who as recently as 1979 at an Executive Board meeting said how blessed she was to be alive to see the growth of the organization, lies in a coma. Eliza Shippen, who in 1980 was present for the ground breaking of Delta Towers, a 150-unit apartment building for the elderly and handicapped, realized through the efforts of her D.C. Alumnae Chapter, passed away the following year. Osceola Adams, who lived to see a Delta arts award, "the Osceola," established in her name, died in 1983. Winona Cargile Alexander, present at the 1981 conference where sorors marched down Pennsylvania Avenue, died in 1984. Past president Lillian Benbow succumbed to breast cancer in the same year, and in 1985, Patricia Roberts Harris, who just four years before reminisced about her early Delta years, also was felled by the disease.

The two remaining founders, Bertha Campbell—who is expected at the 1988 Diamond Jubilee celebration and national convention of the sorority in San Francisco—and Naomi Richardson, who, until his death this year, took care of an *older* brother in Washingtonville, New York; as well as the past presidents, have surely seen phenomenal gains in every aspect of the sorority's activity. It has stretched, after all, throughout the United States as well as Africa, the Caribbean, and more recently, West Germany, to the tune of 125,000 members. And emblematic of that evolution is the growth of aid to the higher education of Black youth—its first national program. Between 1982 and 1983, 2,000 students were given some $800,000 in scholarship aid. And the Endowed Chairs given in the last two years to Hampton Institute and Spelman College, now represent $50,000-a-year stipends.

Of course, challenges remain. Hortense Canady's theme for the 1985 convention that stressed equity through education, employment, and empowerment is yet to be realized. And there are internal problems of management and the need to increase the percentage of active sorors. Too many chapters still carry on business as usual, and there is the need to develop the pledging process so that it becomes a boon rather than an impediment to maintaining grade-point averages. But one must conclude that the organization's struggle for sisterhood, for identity, for the realization of their obligations as educated Black women, has been extraordinary. Delta has made a difference in people's lives. This was never more evident than when President Canady met recently with a number of the women who had lived at the Delta Home for Girls founded more than forty years ago. Directly due to the efforts of the organization many had gone on to college.

Nevertheless, the organization is never satisfied with itself and has never been afraid to engage in the continual "appraisal and reappraisal of its purpose," as Lillian Benbow once noted. "We must begin to do it again," stressed Hortense Canady, who will be leaving office in 1988. "It is an agonizing process, but one which may result in us not only coming closer together, but in redefining public service in such a way that it not only has a major impact on our community but on the national purpose, on the national commitment of Black people in this nation."[17] In its seventy-fifth year, Delta Sigma Theta, Inc., has much to celebrate and much to do.

Notes

PREFACE

1. See Mayer N. Zald and Roberta Ash, "Social Movement Organizations: Growth, Decay and Change," in *Social Forces,* Vol. 44, No. 3, pp. 327–341, for the references to social movement organizations.
2. Ibid., p. 330.
3. Ibid.
4. Ibid., p. 334

INTRODUCTION

1. Proceedings, 28th National Convention, 1965. p. 115.
2. Charles H. Wesley, *The History of Alpha Phi Alpha: A Development in College Life* (Washington, D.C.: Foundation Publishers, 1929, 1950), p. xix.
3. Charles S. Johnson, *The Negro College Graduate* (Durham, N.C.: University of North Carolina Press, 1938), p. 8.
4. Jeanne L. Noble, "The Negro Woman's College Education," Ph.D. dissertation, Columbia University, 1942, p. 4.
5. Rayford Logan, "Social Action, Health Projects Sponsored by 'Greek' Organizations," in "50 Years of Progress Series," *Pittsburgh Courier,* 1947, p. 2.
6. Quoted in Benjamin Quarles, *The Negro in the Making of America* (New York: Collier Books, 1964), p. 169.
7. Noble, op. cit., p. 23.

CHAPTER 1. WORLD OF THE FOUNDERS

1. Much of the biographical information came from Pauline Anderson Simmons Hill and Sherrilyn Johnson Jordan, *Too Young to Be Old: Bertha Pitts Campbell* (Seattle: Peanut Butter Publishing, 1981)

2. Interview, Bertha Pitts Campbell, October 4, 1986.

3. *Howard University Record,* Vols. 3 and 4, 1903–1907, p. 18.

4. Ibid., p. 20.

5. Ibid., p. 21.

6. Rayford W. Logan, *Howard University: The First Hundred Years, 1867–1967* (New York: New York University Press, 1969), p. 101.

7. Ibid., p. 122.

8. Interview, Naomi Sewell Richardson, June 23, 1986.

9. *Howard University Journal,* March 16, 1914, p. 7.

10. Logan, op. cit., p. 113.

11. Ibid., p. 56.

12. Ibid., p. 113.

13. *Howard Record,* op. cit., pp. 59–60.

14. Ibid., p. 56.

15. *Howard University Journal,* October 11, 1912.

16. Interview, Campbell, op. cit.

17. Interview, Naomi Sewell Richardson, June 23, 1986.

18. Many biographical details about Dodd come from Julia K. Gibson Jordan and Charlie Mae Brown Smith, *Beauty and the Best: Frederica Chase Dodd, The Story of Love and Dedication* (Dallas: n.p., 1985).

19. Interview, Campbell, op. cit.

20. Logan, op. cit., p. 216.

21. Raymond Wolters, *The New Negro on Campus: Black College Rebellions of the 1920s* (Princeton: Princeton University Press, 1975), p. 88.

22. Interview, Campbell, op. cit.

23. Interview, Elsie Brown Smith, June 14, 1987.

24. Many of the biographical details about Murphy come from Elizabeth Murphy Moss, *Be Strong! The Life of Vashti Turley Murphy* (Baltimore: n.p., 1980), p. 4.

25. Logan, op. cit., p. 167.

26. *Howard Record,* op. cit., p. 25.

27. Ibid., p. 26.

28. Helen G. Edmonds, "The History of Delta Sigma Theta," unpublished manuscript, 1954, p. 32.

29. *Howard University Journal,* January 16, 1914, p. 6.

30. Ibid., February 7, 1913, p. 6.

31. Ibid., December 20, 1912, p. 8.

32. Ibid., March 6, 1914, p. 7.

33. *The Crisis,* July 1914, p. 133.

34. Wolters, op. cit., p. 88.

35. Ibid., p. 89.

36. "Founders' Greetings," in *The Delta,* May 1963, p. 19.

37. Charles S. Johnson, *The Negro College Graduate* (Durham, N.C.: University of North Carolina Press, 1938), p. 8.

38. *The Crisis,* August 1915, p. 208.

39. *Howard University Journal,* November 15, 1912, p. 1.

40. Ibid., April 17, 1914, p. 2.
41. Logan, op. cit., p. 170.
42. Ibid.
43. Marjorie Parker, *Alpha Kappa Alpha: In the Eye of the Beholder* (Washington, D.C.: n.p., 1979), p. 13.
44. Charles H. Wesley, *The History of Alpha Phi Alpha: A Development in College Life* (Washington, D.C.: Foundation Publishers, 1929, 1950), p. xix.
45. *From These Roots*, edited by Raleigh Alumnae Chapter (n.p., n.d.) p. 32.
46. Parker, op. cit., p. 71.
47. Interview, Campbell, op. cit.

CHAPTER 2. THE FOUNDING

1. *Howard University Journal*, October, 18, 1912, p. 1.
2. Ibid., pp. 1, 8.
3. Edna Johnson Morris, *The History and Development of Delta Sigma Theta Sorority* (Gary, Ind.: Gary American Publishing Company, 1944), p. 12.
4. *From These Roots*, edited by Raleigh Alumnae Chapter (n.p., n.d.), p. 34.
5. Interview, Naomi Sewell Richardson, June 23, 1986.
6. Quoted in "Deltas' Dawning Honored," *The Washington Post*, August 31, 1981, p. C-8.
7. Morris, op. cit., p. 12.
8. *From These Roots*, op. cit., p. 34.
9. Interview, Ethel Cuff Black, n.d. unnamed interviewer.
10. *From These Roots*, op. cit., p. 34.
11. Marjorie Parker, *Alpha Kappa Alpha: In the Eye of the Beholder* (Washington, D.C.: n.p., 1978), p. 30.
12. Interview, Ethel Cuff Black, op. cit.
13. Interview, Elsie Brown Smith, June 14, 1987.
14. Helen G. Edmonds, "The History of Delta Sigma Theta Sorority," unpublished manuscript, 1954, p. 33.
15. Ibid., p. 28.
16. Morris, op. cit., p. 13.
17. Ibid., p. 13.
18. Rayford W. Logan, *Howard University: The First Hundred Years, 1867–1967* (New York: New York University Press, 1969), p. 165.
19. Edmonds, op. cit., p. 34.
20. Interview, Naomi Sewell Richardson, 1976, conducted by Mid-Hudson Alumnae Chapter
21. Mary Elizabeth Vroman, *Shaped to Its Purpose: Delta Sigma Theta—The First Fifty Years* (New York: Random House, 1965), p. 15.
22. Edmonds, op. cit., p. 31.
23. *Howard University Journal*, February 13, 1913, p. 3.
24. Ibid.
25. *Howard University Journal*, October 24, 1913, p. 6.
26. Edmonds, op. cit., p. 37.
27. Vroman, op. cit., p. 15.
28. Quoted in *The Crisis*, August 1915, p. 206.
29. Ibid., p. 187

30. Ibid., p. 176.
31. Logan, op. cit., p. 97.
32. *From These Roots,* op. cit., p. 34.
33. "Deltas' Dawning Honored," *The Washington Post,* op. cit.
34. Quoted in Paula Giddings, *When and Where I Enter: The Impact of Black Women on Race and Sex in America* (New York: William Morrow and Co., 1984), p. 370.
35. "Founders' Greetings," in *The Delta,* May 1963, p. 18.
36. Interview, Naomi Sewell Richardson, June 23, 1986.
37. Interview, Bertha Pitts Campbell, op. cit.
38. Quoted in Eleanor Flexner, *Century of Struggle: The Woman's Rights Movement in the United States* (Cambridge, Mass.: Harvard University Press, 1959, 1975), p. 273.
39. Ibid.
40. *The Delta,* op. cit., p. 18.
41. Ibid.
42. Ibid.
43. *The Crisis,* April 1913, p. 298.

CHAPTER 3. EXTENDING THE VISION: NATIONALIZING AN IDEA

1. Edna Johnson Morris, *The History and Development of Delta Sigma Theta Sorority* (Gary, Ind.: Gary American Publishing Co., 1944), p. 16.
2. *NIKH Yearbook,* Howard University, 1915, p. 44.
3. *Howard University Journal,* December, 1913, p. 6.
4. Ibid.
5. Ibid., January 13, 1914, p. 5.
6. Ibid.
7. *The Crisis,* June, 1914, p. 133.
8. Charles S. Johnson, *The Negro College Graduate* (Durham, N.C.: University of North Carolina Press, 1938), p. 8.
9. Interview, Naomi Sewell Richardson, 1976, by Mid-Hudson Alumnae Chapter
10. Ibid.
11. *The Delta,* May 1971, p. 14.
12. Ibid., p. 13.
13. Biography submitted by Ethel Carr Watson, n.d.
14. Helen G. Edmonds, "The History of Delta Sigma Theta Sorority," unpublished manuscript, 1954, p. 33.
15. John Hope Franklin, *From Slavery to Freedom: A History of Negro Americans* (New York: Knopf, 1967), p. 231.
16. Morris, op. cit., pp. 16–17.
17. Edmonds, op. cit., p. 40.
18. Interview, Anna Johnson Julian, February 6, 1986.
19. Quoted in Proceedings, 34th National Convention, 1977, p. 51.
20. Ibid.
21. Ibid.

22. "A Memorable Page in Iowa's Black History," in *The Des Moines Register,* November 20, 1977, p. 4E.

23. John Harrison Thornton, "Co-Education at the State University at Iowa," in *Iowa Journal of History and Politics,* October 1947, p. 45.

24. Mary Constance Murray, "The Negro Student at the University of Iowa," Iowa City, 1945. Misc. Papers.

25. Numa P. G. Adams, "The Place of the Fraternity in Negro College Life," *Howard University Record,* Vol. 3., 1919, p. 17.

26. Ibid., p. 18.

27. Quoted in Proceedings, 1977, op. cit., p. 51.

28. Ibid.

29. Ibid.

30. Morris, op. cit., p. 18.

31. Proceedings, 1977, op. cit., p. 50.

32. Morris, op. cit., p. 18.

33. Ibid., p. 19.

CHAPTER 4. GROUNDS FOR A MOVEMENT

1. Raymond Wolters, *The New Negro on Campus: Black College Rebellions of the 1920s* (Princeton: Princeton University Press, 1975), p. 313.

2. Charles S. Johnson, *The Negro College Graduate* (Durham, N.C.: University of North Carolina Press, 1938) p. 9.

3. Ibid.

4. Aptheker, op. cit., p. 186.

5. Numa P.G. Adams, "The Place of the Fraternity in Negro College Life," *Howard University Record,* Vol. 3. 1919, p. 17.

6. Ibid.

7. Wolters, op. cit., p. 315.

8. Ibid., p. 316.

9. Ibid., p. 319.

10. Ibid., p. 317.

11. Ibid., p. 318.

12. Interview, Elsie Brown Smith, June 14, 1987.

13. Wolters, op. cit., p. 317.

14. Interview, Anna Johnson Julian, February 6, 1986.

15. Ibid.

16. Edna Johnson Morris, *The History and Development of Delta Sigma Theta Sorority* (Gary, Ind.: Gary American Publishing Co., 1944) p. 19.

17. Quoted from Proceedings, 34th National Convention, 1977, p. 50.

18. Ibid.

19. *Howard University Record,* 1922, p. 490.

20. Interview, Louise Thompson, January 14, 1987.

21. Arnold Rampersand, *The Life of Langston Hughes, Vol. I, 1902–1941: I, Too, Sing America* (New York: Oxford University Press, 1986), p. 162.

22. Gloria T. Hull, ed., *Give Us Each Day: The Diary of Alice Dunbar-Nelson* (New York: W. W. Norton & Co., 1984), p. 134.

23. Ibid.

24. *Howard University Record,* February 22, 1923, p. 233.
25. Edmonds, op. cit., p. 303.
26. Ibid., p. 302.
27. Ibid., p. 303.
28. John Hope Franklin, *From Slavery to Freedom: A History of Negro Americans* (New York: Knopf, 1967), p. 401.
29. Edmonds, op. cit., p. 66.
30. Ibid.
31. Morris, op. cit., p. 27.

CHAPTER 5. NEW ERA, NEW CHALLENGE

1. *The Delta,* February 1925, p. 7.
2. Edna Johnson Morris, *The History and Development of Delta Sigma Theta Sorority* (Gary, Ind.: Gary American Publishing Co., 1944) p. 30.
3. Ibid.
4. *The Delta,* op. cit., p. 9.
5. Ibid.
6. Proceedings, 34th National Convention, 1977. p. 51.
7. *The Delta,* op. cit., p. 5.
8. Helen G. Edmonds, "The History of Delta Sigma Theta," unpublished manuscript, 1954, p. 268.
9. *The Delta Bulletin,* February 2, 1925, p. 1.
10. Ibid., p. 2.
11. Ibid.
12. *The Delta Journal,* August 3, 1925, p. 3.
13. Ibid., p. 10.
14. *The Delta Bulletin,* op. cit.
15. Ibid., p. 2.
16. Ibid., p. 1.
17. Ibid., p. 1.
18. Morris, op. cit., p. 35.
19. *The Delta Bulletin,* op. cit., p. 1.
20. Quoted in Marjorie Parker, *Alpha Kappa Alpha: In the Eye of the Beholder* (Washington, D.C.: n.p., 1978), p. 33.
21. Herbert Aptheker, *Afro-American History: The Modern Era* (Secaucus, N.J.: Citadel Press, 1971), p. 295.
22. *Howard University Record,* February 1925, p. 90.
23. Ibid.
24. Aptheker, op. cit., p. 189.
25. Morris, op. cit., pp. 32–33.
26. Ibid., p. 37.
27. Gloria T. Hull, *Give Us Each Day: The Diary of Alice Dunbar-Nelson* (New York: W. W. Norton & Co., 1984), p. 273.
28. Proceedings, 10th National Convention, Report of the First Vice-President, 1929, p. 2.
29. Ibid.
30. Ibid., p. 7.

31. Ibid., Report of the Journalist, p. 1.
32. Proceedings, op. cit., p. 15.
33. Ibid., p. 10.
34. Ibid.
35. Ibid., p. 15.
36. Ibid., p. 38.
37. Ibid., p. 7.

CHAPTER 6. STRENGTHENING WITHIN—LOOKING WITHOUT

1. Interview, Anna Johnson Julian, February 6, 1986.
2. Helen G. Edmonds, "The History of Delta Sigma Theta," unpublished manuscript, 1954, pp. 84–84.
3. Edna Johnson Morris, *The History and Development of Delta Sigma Theta Sorority* (Gary, Ind.: Gary American Publishing Co., 1944), p. 41.
4. Letter from Anna Johnson Julian to Norlishia Jackson, May 21, 1973.
5. Edmonds, op. cit., p. 167.
6. Quoted in Benjamin Quarles, *The Negro in the Making of America* (New York: Collier Books, 1964, 1987), p. 208.
7. Edmonds, op. cit., p. 169.
8. Ibid., p. 168.
9. Ibid., p. 171.
10. Ibid.
11. Ibid., p. 160.
12. Ibid.
13. Ibid.
14. Ibid., p. 166.
15. Ibid., p. 118.
16. Ibid., p. 120.
17. Morris, op. cit., p. 41.
18. Minutes, Central Regional Council, May 14, 1932, p. 2.
19. Ibid.
20. Letter from Thyrsa W. Amos to Mrs. J. H. Peele, May 9, 1934.
21. Letter from Mary Johnson Yancey to Dorothy P. Harrison, August 5, 1958.
22. Edmonds, op. cit., p. 172.
23. Letter from Ethel LaMay Calimese to Cora K. Miller, April 15, 1927.
24. Memo from Cora K. Miller, April 30, 1927.
25. Letter from Ethel LaMay Calimese to Miss Leonard, May 19, 1927.
26. *The Delta Bulletin,* May 1932, p. 5.
27. Interview, Anna Johnson Julian, op. cit.

CHAPTER 7. "ONE BLOOD, ONE TRADITION"

1. John Hope Franklin, *From Slavery to Freedom: A History of Negro Americans* (New York: Knopf, 1967), p. 496.

2. Letter to Claude Barnett from Melissa, June 6, 1933, Claude Barnett Papers, Chicago Historical Society.
3. Letter from Anna Johnson Julian to Norlishia Jackson, May 21, 1973.
4. Franklin, op. cit., p. 497.
5. Ibid., p. 496.
6. Quoted in *When and Where I Enter: The Impact of Black Women on Race and Sex in America* (New York: William Morrow and Co., 1984), p. 197.
7. *Norfolk Journal and Guide*, December 28, 1935, p. 10.
8. *The Delta*, May 1935, p. 3.
9. Helen G. Edmonds, "The History of Delta Sigma Theta," unpublished manuscript, 1954, p. 93.
10. *The Delta*, April 1933, p. 23.
11. Ibid., p. 22
12. Ibid., p. 23.
13. Mary Elizabeth Vroman, *Shaped to Its Purpose: Delta Sigma Theta—The First Fifty Years* (New York: Random House, 1964), pp. 33–34.
14. *The Delta*.
15. Carter G. Woodson, *The Mis-Education of the Negro* (Washington, D.C.: AMS Press, Inc., 1933, 1977), p. 52.
16. Interview, Anna Johnson Julian, February 6, 1986.
17. Rayford Logan, *Howard University: The First Hundred Years, 1867–1967* (New York: New York University Press, 1969), pp. 310–311.
18. Charles S. Johnson, *The Negro College Graduate* (Durham, N.C.: University of North Carolina Press, 1938), p. 8.
19. Logan, op. cit., pp. 316–317.
20. Johnson, op. cit., pp. 56, 57.
21. *The Delta*, August 1935, p. 11.
22. *The Delta Bulletin*, November 1933, p. 4.
23. *The Delta*, August 1935, p. 23.
24. John W. Davis, "The Negro Land-Grant College," *Journal of Negro Education*, 1933, p. 328.
25. Ibid., p. 314.
26. Ibid., p. 319.
27. Ibid., p. 325.
28. Franklin, op. cit., p. 550.
29. Davis. op. cit., p. 322.
30. Johnson, op. cit., p. 80.
31. *The Delta Bulletin*, November, 1933, p. 3.
32. Edmonds, op. cit., p. 87.
33. *The Delta Bulletin*, op. cit., p. 4.
34. Edmonds, op. cit., p. 90.
35. Ibid.
36. *The Delta Bulletin*, May 1934, p. 2.
37. *The Delta*, August 1935, p. 23.
38. Ibid.
39. Edmonds, op. cit., p. 304.
40. Harvard Sitkoff, *A New Deal for Blacks* (New York: Oxford University Press, 1978), p. 47.
41. Edmonds, op. cit., p. 41.
42. *The Delta Bulletin*, February, 1933, p. 3.
43. Letter from Jeannette Triplett Jones to Louise Thompson, June 1, 1934.
44. *The Delta Bulletin*, October 1935, p. 1.
45. *The Delta*, August 1935, p. 2.

CHAPTER 8. FROM COALITION TO AUTONOMY

1. Quoted in Paula Giddings, *When and Where I Enter: The Impact of Black Women on Race and Sex in America* (New York: William Morrow and Co., 1984), p. 224.
2. Quoted in *The Delta Journal,* May 1945, p. 44.
3. Helen G. Edmonds, "The History of Delta Sigma Theta," unpublished manuscript, 1954, pp. 190, 191.
4. Mary Elizabeth Vroman, *Shaped to Its Purpose: Delta Sigma Theta—The First Fifty Years* (New York: Random House, 1964), p. 47.
5. Edmonds, op. cit., p. 204.
6. Ibid., p. 206.
7. Vroman, op. cit., p. 45.
8. Ibid., p. 53.
9. Biennial Report, January 1, 1938–August 26, 1939, pp. 10–11.
10. Ibid.
11. Letter from Osceola Macarthy Adams to Vivian Osborne Marsh, April 16, 1947.
12. Biennial Report, op. cit., p. 11.
13. Edmonds, op. cit., p. 145.
14. Marjorie Parker, *Alpha Kappa Alpha: In the Eye of the Beholder* (Washington, D.C.: Foundation Publishers, 1979), p. 36.
15. Interview, Elsie Austin, April 14, 1985.
16. Giddings, op. cit., p. 234.

CHAPTER 9. COMING OF AGE

1. Helen G. Edmonds, "The History of Delta Sigma Theta Sorority," unpublished manuscript, 1954, p. 230.
2. Ibid., p. 233.
3. Ibid., p. 236.
4. Ibid., p. 238.
5. Ibid., p. 239.
6. Ibid., p. 238.
7. Proceedings, 16th National Convention, 1971, p. 41.
8. Quoted in Paula Giddings, *When and Where I Enter: The Impact of Black Women on Race and Sex in America* (New York: William Morrow and Co., 1984), p. 229.
9. Helen Edmonds, op. cit., p. 99.
10. Ibid., p. 98.
11. Ibid., p. 99.
12. Ibid., p. 103.
13. Ibid., p. 99.
14. *The Delta Bulletin,* November 1944, p. 4.
15. Ibid.

16. Edmonds, op. cit., p. 323.
17. Ibid., p. 242.
18. Ibid., p. 245.
19. Ibid.
20. Ibid., p. 244.
21. Ibid., p. 256.
22. Quoted in John Hope Franklin, *From Slavery to Freedom: A History of Negro Americans* (New York: Knopf, 1967), p. 605.
23. Edmonds, op. cit., p. 328.
24. *The Delta Bulletin,* January 1945, p. 1.
25. Rayford Logan, "Social Action, Health Projects Sponsored by Greek Organizations," *Pittsburgh Courier,* February 9, 1947, p. 5.
26. *The Delta,* June 1948, p. 49.
27. Letter from Beatrice Penman to Mae Wright Downs, January 4, 1948.
28. Ibid.

CHAPTER 10. THE MODERN SISTERHOOD

1. *The Delta,* July 1947, p. 8.
2. Quoted in Pauli Murray, *Song in a Weary Throat: An American Pilgrimage* (New York: Harper & Row Publishers, 1987), p. 79.
3. Interview, Jeanne Noble, June 25, 1986.
4. Helen G. Edmonds, "A History of Delta Sigma Theta," unpublished manuscript, 1954, p. 215.
5. Ibid.
6. Ibid., p. 378.
7. Summary of Report from ACHR, presented at 23rd National Convention, 1954.
8. Interview, Noble, op. cit.
9. Edmonds, op. cit., p. 367.
10. Ibid., p. 136.
11. Ibid., p. 135.
12. Interview, Noble, op cit.
13. Edmonds op. cit., p. 137.
14. Ibid., p. 357.
15. Ibid., p. 355.
16. *The Delta Newsletter,* April 1953, p. 4.
17. Edmonds, op. cit., p. 361.
18. Proceedings, 22nd National Convention, 1952, "Report of the Treasurer of Grand Chapter."
19. Letter from Frederica Chase Dodd to Myra Davis Hemmings, May 22, 1950.
20. Proceedings, op. cit., p. 15.
21. Interview, Anna Johnson Julian, February 6, 1986.
22. Minutes, Executive Board meeting, August 1953, p. 11.
23. *The Delta Journal,* August 1954, p. 19.
24. Minutes, op. cit., p. 36.
25. Ibid., p. 37.
26. Proceedings, op. cit., p. 47.

27. Ibid.
28. Ibid., p. 49.
29. Letter from Catherine Middleton to Dorothy Height, September 3, 1954.
30. Ibid.
31. Proceedings, 24th National Convention, 1956, pp. 10–11.
32. Ibid., p. 19.
33. Proceedings, 23rd National Convention, 1954, p. 18.
34. Proceedings, 24th National Convention, 1956, p. 19.
35. Ibid., p. 20.
36. Ibid., p. 45.

CHAPTER 11. DELTA IN THE MOVEMENT YEARS

1. Interview, Jeanne Noble, June 25, 1986.
2. Interview, Dorothy Penman Harrison, February 7, 1986.
3. Ibid.
4. Ibid.
5. Quoted in *The Washington Post,* August 3, 1981, p. C-8.
6. Interview, Noble, op. cit.
7. Ibid.
8. Mary Elizabeth Vroman, *Shaped to Its Purpose: Delta Sigma Theta—The First Fifty Years* (New York: Random House, 1964), p. 116.
9. Ibid., p. 122.
10. Proceedings, 25th National Convention, 1958, p. 17.
11. Ibid., p. 43.
12. Letter from Mary Johnson Yancey to Dorothy P. Harrison, August 5, 1958.
13. *The Delta,* October 1958, p. 35.
14. Proceedings, op. cit., p. 56.
15. Interview, Noble, op. cit.
16. Proceedings, op. cit., p. 18.
17. Ibid.
18. Letter from Christine M. Taylor to Jeanne Noble, October 2, 1958.
19. *The Delta,* February 1960, p. 9.
20. Vroman, op. cit., p. 164.
21. *The Delta,* op. cit., p. 10
22. "The Delta Undergraduate: Her Activities, Her Values, Her Goals—Digest of the Study of the Yancey Commission," 1963, p. 21.
23. Interview, Noble, op. cit.
24. Interview, Lynnette Taylor, December 11, 1985.
25. Interview, Noble, op. cit.
26. Interview, Taylor, op. cit.
27. Proceedings, 28th National Convention, 1965, p. 80.
28. Interview, Noble, op. cit.

CHAPTER 12. CHALLENGE AND CHANGE

1. Proceedings, 27th National Convention, 1963, p. 19.
2. *The Delta,* March 1964, p. 55.
3. Interview, Jeanne Noble, June 25, 1986.
4. Ibid.
5. Interview, Geraldine P. Woods, June 11, 1986.
6. Ibid.
7. Ibid.
8. Interview, Lynnette Taylor, December 12, 1985.
9. Interview, Woods, op. cit.
10. Interview, Taylor, op. cit.
11. Ibid.
12. Interview, Woods, op. cit.
13. Proceedings, 28th National Convention, 1965, p. 118.
14. Ibid.
15. Ibid., p. 27.
16. Interview, Woods, op. cit.
17. Interview, Taylor, op. cit.
18. Ibid.

CHAPTER 13. TOWARD A NEW IDENTITY

1. Proceedings, 31st National Convention, 1971.
2. Interview, Lynnette Taylor, December 12, 1985.
3. Ibid.
4. Minutes, Executive Board meeting, 1968, p. 3.
5. Interview, Frankie Freeman, February 1, 1986.
6. Letter from Patricia Press to Frankie Freeman, March 15, 1968.
7. Ibid.
8. Proceedings, 30th National Convention, 1969, "Call to Convention."
9. Ibid., p. 38.
10. Proceedings, 30th National Convention, 1969, p. 191.
11. Ibid., p. 70.
12. Ibid., p. 118.
13. Ibid., p. 172.
14. Ibid., p. 138.
15. Ibid., p. 82.
16. Ibid., p. 95.
17. Ibid.
18. Ibid., p. 83.
19. Ibid., p. 216.
20. Ibid.

21. Ibid., p. 220.
22. Ibid., p. 56.
23. Interview, Jeanne Noble, op. cit.
24. Ibid.
25. *The Delta,* 1973 Preconvention Issue, p. 70.
26. Ibid.
27. Quoted in *Houston Post,* August 14, 1971, p. 15A.
28. Proceedings, 31st National Convention, 1971, "Address of Lillian Benbow."
29. Ibid.
30. Ibid.
31. *The Delta Journal,* May 1961, p. 28.
32. Proceedings, 32nd National Convention, 1973, p. 6.
33. *The Delta,* Summer 1975, p. 18.
34. Ibid., 1973 Preconvention Issue, p. 2.
35. Ibid.
36. Interview, Jeanne Noble, June 25, 1986.
37. *The Delta Newsletter,* September-October 1975, p. 1.
38. Ibid.
39. Ibid., p. 4.
40. *The Washington Post,* August 9, 1974.
41. Interview, Noble, op. cit.
42. Interview, Taylor, op. cit.
43. *The Delta,* Fall-Winter, 1976, p. 68.

CHAPTER 14. DELTA SIGMA THETA, INC.: THE CONTEMPORARY YEARS

1. Interview, Thelma Daley, December 12, 1985.
2. *The Delta Newsletter,* Summer issue, 1977, p. 2.
3. Ibid.
4. "The Corporate Report, 1977–1979," *The Delta,* August 1979, p. 22.
5. Proceediings, 36th National Convention, 1981, p. 4.
6. Ibid., p. 6.
7. Ibid.
8. Interview, Mona Bailey, October 6, 1985.
9. Proceedings, op. cit., p. 37.
10. Interview, Hortense Canady, January 18, 1987.
11. *U.S.A. Today,* March 12, 1984, p. 11A.
12. Ibid.
13. *Summit II: A Call to Action in Support of Black Single Mothers,* p. 6.
14. Ibid., p. 7.
15. Ibid., p. 57.
16. Interview, Canady, op. cit.
17. Ibid.

A P P E N D I X

FOUNDERS OF DELTA SIGMA THETA

Osceola Macarthy Adams
Marguerite Young Alexander
Winona Cargile Alexander
Ethel Cuff Black
Bertha Pitts Campbell
Zephyr Chisom Carter
Edna Brown Coleman
Jessie McGuire Dent
Frederica Chase Dodd
Myra Davis Hemmings
Olive C. Jones
Jimmie Bugg Middleton
Pauline Oberdorfer Minor
Vashti Turley Murphy
Naomi Sewell Richardson
Mamie Reddy Rose
Eliza P. Shippen
Florence Letcher Toms
Ethel Carr Watson
Wertie Blackwell Weaver
Madree Penn White
Edith Motte Young

NATIONAL PRESIDENTS

Sadie T. M. Alexander 1919–1923
Dorothy Pelham Beckley 1923–1926
Ethel LaMay Calimese 1926–1929
Anna Johnson Julian 1929–1931
Gladys Byram Shepperd 1931–1933
Jeannette Triplett Jones 1933–1935
Vivian Osborne Marsh 1935–1939
Elsie Austin 1939–1944
Mae Wright Downs 1944–1947
Dorothy I. Height 1947–1956
Dorothy P. Harrison 1956–1958
Jeanne L. Noble 1958–1963
Geraldine P. Woods 1963–1967
Frankie M. Freeman 1967–1971
Lillian P. Benbow 1971–1975
Thelma P. Daley 1975–1979
Mona H. Bailey 1979–1983
Hortense G. Canady 1983–1988

NATIONAL CONVENTIONS

1st	Washington, D.C.	December 1919
2nd	Wilberforce, Ohio	December 1920
3rd	Philadelphia, Pennsylvania	December 1921
4th	Chicago, Illinois	December 1922
5th	Columbus, Ohio	December 1923
6th	New York, New York	December 1924
7th	Des Moines, Iowa	December 1925
8th	Cincinnati, Ohio	December 1926
9th	Washington, D.C.	December 1927
10th	Pittsburgh, Pennsylvania	December 1929
11th	Nashville, Tennessee	December 1931
12th	Chicago, Illinois	August 1933
13th	Los Angeles, California	August 1935
14th	Cleveland, Ohio	December 1937
15th	New York, New York	August 1939
16th	Detroit, Michigan	December 1941
17th	Wilberforce, Ohio	August 1944
18th	Richmond, Virginia	December 1945

19th	San Antonio, Texas	December 1947
20th	St. Louis, Missouri	August 1948
21st	Berkeley, California	August 1950
22nd	Cleveland, Ohio	December 1952
23rd	New York, New York	August 1954
24th	Detroit, Michigan	December 1956
25th	Washington, D.C.	August 1958
26th	Chicago, Illinois	August 1960
27th	New York, New York	August 1963
28th	Los Angeles, California	August 1965
29th	Cincinnati, Ohio	August 1967
30th	Baltimore, Maryland	August 1969
31st	Houston, Texas	August 1971
32nd	Atlanta, Georgia	August 1973
33rd	Seattle, Washington	August 1975
34th	Denver, Colorado	August 1977
35th	New Orleans, Louisiana	August 1979
36th	Washington, D.C.	August 1981
37th	Detroit, Michigan	August 1983
38th	Dallas, Texas	August 1985
39th	San Francisco, California	July 1988

THE DELTA OATH

BY MARY CHURCH TERRELL
(1914)

I will strive to reach the highest educational, moral, and spiritual efficiency which I can possibly attain.

I will never lower my aims for any temporary benefit which might be gained.

I will endeavor to preserve my health, for however great one's mental and moral strength may be, physical weakness prevents the accomplishment of much that otherwise might be done.

I will close my ears and seal my lips to slanderous gossip.

I will labor to ennoble the ideals and purify the atmosphere of the home.

I will always protest against the double standard of morals.

I will take an active interest in the welfare of my country, using my influence toward the enactment of laws for the protection of the unfortunate and weak, and for the repeal of those depriving human beings of their privileges and rights.

I will never belittle my race, but encourage all to hold it in honor and esteem.

I will not shrink from undertaking what seems wise and good because I labor under the double handicap of race and sex but, striving to preserve a calm mind with a courageous spirit, barring bitterness from my heart, I will strive all the more earnestly to reach the goal.

THE DELTA HYMN

Delta Sigma Theta

Alice Dunbar Nelson

Florence Cole-Talbert

Mod. Marziale

1. Del - ta! With glowing hearts we praise thee For the strength thy love bestows, For the glow-ing
2. Del - ta! With loy-al hearts we gath-er To re-new our vows of love; In the force-ful

grace of thy sis-ter-hood, And the pow'r that from it flows. Keep in us a strong en-deav-or,
bond of de-vot-ed trust, As our woman-hood moves on. Strengthen in us, old or young-er,

And our souls to rap-ture raise. Del - ta lights the flame, and ev-er Warms our hearts her bond to praise.
As our ranks increase and grow; Del-ta's i-deals, ev - er stronger, Glo-rious in tri-um-phant pow'r.

CHORUS. *Con moto*

Del-ta Sig-ma The-ta! We re-joice in thee! Del-ta Sig-ma The-ta! We pledge thee lo-yal-ty. De-

vot - ed to truth; a bond of our youth That keeps our hearts clean and pure to the end; The

bright gleam of thy vi - sion has light - ed the world; Del-ta Sig-ma The-ta! Our own!

INDEX